The Three Economic Enlightenments

When people wonder about the appropriate course of action in a given situation, they might already be engaging in moral reasoning. This also applies to the field of business, where an understanding of ethics could help businesspeople and market participants make morally informed decisions. This book aims to enlarge the body of ethical theories available in business ethics by illustrating three moral principles relevant to economic agents based on the ideas of Immanuel Kant, Antonio Genovesi, and Adam Smith. All three authors were prominent figures in the eighteenth-century European Enlightenment movement and have much to teach us about the origins of modern economics. Additionally, the book provides specific examples relating to contemporary business situations, focusing on the ethical challenges posed by incomplete contracts. Overall, this book demonstrates that the historical evolution of economic and philosophical concepts remains pertinent to current dialogues in business ethics.

PAOLO SANTORI is an assistant professor in the philosophy department at Tilburg University, the Netherlands, and the Chair of the Scientific Committee of the Economy of Francesco Foundation. He is the author of *Thomas Aquinas and the Civil Economy Tradition* (2021) and several articles in scientific journals.

The Three Economic Enlightenments

Old-New Lessons for Business Ethics

PAOLO SANTORI
Tilburg University

Shaftesbury Road, Cambridge CB2 8EA, United Kingdom

One Liberty Plaza, 20th Floor, New York, NY 10006, USA

477 Williamstown Road, Port Melbourne, VIC 3207, Australia

314–321, 3rd Floor, Plot 3, Splendor Forum, Jasola District Centre, New Delhi – 110025, India

103 Penang Road, #05–06/07, Visioncrest Commercial, Singapore 238467

Cambridge University Press is part of Cambridge University Press & Assessment, a department of the University of Cambridge.

We share the University's mission to contribute to society through the pursuit of education, learning and research at the highest international levels of excellence.

www.cambridge.org
Information on this title: www.cambridge.org/9781009620949

DOI: 10.1017/9781009620925

© Paolo Santori 2025

This publication is in copyright. Subject to statutory exception and to the provisions of relevant collective licensing agreements, no reproduction of any part may take place without the written permission of Cambridge University Press & Assessment.

When citing this work, please include a reference to the DOI 10.1017/9781009620925

First published 2025

A catalogue record for this publication is available from the British Library

A Cataloging-in-Publication data record for this book is available from the Library of Congress

ISBN 978-1-009-62094-9 Hardback
ISBN 978-1-009-62091-8 Paperback

Cambridge University Press & Assessment has no responsibility for the persistence or accuracy of URLs for external or third-party internet websites referred to in this publication and does not guarantee that any content on such websites is, or will remain, accurate or appropriate.

For EU product safety concerns, contact us at Calle de José Abascal, 56, 1°, 28003 Madrid, Spain, or email eugpsr@cambridge.org

To my niece Larissa Croci and my grandmas Giuseppa Marchetti and Elvira Capretta

Contents

Acknowledgments		*page* ix
1	Introduction	1
	1.1 Prologue	1
	1.2 Business Ethics and Normative Ethical Theories	3
	1.3 Aims and Scope	7
	1.4 Application	10
	1.5 Roadmap	13

Part I Political Economy, Civil Economy, Moral Economy

2	Genovesi, Kant, and Smith	23
	2.1 One, No One, and One Hundred Thousands	23
	2.2 Similarities	25
	2.3 Differences	34
	2.4 Visible and Invisible Ties	41
	2.5 Smith's Political Economy	47
	2.6 Genovesi's Civil Economy	53
	2.7 Kant's Moral Economy	57
3	The Three Economic Enlightenments	73
	3.1 From History to Theory	73
	3.2 Inclination and Reason	75
	3.3 Smith's Political Economy: Self-Interest and Non-Tuism	79
	3.4 Genovesi's Civil Economy: Mutual Assistance	84
	3.5 Kant's Moral Economy: Honoring the Spirit of Mutually Beneficial Contracts	87
	3.6 Similarities and Contrasts	92

Part II Application

4	A Contractor under the Rain	105
	4.1 Motivations before Actions	105
	4.2 Complete and Incomplete Contracts	107
	4.3 Case Study	109

		4.3.1 The Story	109
		4.3.2 The Moral Problem	111
	4.4	Applying the Three Economic Enlightenments	112
		4.4.1 Contractor	113
		4.4.2 House Owners	116
	4.5	Discussion	117
5	Unreliable Questionnaires		122
	5.1	Research Approaches	122
	5.2	Case Study	125
		5.2.1 The Story	125
		5.2.2 The Moral Problem	126
	5.3	Applying the Three Economic Enlightenments	127
		5.3.1 Researcher	128
		5.3.2 Participants	131
	5.4	Discussion	133
6	Armed Banks		137
	6.1	Banks and Morality	137
	6.2	Case Study	140
		6.2.1 The Story	140
		6.2.2 The Moral Problem	142
	6.3	Applying the Three Economic Enlightenments	143
		6.3.1 Customer	144
		6.3.2 Bank's Managers	146
	6.4	Discussion	148
7	Conclusion: The Fourth Economic Enlightenment		154
	7.1	Beyond the Three Economic Enlightenments	154
	7.2	Expanding the Framework	156
		7.2.1 Third Parties and Externalities	156
		7.2.2 Initial Conditions	159
		7.2.3 What Are We Trading?	160
		7.2.4 Inclinations and Sociality	161
		7.2.5 The Shadows of the Enlightenments	163
	7.3	Alternative Frameworks	166
		7.3.1 Masculine and Feminine Approaches	166
		7.3.2 Base and Superstructure	168
		7.3.3 Non-Western Approaches	169

Bibliography 175
Index 191

Acknowledgments

This book is the culmination of many years of dedicated research, and I am truly grateful to so many people, far more than I can mention here. To begin, I would like to express my deepest gratitude to my fiancée, Diana Salgado. She plays an integral role in all my endeavors. Her constant encouragement has been essential in moving this project forward. Additionally, her passion and dedication to justice issues, particularly in the realms of diversity and inclusion, continuously serve as a profound source of inspiration. My parents also deserve a special mention, as they have always been a steady reference point in my life. In due course, I shall also publish books in Italian, with the hope that they may appreciate every time I mention them in the acknowledgments.

As I transition to academia, I deeply feel the need to express my gratitude to Luigino Bruni. Over the past ten years since our first meeting, he has been not just a supervisor but also a mentor and a genuine friend. If I can become even half the person and scholar he is, I would be truly fulfilled. I also want to express my heartfelt thanks to my wonderful colleagues at the Department of Philosophy at Tilburg University. I am not just talking about their invaluable advice and thoughtful comments during our weekly seminar when I shared the core ideas of this manuscript. I truly admire each of them for being such dedicated, knowledgeable, and passionate researchers and teachers. If there is something valuable in this book, they should take credit for the inspiring example they set every day. Among them, special mention goes to Roos Slegers, whom I referenced multiple times during the writing process. Her patience and wisdom have been a tremendous help.

Vittorio Pelligra and Enea Bianchi contributed to this project in various ways. I am grateful to them, as well as to the international networks of Adam Smith scholars and civil economy scholars.

I am also thankful to the editors at Cambridge University Press, especially Valerie Appleby and Carrie Parkinson, for their invaluable support throughout every stage of the writing process, from the book proposal to manuscript preparation.

I will not name every scholar who supported me during my research journey. I have already recognized them in the acknowledgments of my first book, and while the list may vary slightly, it remains more or less the same. The same applies to my friends and relatives. I wish to convey the final acknowledgment of people involved in the Economy of Francesco (EoF) movement. I regard this book as an integral component of the EoF initiative that aspires to transform the global economy and economic paradigms to pursue a more equitable and sustainable future.

1 Introduction

1.1 Prologue

Ebenezer Scrooge stands out as one of the most beloved characters created by Charles Dickens's pen and genius. Originally published in 1843, *A Christmas Carol* has woven itself into the fabric of holiday customs worldwide. There are many reasons behind this success, but one is the presence of another much loved character in the novella: Bob Cratchit, Scrooge's counting house clerk. Dickens depicts him as a faithful employee, a loving father and husband,[1] and a person who profoundly loves the good sentiments aroused during Christmastime in particular[2] – unforgettable is the scene in which "the clerk in the tank involuntarily applauded,"[3] the Christmas laudation made by Scrooge's nephew, later to be reproached by Scrooge himself ("Let me hear another sound from you and you'll keep your Christmas by losing your situation"[4]). In the novella, Scrooge undergoes a transformative journey that significantly alters, among many other things, his relationship with Cratchit.

Scrooge paid his employee a mere fifteen shillings a week, which he admitted was insufficient, barely enabling the clerk to support his large family. In addition, Dickens vividly illustrates Scrooge as a rather stern and unsympathetic employer. He would deny Cratchit the warmth of a cozy fire to save on coal costs and even scold him for taking a much-deserved paid day off on December 25th: "If I was to stop half-a-crown for it, you'd think yourself ill-used … and yet, you don't think *me* ill used, when I pay a day's wage for no work."[5] Things change after the Ghost of Christmas Present and the Ghost of Christmas Yet to Come show him the poor conditions in which Cratchit's family celebrates Christmas and the sad ending of Tiny Tim, who dies of an illness that his father is unable to cure with his insufficient salary. One of the more tangible signs of Scrooge's transformation from a greedy and insensible man into a heartful and kind person is the dialogue with his clerk on December 26th:

"Now, I'll tell you what, my friend," said Scrooge, "I am not going to stand this sort of thing any longer. And therefore," he continued, leaping from his stool, and giving Bob such a dig in the waistcoat that he staggered back into the Tank again: "and therefore I am about to raise your salary!" ... "A merry Christmas, Bob!" said Scrooge, with an earnestness that could not be mistaken, as he clapped him on the back. "A merrier Christmas, Bob, my good fellow, than I have given you, for many a year! I'll raise your salary, and endeavour to assist your struggling family, and we will discuss your affairs this very afternoon, over a Christmas bowl of smoking bishop, Bob! Make up the fires, and buy another coal-scuttle before you dot another i, Bob Cratchit!"[6]

The happy ending of *A Christmas Carol* is favored by the supernatural intervention of three ghosts who reawaken Scrooge's dormant conscience and sense of generosity. But in our nonfictional lives, this is not something we can count on. If we envision an alternate version of Dickens's tale, stripped of its magical elements, it's reasonable to suggest that Cratchit ought to have directly confronted Scrooge to negotiate a salary increase. After all, he would have good reasons to do so. He was a faithful employee, facing difficult circumstances due to Tiny Tim's health conditions, and the first contract signed with Scrooge had to be reviewed to account for the changing circumstances. I am not claiming that Cratchit would have been inherently entitled to a raise or that he would have undeniable reasons for requesting one. However, I believe everyone would concur that addressing the matter with his employer, as unsympathetic and cold as Scrooge's attitude might have been, would be the right thing to do.

If we agree with this last statement, we can take a step further and wonder about the content of the meeting between Scrooge and Cratchit. Although renegotiating a contract is an economic matter, it inherently encompasses moral considerations. Both Scrooge and Cratchit might be interested in making what, from their perspective, is the fair choice. The problem is that morality is not that simple, and what counts as "fair" or "just" cannot be univocally or definitively determined. Before the meeting, Scrooge and Cratchit might wonder what course of action they should follow, which moral principles should guide them, and what moral reasons they should put forward to support their choices. If, for any given situation, there was just one all-inclusive moral package (principles, reasons, courses of action), then the task of people interested in doing the right thing would be simply to discover it. The history of ethics shows us that this is not the case. There is no unique moral system nor conclusive agreement on the primacy of one of the many available. In their renegotiation, Scrooge and Cratchit are reading a menu of moral principles. Each principle suggests a course of action and good moral reasons to go that way. Ultimately, it is their choice.

This book aims to enrich Scrooge and Cratchit's moral options by providing three moral principles that can be applied to cases similar to theirs. If you find these economic and moral issues intriguing, I encourage you to keep reading. Otherwise, there is still the hope that the three ghosts might do the work for us.

1.2 Business Ethics and Normative Ethical Theories

Normative ethical theories are pillars of research and teaching in business ethics (BE, henceforth). Western approaches to BE revolve around the triad of consequentialism, deontology, and virtue ethics, as can be seen in hundreds of BE textbooks[7] and course materials.[8] The starting point is common to every approach, and it consists of the refusal of the market as a "morally free zone,"[9] which means that the debate on what is right and wrong, good and bad, cannot be separated from analyses of the business world. Normative ethical theories attract students and researchers not by detailing common patterns of actions or business habits but by encouraging everyone to explore what "should" happen independently of what "usually" happens. Consequentialism, deontology, and virtue ethics provide three distinct perspectives to tackle normative business queries. While these normative ethical theories were developed during various eras of Western history, they still offer insights valuable in addressing modern challenges.

Many BE courses begin with an introductory lecture on consequentialism, deontology, and virtue ethics. In one of my courses at Tilburg University (the Netherlands), titled "Morality of Commercial Life," for third-year international business administration students, the first lecture focuses on these normative ethical theories. This should not come as a surprise. As shown in the chapter devoted to the Netherlands in the *Global Survey of Business Ethics 2022–2024: Teaching,*

Research and Training,[10] the three theories are commonly studied in Dutch universities:

Table 4 shows results derived from respondents in academia and training. In both areas, most respondents can be seen to use variations of consequentialism/utilitarianism, deontology, and virtue ethics as the standard theoretical foundation for their approach to business ethics. Note that the use of these three normative ethical theories is not specific to Dutch business ethics; proponents of U.S. approaches to business ethics typically use a similar "traditional trifecta" of normative ethical theories, and it may well be that the theoretical foundation of Dutch business ethics is partly derived from its North American counterpart.[11]

The triad is then further elaborated in each of its three components. Consequentialism is frequently illustrated through utilitarianism, which assesses the morality of an action or policy based on its outcomes. This necessitates consideration of which consequences are significant. The utilitarianism of Jeremy Bentham (1748–1832) is anchored in the principle of utility, focusing on maximizing pleasure and minimizing pain for everyone affected by an action or policy.[12] Though this serves as a common foundation, explanations of consequentialism may vary. Some educators delve into historical expansions of Bentham's perspective, including John Stuart Mill's (1806–1873) differentiation of higher and lower pleasures[13] or Henry Sidgwick's (1838–1900) distinctions between egoistic and universal hedonism.[14] Others explore modern applications of utilitarianism, like Peter Singer's argument for animal ethics in critiquing the meat industry.[15] There are other routes to discuss consequentialism without necessarily referring to utilitarianism. A very recurrent one is the distinction between act-consequentialism, focused on case-by-case calculus of the consequences of an action, and rule-consequentialism, which claims "that an act is morally wrong if and only if it is forbidden by rules justified by their consequences."[16] Alternatively, the reflection can refer to the impartiality of consequentialist theories, which entails, for example, assessing if consequences should refer to present or future generations.

Deontology operates similarly. Deontological normative ethical theories typically emphasize rights and duties when evaluating the morality of actions, prioritizing intentions over outcomes. A key figure is Immanuel Kant (1724–1804). With his concepts of duty and the categorical imperative, educators help students grasp the significance of universal moral principles in ethical reasoning and highlight the need to avoid treating others merely as means to an end and recognizing that acting rightly may not always lead to favorable results for oneself or others.[17] Nonetheless, lectures vary widely. Some explore the argument that Kant's philosophy is not entirely deontological, as it involves making judgments based not only on universal principles but also on contextual factors.[18] Some distinguish between duty ethics and rights and justice ethics. Within the rights and justice ethics category, references include human rights theory[19] and the contractualist perspective[20] of John Rawls (1921–2002). In this latter view, morality is seen as a mutual agreement among individuals on the principles of justice that should underpin societal institutions such as the state or market.

Virtue ethics is frequently viewed as a counterpoint to both consequentialism and deontology. While the latter normative ethical theories focus on the moral evaluation of individual actions, virtue ethics emphasizes the character traits that contribute to human flourishing. A foundational aspect of this tradition is the perspective of Aristotle (384–322 BCE) on virtues, which he sees as habits that represent human excellence in the pursuit of eudaimonia (the good life).[21] Justice, in this framework, is not merely about actions; rather, it is a virtue that must be cultivated through deliberate practice, enhancing our ability to flourish. Contemporary discussions on virtue ethics sometimes arise in BE lectures. Among them is Alasdair MacIntyre's theory of virtues as connected to practices. According to MacIntyre, a practice is "any coherent and complex form of socially established cooperative human activity through which goods internal to that form of activity are realized in the course of trying to achieve those standards of excellence which are appropriate to, and partially definitive of, that form of activity."[22] Can the market be considered a practice with its annexed virtues? While MacIntyre seems to exclude this possibility, others admit it and list market virtues.[23] These can be topics that connect virtue ethics to BE and, as such, might be the object of BE lectures.[24]

While some scholars and educators explore alternative paths within the triad, others seek to transcend it by examining substitutes. For instance, care ethics has gained substantial recognition in BE research and can be seen as the "fourth" pillar of this framework. Care ethics emphasizes significant personal relationships over abstract rules or universal principles, prioritizes dependence and mutual support instead of independence and autonomy, values partiality as attentiveness to individuals' needs rather than impartiality, and underscores the importance of emotions and passions over rationality and calculation. The objective is not just to act rightly but to foster meaningful and authentic relationships founded on cooperation and mutual assistance. The workplace and marketplace are two areas where reciprocal care can be practiced. Care ethics emerged as a feminist critique of the masculine character of normative ethical theories,[25] and today, the discussion of the possibility of theorizing and applying a "feminist business ethics" is vivid and ongoing.[26]

A different way to overcome the triad involves decolonizing normative ethical theories by examining non-Western ethical accounts. Confucian ethics is among those explored in the literature.[27] Aside from similarities to Aristotelian virtue ethics, Confucian ethics emphasizes family relations, hierarchy, and social traditions, as well as rituals as meaningful organizational practices. Another interesting project in the decolonization (or de-Westernization) of BE is represented (not exclusively) by the publication of the volume *Tribal Wisdom for Business Ethics*.[28] In it, contributors highlight several elements from Indigenous knowledge and practices that could enhance both the theory and practice of BE. One significant aspect is the role of stories and storytelling as tools for sharing knowledge and wisdom. Unlike conventional Western narratives, tribal stories often do not adhere to a linear format (beginning, middle, and end); rather, they are considered "living" tales that reflect the connections among all natural elements, with humans being just one of them. These stories are specific to particular territories and communities and convey knowledge that extends beyond science and rationality. Scholars argue that because businesses function within distinct communities and locales, BE should embrace indigenous knowledge. They advocate for re-evaluating the concept of "global business ethics," which often hinges on the dominance of Western normative ethical theories, including the triad.[29]

My book can be considered another attempt to look for alternatives to the triad of normative ethical theories. However, my aim is not to find substitutes for but rather integrations of consequentialism, deontology, and virtue ethics. In other words, I will not provide any arguments for abandoning the triad. Instead, I aim to add a new section to the chapters devoted to normative ethical theories in BE textbooks. To explain how I intend to do so, I will now turn to the aims and scope of this book.

1.3 Aims and Scope

The triad signifies a productive intersection between BE and the Western history of ideas. Aristotle developed his concepts in ancient Greece, whereas Kant and Bentham formed their own within a European landscape influenced by the Enlightenment of the eighteenth century. Still, we find their ideas relevant in addressing contemporary moral issues, including those that emerge in the economic sphere.

My book seeks to contribute to the existing triad of normative ethical theories – consequentialism, deontology, and virtue ethics – by introducing another triad. I plan to achieve this by recreating the productive intersection of the Western history of ideas and BE. The triad of normative ethical theories I propose comprises political economy, civil economy, and moral economy. Under these labels, I include the moral principles for economic agents[30] elaborated by Adam Smith (1723–1790), Antonio Genovesi (1713–1769), and Kant. In the eighteenth century, these Enlightenment philosophers provided, more or less explicitly, different answers to the same two questions: What is the moral principle to adopt when engaging in a market transaction? What are the moral reasons to follow it?

Smith combined self-interest with the concept of the invisible hand. From this standpoint, I will outline the moral "principle of self-interest and non-tuism." In contrast, Genovesi argued that reciprocity, which he viewed as a natural tendency toward mutual assistance, provides ethical guidance for market participants. This is why I refer to his ideas as the moral "principle of mutual assistance." Unlike those of Smith and Genovesi, Kant's writings and lectures from 1784 and 1785 framed a market within the kingdom of ends, where mutual assistance shifts from the empirical to the a priori realm. For Kant, morality is centered on duties grounded in universal principles. Concerning the market sphere, I assert that he was discussing the moral principle of "honoring the spirit of mutually beneficial contracts." Readers need not be concerned if these principles seem unclear; nearly all the chapters in this book will define and explore them. At this point, it is necessary to determine the boundaries of this book by offering some clarifications.

First, it's important to distinguish between the moral principles underlying the two triads of normative ethical theories. While consequentialism, deontology, and virtue ethics address various aspects of social life, the principles of political economy, civil economy, and moral economy focus on market transactions – particularly voluntary exchanges between individuals in a free market. My triad does not extend to issues in law, education, ecology, politics, family, bioethics, gender, or other domains. For example, while we might explore the implications of consequentialist thought on terrorism, applying the principle of mutual assistance in that context wouldn't make sense. Similarly, though virtue ethics can inform the virtues that a specific institution, like a school, should promote, the concepts of self-interest and non-tuism have little relevance there. The list of excluded domains could continue. Even within the economic sphere, my new triad has a narrower focus than traditional frameworks. Economic inequalities can indeed be assessed from utilitarian or deontological perspectives. However, the three principles I will outline assume a certain equality among the parties involved in the exchange, or at least that any inequality is not so extreme as to compel someone to engage in market transactions out of necessity. While this may seem like a limitation, it actually sets a pragmatic scope for my analysis. If I can demonstrate the utility of this new triad within its defined limits, that will already mark a significant achievement.

The second clarification concerns the terminology I have chosen. Political economy and civil economy are two schools of economic thought that emerged in the eighteenth century, namely in the UK and Italy.[31] When historians refer to schools, they do not imply a physical place or a tight-knit group of instructors and pupils. Instead, the term encompasses theorists who share a fundamental understanding of a specific research topic. Thus, it can be asserted that both Smith and Genovesi were pivotal figures for their respective schools. However, in this book, I will use political economy and civil economy in a more general sense. My goal is not to demonstrate that their respective moral principles apply universally to all authors typically categorized under these labels. At the same time, it is also false to claim that these moral principles are entirely separate from their associated schools of economic thought. My modest objective is to suggest that these moral principles derive from the theories of Smith and Genovesi and can, therefore, be classified as political economy and civil economy, respectively. To clarify this usage, I categorize the moral principle connected to Kant as "moral economy." Everyone knows there has never been an established school of economic thought named thus. This serves to caution readers to establish precise associations between my labels and historical schools of thought. I adopt this terminology to reflect what occurs within the classic triad of normative ethical theories. While I illustrate the diversity within each part of the triad, it is commonplace to link consequentialism with Bentham, deontology with Kant, and virtue ethics with Aristotle. I aim to provide compelling arguments that connect Smith's moral principle to political economy, Kant's moral principle to moral economy, and Genovesi's moral principle to civil economy. This is with the hope that researchers will further explore this new triad as it applies to BE.

Next, I would like to clarify the title of my book. Smith, Kant, and Genovesi were prominent figures of the eighteenth century, all key protagonists of the Enlightenment era. As philosophers, they championed the advancement of reason and science, viewing these as foundational elements of modern societies. The market sphere was no different. In contrast to the hierarchies and privileges of feudal societies, where many individuals lacked the freedom to choose their trading partners, commercial societies founded on voluntary exchanges marked a significant advancement in human history. Freedom, equality, and fraternity were principles that these philosophers acknowledged and supported in their theories. Nonetheless, viewing the Enlightenment as a single entity would be erroneous, even in the context of Western history. Instead, we should think of it in the plural, as "Enlightenments." For instance, Smith belonged to the Scottish Enlightenment, Genovesi was part of the Italian (specifically Neapolitan) Enlightenment, and Kant represented one development in the German Enlightenment. This book does not aim to detail the distinctions among the three Enlightenments. Instead, its goal is to highlight the pluralism found in Western thought by discussing the different moral principles relevant to market transactions elaborated within the three Enlightenments. It is evident that a multitude of authors and moral principles associated with various Enlightenment movements (e.g., French Enlightenment or British Enlightenment) could also be examined. My analysis represents just one of many contributions aiming to prevent reductionism in the history of ideas, particularly in the history of Western philosophical and economic thought.[32]

A final, brief clarification concerns the connection between the three moral principles and the theories of Smith, Genovesi, and Kant. Notably, these authors do not directly mention these principles or apply them to voluntary market exchanges between individuals. However, I assert that they can be inferred from their theories. This is what I do in this book. I outline the moral principles through an analysis and interpretation of the theories of the three philosophers. My intention is for readers to apply their timeless ideas to contemporary debates in BE revolving around moral issues. I believe these moral principles align with the essence of the theories of Smith, Genovesi, and Kant. However, for readers who may not be well versed in the history of Western philosophical and economic thought, it's important to clearly distinguish between their theories and *my interpretation* of them.

These considerations lead me to the focus of the next section. I have outlined my intentions and aspirations for this book. However, I have not clearly articulated why it is worthwhile. For scholars of BE, the overarching goal may be apparent. Research in BE, including studies on the history of ideas, seeks practical application. We study ancient authors to uncover answers or rediscover neglected questions, applying their insights to current business challenges. While this is certainly the aim of the book, it's essential to elaborate on what "application" entails regarding the moral principles of normative ethical theories.

1.4 Application

Applying normative ethical theories to specific cases is not straightforward or self-evident. Challenges frequently emerge when moving from general principles to real-world scenarios, and BE is no exception. Scholars, for instance, have debated the application of Kant's moral philosophy. Some critics[33] designate particular authors as "moral purists" for contending that Kant's duty-based perspective on morality should be regarded as a critique of all market scenarios. Moral purists interpret Kant as suggesting that when self-interest is involved, duty ceases to exist, thus leaving no room for morality in free markets. However, these authors often overlook Kant's important distinction between morality and ethics, the latter of which mixes general rational principles with empirical aspects of human inclinations and desires. While Kant emphasizes that moral law, framed as duty, should dominate our motivations, this does not inherently conflict with the self-interested aims of individuals. I delve into the shortcomings of moral purism in Chapter 2, but I mention them here to illustrate the challenges that can arise when trying to apply moral principles to specific situations.

The challenges are heightened when examining the normative ethical theories of ancient authors. For instance, consider Aristotle's virtue ethics. His concept of virtues as character traits guiding individuals toward eudaimonia was relevant in a society with minimal disagreement about what happiness entails. Thus, we can interpret Aristotle's *Nicomachean Ethics* as a father (Aristotle) instructing his son (Nicomachus) on the virtues essential for a fulfilling life. However, scholars aiming to apply Aristotle's virtues to modern market issues might overlook that in today's Western societies, we experience "reasonable pluralism."[34] Rawls used this term to indicate that citizens in liberal democracies hold diverse beliefs about what constitutes a good life and prefer that social institutions, including the market, not be governed by a singular perspective. In essence, we have varying opinions on which virtues matter. As such, any attempt to adapt Aristotle's virtue ethics to contemporary contexts must recognize this divergence – and many others.[35]

My book analyzes three Enlightenment authors from the eighteenth century by elaborating on three moral principles derived from their theories. As a result, I encounter the same challenges and risks regarding application. How should I address them? The solution is to articulate the same rules of engagement I usually discuss in the lecture on normative ethical theories in my BE course. The first rule concerns the temptation to tick boxes. When presented with moral principles, we might be tempted to think of them as self-explanatory guidelines to be uncritically applied to people's conduct. For example, if an action aligns with the utilitarian principle of maximizing pleasure and minimizing suffering, it can be considered moral. This approach is not advisable. Moral principles may, and indeed should, be subject to scrutiny. In the context of utilitarianism, one might consider what constitutes pleasure and for whom it is applicable. In essence, I encourage students to view normative ethical theories not as definitive conclusions but as foundational starting points for contemplating moral problems or dilemmas in particular cases.

The second rule is to value pluralism and freedom of choice. When considering three normative ethical theories – whether the classical versions or the ones I discuss in this book – the aim isn't to choose a single preferred theory. Each theory presents its own set of moral principles, each with distinct values and limitations. The objective of my lecture (and this book) is to provide an ethical toolkit made up of various normative ethical theories that students (and readers) can use to make their own moral judgments in specific situations. I believe that having multiple alternatives enhances our freedom of choice. By selecting one moral principle and comparing it to others, our decision becomes more informed (and freer) because it encompasses all the reasons we consider other moral principles to be inadequate. This section presents the overarching aim of this book, that is, the rationale behind writing (and reading) a book focusing on the three economic enlightenments. I intend to diversify the wellspring of ethical theories available to students and scholars by introducing an alternative set of normative ethical theories. My approach involves exploring the history of Western thought to accomplish this objective. To enhance readers' freedom of choice, I refrain from showing any preference for the three authors or the moral principles I examine. Political economy, civil economy, and moral economy offer three perspectives from which to frame contemporary business issues. The final choice for one over the other can emerge only from the reader's own reflections based on their basic moral understanding.

The third and final rule emphasizes the connection between moral principles and their application. In Chapter 4, I delve into how these principles outline broad guidelines for conduct while providing the moral reasons for adhering to them. However, moral principles do not necessarily automatically become motivations for action. Motivations are the ultimate reasons why we act in a certain way. However, they can consist of various factors. I can find motivation in the traditions and customs of my surroundings, the guidance of others, my instincts, or my passions, among other influences. Moral reasons, as expressed by moral principles, can be one motivation among others. I propose that motivation transforms into a moral motivation when it is linked to at least one moral reason reflected by a moral principle. Moreover, human actions cannot be explained just by relying on their motivations. Sometimes, we want to act in a certain way but find ourselves doing something different because of the circumstances. Not everything is in our control or unfolds as expected. And yet, it is still valuable to reflect on what we can control. I believe most people want to understand whether their motivations for acting are right or wrong and, thus, seek various perspectives to assess those motivations. Understanding the distinction between courses of action, moral reasons, and motivations is necessary to accurately apply the moral principles outlined in political economy, civil economy, and moral economy discussed in this book. I am not offering ready-made recipes to act morally but rather three alternatives to ground and structure our reflections on the morality of our own or others' behavior. By establishing clear boundaries for what readers can expect from the application part of this book, I aim to mitigate the risks and challenges associated with using normative ethical theories in BE.

Up to this point, I've discussed *how* the three moral principles should be applied. Another aspect of applying normative ethical theories involves the *specific contexts* in which they are applied. I've indicated a focus on market transactions and voluntary exchanges. However, these terms are broad and can encompass a variety of situations. In order to further delimit the scope of the application, I will address the issue of incomplete contracts. In the field of economics, contracts represent the terms of a mutually beneficial agreement between two or more parties. Contracts are considered incomplete due to their inability to anticipate all present and future contingencies that may alter the mutually beneficial nature of a market transaction. I have selected three fictional examples inspired by real-life stories of incomplete contracts to illustrate how the moral dilemmas they present can be analyzed using the moral principles from the three economic enlightenments. In Chapter 4, I provide a detailed explanation of this. For now, I will guide the reader through the book's structure by presenting a roadmap.

1.5 Roadmap

I have structured this book with the intended audience in mind. Readers may be divided into two groups: those interested in historical and philosophical analysis and those more focused on applying moral principles to practical situations. I hope that both groups will move beyond their specific interests and engage with the entire book. Acknowledging that this is not guaranteed, I will now outline the book's structure by offering a reader's guide.

The book consists of two parts. Part I, titled "Political Economy, Civil Economy, Moral Economy," is followed by Part II, titled

"Application." Each part includes an introductory text that outlines what to expect in the subsequent chapters. I will now summarize the content of each chapter.

Part I consists of two chapters. Chapter 2 focuses on the evolution of economic and philosophical ideas, exploring the perspectives of Smith, Genovesi, and Kant regarding the morality of commercial society. To enhance understanding of these authors' ideas, relevant historical and contextual information is included. However, the chapter mainly emphasizes part of the existing secondary literature, addressing both Smith and Kant – two prominent figures in Western philosophy – and Genovesi. The latter's works, despite being untranslated into English, are increasingly sparking international discussions, particularly among scholars of economic thought.[36] I aim to illustrate the diverse interpretations of each philosopher's thoughts. Even within the specific area of markets and morality, multiple perspectives exist regarding the core message of their reflections. I believe it's unfeasible to arrive at conclusive answers regarding the "correct" interpretations. Nevertheless, without the pretense of covering everything, it is essential to acknowledge the plurality and diversity of secondary literature prior to presenting one's own interpretation.

Chapter 2 sets the stage for Chapter 3, where I unveil the moral principles behind the three economic enlightenments. I will describe Smith's perspective using the ideas of self-interest, the invisible hand, and non-tuism (the latter concept originated from his later interpreters). In contrast to Smith, Genovesi posits that within the civil economy framework, self-interest is a key motivation driving economic agents, alongside the inclination to assist one another. The moral foundation for economic agents is rooted in the principle of mutual assistance, understood as intended mutual benefit. Kant's stance appears to align more with Genovesi than with Smith. However, for Kant, mutual assistance is not an innate inclination of economic agents but a mandate of pure practical reason. Thus, Kant's position will be elaborated through the notion of the imperfect duty to uphold the spirit of mutually beneficial contracts.

Chapter 3 is the central one in the book. Readers who focus solely on "application" – those who aren't interested in the origins of ideas and the debates surrounding them – might be able to skip Chapter 2, but Chapter 3 is essential to grasp what happens in Part II. This does not imply that Chapter 2 is optional. As a philosopher trained in the history of Western thought, I assert that effective application relies on sound theorization, which in turn requires a historical analysis of past authors' ideas, including secondary literature. Still, I acknowledge the diverse interests of potential readers. Consequently, I have structured each chapter of Part I as a self-contained learning unit. Readers who wish to grasp the big picture must refer to both chapters, but it is possible to consider Chapter 3 the starting point for the subsequent application.

Part II is divided into three chapters. In them, the moral principles of the three economic enlightenments will be applied to three fictional case studies[37] of incomplete contracts. Chapter 4 introduces the first fictional case study. A contractor is engaged to renovate the façade of the house. The contract stipulates that work must halt during rain. The contractor utilizes uncertain weather forecasts to delay the project for a week. In response, the clients convene a meeting to challenge the decision. The three economic enlightenments offer distinct answers to the questions both the contractor and the clients ponder before the meeting: How should I engage in the discussion? What moral principle should become my motivation for action?

Chapter 5 explores the case of a researcher tasked with conducting a survey. The agreement specifies that participants receive payment in the form of a gift card for completing a survey with open-ended questions. During the analysis of responses, the researcher discovered that 20 percent of participants provided unsatisfactory responses. Frustrated, she raised concerns and organized a meeting with a random selection of those participants to address their responses. The three economic enlightenments offer distinct angles from which the researcher can argue that the participants should have engaged with the survey more carefully despite the lack of more explicit instructions in the contract. Interestingly, participants can also reference these perspectives to explain and justify their own actions.

Chapter 6 focuses on the third fictional case involving an incomplete contract. It tells the story of an individual grappling with an ethical dilemma regarding his bank deposits. Years after depositing his funds, he realizes that the bank invests in the arms and gambling industries. He seeks to move his savings to a different bank without incurring the costs outlined in the contract with the "armed" bank. I will demonstrate how he can leverage the moral principles from the three economic enlightenments to articulate his moral reasons and motivations for altering the contract terms, while also showing how the bank managers can implement a similar approach.

Readers may perceive the inclusion of three fictional case studies to illustrate the same three moral principles as redundant. While this might have some validity, I contend that the distinct contexts of these stories can effectively demonstrate the application of the moral principles I delineate in Part I. Exploring whether the three economic enlightenments can extend to other cases or issues beyond incomplete contracts is not within the scope or objectives of this book.

Chapter 7 will examine the framework of my analysis. I will discuss areas needing further development, such as the impact of the institutional contexts affecting exchanges, and different frameworks, like feminist perspectives, which can be suitably compared and contrasted with the three economic enlightenments. My goal is to diversify the normative ethical theories accessible to scholars and students of BE. One may question whether it is appropriate to reference the theories of three European Enlightenment philosophers as the most effective method to accomplish this objective. This book may be subjected to critiques rooted in feminist or decolonial perspectives on BE. While I cannot offer definitive counterarguments to these objections, there is much to be said about the value of revisiting the history of Western ideas to uncover diversity and plurality. A fundamental aspect of decolonizing knowledge and curricula is to question the prevailing narratives surrounding the Western philosophical "canon."[38] I view this book as contributing to that objective, fitting into a larger effort that encompasses various perspectives extending beyond the canon.

Notes

1. According to Regina Hansen, Cratchit's family can be interpreted as Dickens's challenge to the dominant domestic ideal of Victorian times. See Hansen, R. (2011). The Cratchits on film: Neo-Victorian visions of domesticity. In Kohlke, M., & Gutleben, C. (eds.), *Neo-Victorian Families*. Amsterdam, Rodopi, 175–196.
2. Paul Davis argues that Bob Cratchit and his family truly embody the heart of the story. Their simple yet warm Christmas dinner and Tiny Tim's infectious joy create some of the most heartfelt moments in the book. See Davis, P. (1990). *Lives and Times of Ebenezer Scrooge*. New Haven, Yale University Press.

3. Dickens, C. (2010). *A Christmas Carol and Other Christmas Writings*. London, Penguin, 37.
4. Ibid.
5. Ibid., 40.
6. Ibid., 116.
7. To mention a few recent examples, see Crane, A., Matten, D., Glozer, S., & Spence L. (2019). *Business Ethics: Managing Corporate Citizenship and Sustainability in the Age of Globalization*. Oxford, Oxford University Press, chap. 3; Melé, D. (2020). *Business Ethics in Action*. London, Bloomsbury; Weiss, J. W. (2021). *Business Ethics: A Stakeholder and Issues Management Approach*. Oakland, Westchester Publishing Services; Graafland, J. (2022). *Ethics and Economics: An Introduction to Free Markets, Equality and Happiness*. Abingdon, Routledge; Gibson, K. (2023). *Ethics and Business: An Introduction*. Cambridge, Cambridge University Press; Shaw, W., & Miller, D. (2024). *Business Ethics: A Textbook with Cases*. Boston, Cengage Learning; De Cruz, A. F. (2024). *Business Ethics: An Institutional Governance Approach to Ethical Decision Making*. Singapore, Springer Nature Singapore. The same can be seen in surveys on normative ethical theories in BE textbooks: Derry, R., & Green, R. M. (1989). Ethical theory in business ethics: A critical assessment. *Journal of Business Ethics*, 8, 521–533.
8. See Robinson, B., & Enderle G. (2024). *Global Survey of Business Ethics 2022–2024: Teaching, Research and Training*, vol. 3, *Europe*. Geneva, Globethics Publications. Instead of providing additional literature sources, I encourage readers to conduct a simple experiment. Use an online search engine and enter the keywords "normative ethical theories," "business ethics," "courses," and "teaching." This search will reveal the scattered references to normative ethical theories in the course materials (learning goals, methodologies, lectures) of business ethics courses delivered globally.
9. The expression comes from Gauthier, D. (1986). *Morals by Agreement*. Oxford, Oxford University Press.
10. See Robinson & Enderle (eds.), *Global Survey of Business Ethics*.
11. Meijer, K., & Smit, M. (2024). The status of business ethics teaching, research and training: The Netherlands. In Robinson, B., & Enderle, G. (eds.), *Global Survey of Business Ethics: 2022–2024: Teaching, Research and Training: Volume 3: Europe*. Geneva: Globethics Global Series, 349. In the same volume, something similar is shown regarding Sweden: "Academia explores frameworks and approaches for ethical decision-making in business contexts. This includes examining topics such as moral reasoning, ethical dilemmas, ethical relativism, ethical frameworks (e.g. utilitarianism, deontology, virtue ethics) and the role

of personal values and biases in decision-making processes)" (Ibid., 391). See also Freeman, R. E. (2023). Foreword. In Painter-Morland, M., & Ten Bos, R. (eds.), *Business Ethics and Continental Philosophy*. Cambridge, Cambridge University Press.
12. See Bentham, J. ([1790] 2007). *An Introduction to the Principles of Morals and Legislation*. New York, Dover Philosophical Classics.
13. Mill, J. S. ([1861] 2017). *Utilitarianism. With Related Remarks from Mill's Other Writings*, ed. by B. Eggleston. Indianapolis, Hackett Publishing Company.
14. See Schultz, B. (2024). "Henry Sidgwick." *The Stanford Encyclopedia of Philosophy*. https://plato.stanford.edu/archives/fall2024/entries/sidgwick/. Last accessed Oct. 15, 2024.
15. Singer, P. (2023). *Animal Liberation Now: The Definitive Classic Renewed*. New York, Harper Perennial.
16. Hooker, B. (2023). Rule consequentialism. *The Stanford Encyclopedia of Philosophy*, 12. https://plato.stanford.edu/entries/consequentialism-rule/. Last accessed Oct. 15, 2023.
17. See Kant, I. ([1785] 2012). *Groundwork of the Metaphysics of Morals*, ed. by M. Gregor & J. Timmermann. New York, Cambridge University Press.
18. See Herman, B. (2016). *Morality as Rationality: A Study of Kant's Ethics*. London, Routledge; Dubbink, W., & Van Liedekerke, L. (2020). Rethinking the purity of moral motives in business: Kant against moral purism. *Journal of Business Ethics*, 167(3), 379–393.
19. See Brenkert, G. G. (2016). Business ethics and human rights: An overview. *Business and Human Rights Journal*, 1(2), 277–306.
20. See Toenjes, R. H. (2002). Why be moral in business? A Rawlsian approach to moral motivation. *Business Ethics Quarterly*, 12(1), 57–72.
21. See Aristotle (2014). *Nicomachean Ethics*, ed. by R. Crisp. Cambridge, Cambridge University Press.
22. MacIntyre, A. ([1981] 2007). *After Virtue*. London, Duckworth, 187.
23. Bruni, L., & Sugden, R. (2013). Reclaiming virtue ethics for economics. *Journal of Economic Perspectives*, 27(4), 141–164.
24. Virtue ethics in BE is also connected to Christian ethics. See Otte, J. T. (2009). Virtuous enterprises: The place of Christian ethics. *Finance & Bien Commun*, 33(1), 87–98; Melé, D. (2024). *The Humanistic Person-Centered Company*. Cham, Springer International Publishing. From this perspective, a new field of study under the label "Humanistic Management" emerged. See Pirson, M. (2017). *Humanistic Management: Protecting Dignity and Promoting Well-Being*. Cambridge, Cambridge University Press.

25. For an overview of feminism and care ethics, see Keller, J., & Kittay, E. F. (2017). Feminist ethics of care. In Garry, A., Khader, S. J., & Stone, A. (eds.), *The Routledge Companion to Feminist Philosophy*. New York, Routledge, 540–555.
26. See Liedtka, J. M. (1996). Feminist morality and competitive reality: A role for an ethic of care? *Business Ethics Quarterly*, 6(2), 179–200; Borgerson, J. L. (2023). On the harmony of feminist ethics and business ethics. In Panter, M., & Werhane, P. H. (eds.), *Leadership, Gender, and Organization*. Cham, Springer International Publishing, 37–62.
27. See Chan, G. K. Y. (2008). The relevance and value of Confucianism in contemporary business ethics. *Journal of Business Ethics*, 77, 347–360; Provis, C. (2020). Business ethics, Confucianism and the different faces of ritual. *Journal of Business Ethics*, 165(2), 191–204.
28. Rosile, G. A. (Ed.). (2016). *Tribal Wisdom for Business Ethics*. Bingley, Emerald Group Publishing.
29. See Michaelson, C. (2010). Revisiting the global business ethics question. *Business Ethics Quarterly*, 20(2), 237–251.
30. In this book, I employ the term "economic agent" to resemble what Dubbink and van der Deijl describe as a market participant: "A market participant is an actor that enters into transactions in the market with full independence, in the sense that the actor is recognized by others as acting independently. In other words, a market participant is an actor to whom we attribute market transactions." See Dubbink, W., & van der Deijl, W. (2023). Corporate responsibility and the morality of the market. In Dubbink, W., & van der Deijl, W. (eds.), *Business Ethics: A Philosophical Introduction*. Cham, Springer, 89.
31. See Bruni, L., & Zamagni, S. (2007). *Civil Economy: Efficiency, Equity, Public Happiness*. Oxford, Peter Lang; Bruni, L. (2012). *The Genesis and Ethos of the Market*. Basingstoke, Palgrave Macmillan; Pabst, A., & Scazzieri, R. (2019). Virtue, production, and the politics of commerce: Genovesi's "civil economy" revisited. *History of Political Economy*, 51(4), 703–729.
32. See, among others, Bruni, L., & Porta, P. L. (2003). Economia civile and pubblica felicità in the Italian Enlightenment. *History of Political Economy*, 35(5), 361–385; Israel, J. (2006). Enlightenment! Which Enlightenment? *Journal of the History of Ideas*, 67(3), 523–545; Sen, A. (2011a). *The Idea of Justice*. Cambridge, The Belknap Press, 5–10.
33. See Dubbink & Van Liedekerke, Rethinking the purity of moral motives; Santori, P. (2024). The market in the kingdom of ends: Kant's moral philosophy for business ethics. *Philosophy of Management*, 23, 239–256.
34. See Rawls, J. (2005). *Political Liberalism*. New York, Columbia University Press, xvii.

35. To be fair, this problem is often discussed in the main applications of Aristotle to BE. See Duska, R. F. (1993). Aristotle: A pre-modern post-modern? Implications for business ethics. *Business Ethics Quarterly*, *3*(3), 227–249; Solomon, R. C. (2004). Aristotle, ethics and business organizations. *Organization Studies*, *25*(6), 1021–1043.
36. To mention one example, in 2018 the *European Journal of the History of Economic Thought* devoted a special issue to Antonio Genovesi's economic thought. See Dal Degan, F. (2018). Antonio Genovesi and Italian economic thought: When ethics matters in economics. *The European Journal of the History of Economic Thought*, *25*(4), 524–530.
37. I refer to stories, cases, case studies, and fictional case studies interchangeably. This is due to the lack of a universally accepted definition of a case study in the literature. For further insights, see Dumez, H. (2015). What is a case, and what is a case study? *Bulletin of Sociological Methodology*, *127*(1), 43–57. The introductory section of Part II elaborates on the characteristics of these stories and their properties, including their representativity and applicability.
38. See Rickless, S. C. (2018). Brief for an inclusive anti-canon. *Metaphilosophy*, *49*(1–2), 167–181; Gordon, L. R. (2019). Decolonizing philosophy. *The Southern Journal of Philosophy*, *57*, 16–36.

PART I

Political Economy, Civil Economy, Moral Economy

Genovesi, Kant, and Smith were not three economists; instead, they were three philosophers who devoted their attention to economic issues in the eighteenth century. Smith was a professor of "Moral Philosophy" at Glasgow University; Genovesi, a professor of "Metaphysics" in Naples, was appointed as the chair of "Commerce and Mechanic" (Commercio e Meccanica) in 1754, and that was one of the first chairs of "Economics" in Europe.[1] Kant never taught economic sciences; however, his books and lectures on moral philosophy and the philosophy of right are replete with references to economic issues.[2]

The thoughts of the three philosophers have a few things in common. To begin with, we are told by their biographers (often former students) that their lectures were highly appreciated. Also, they lived in the Enlightenment period. To the question asked by Kant in his famous pamphlet *What Is Enlightenment?* (*Was ist Aufklärung?*, Kant, 1784),[3] all of them would have offered similar, yet not identical, answers. All three prioritized reason over superstition, critical thinking over dogmatism, and freedom and equality over hierarchy and privileges. The nonidentity of their views of the Enlightenment can be attributed to their cultural and geographical differences. Genovesi was imbued in the Italian Enlightenment, while Smith and Kant were part of the Scottish and German Enlightenments,[4] respectively. One cannot fully grasp one's views on economic issues without referencing their historical period. Therefore, Chapter 2 will be devoted to locating these authors in the intellectual climate of their own time. A complete reconstruction of their thinking is beyond the scope of this book and possibly any book. However, since we are interested in their views on markets and morality, we cannot ignore the philosophical background of their theories. In general, I aim to describe some central elements of their views. As happens with prominent and influential authors in the history of ideas, libraries have been filled with secondary literature. Chapter 2 will mostly focus on this literature, narrowing down the locus of analysis to some studies that addressed their views of markets and morality.

Chapter 2 has both intrinsic and instrumental value. On the one hand, research into the history of ideas remains valuable independent of any expected utility. Pieces of the theories elaborated by Genovesi, Kant, and Smith should be considered valuable in themselves by readers who have devoted their attention to more practical issues. On the other hand, when referring to ancient authors to explore contemporary problems, it remains essential to be aware of their sociocultural background and the many interpretations that subsequent scholars have given. Revealing their three views on morality and markets as the only three possible interpretations would be incorrect. For example, authoritative scholars have interpreted Smith's economic thought very differently; it has been three centuries since scholars debated the so-called Adam Smith Problem.[5] Therefore, Chapter 3 will build upon Chapter 2. In Chapter 3, I expose the three different views of Genovesi, Kant, and Smith on which moral principles should be endorsed by economic agents during a market exchange. There, I will assume that the reader knows both where these ideas come from and what the other alternative interpretations are (Chapter 2). As Part I is functional to Part II, in which I will consider three fictional case studies, Chapters 2 and 3 are inexorably related, and they cannot be fully comprehended in a disjointed manner.

Notes

1. See F. Dal Degan, Antonio Genovesi and Italian economic thought; see also Bruni, L., & Santori, P. (2022b). The other invisible hand: The social and economic effects of theodicy in Vico and Genovesi. *The European Journal of the History of Economic Thought*, 29(3), 548–566.
2. Etzioni, A. (1987). Toward a Kantian socio-economics. *Review of Social Economy*, 45(1), 37–47.
3. Kant, I. ([1784] 1991). An answer to the question: "What is Enlightenment?" In Reiss, H. S., *Kant: Political Writings*. Cambridge, Cambridge University Press.
4. See Fleischacker, S. (2013). *What Is Enlightenment?* London, Routledge.
5. See Montes, L. (2003). The Adam Smith problem: Its origins, the stages of the current debate, and one implication for our understanding of sympathy. *Journal of the History of Economic Thought*, 25(1), 63–90.

2 | Genovesi, Kant, and Smith

2.1 One, No One, and One Hundred Thousands

The years 2023 and 2024 marked significant milestones for two of the three main authors discussed in this book. These years saw the celebration of the three-hundredth anniversary of the births of Smith and Kant, recognizing their remarkable contributions to philosophy and other disciplines. Across the globe, numerous conferences, publications, symposia, and festivities were held. As a young scholar deeply interested in the philosophies of both thinkers, I attended several events where I had a similar initial impression: Kant and Smith have inspired countless scholars and continue to do so within the academic community. A corresponding observation, albeit on a reduced scale, can be made regarding Genovesi, whose contributions have inspired numerous generations of Italian scholars – his three-hundredth anniversary was celebrated in 2013 with numerous conferences and conventions throughout Italy. However, as I have already mentioned in the Introduction, Genovesi has garnered less recognition on a global level due to the absence of translations into the English language of his main works.

The events and publications associated with the three-hundredth anniversaries have unveiled an additional, less apparent, shared characteristic among the three authors: the curious situation in which they have driven their interpreters. What I have observed while attending conferences and reading publications is that scholars generally agree that the authors they are studying – whether Smith, Genovesi, or Kant – possess a coherent line of thought. The interpreter's role is to illuminate the intended meaning that lies hidden within the texts, correspondence, biography, and the historical, political, and economic contexts surrounding the author. As I wrote in an article inspired by my attendance at one of the events of the three-hundredth anniversary of Smith,[1] everyone seems to agree that there is a "true Adam Smith" to be found, and the same can be argued for Genovesi or Kant. The curious element arises from the fact that interpreters frequently assert they've identified the "true Adam Smith" or "true Immanuel Kant," while all the other interpreters are dealing with inaccurate representations. There's nothing surprising about it, as this outcome appears to be closely tied to inquiries into the history of ideas.[2]

This chapter does not aim to uncover the "true" or "real" Genovesi, Smith, and Kant. Instead, I have three more modest objectives. First, I aim to highlight specific aspects of the historical, political, economic, and religious landscape of the eighteenth-century societies where these authors resided, including elements of the Neapolitan-Italian, Scottish, and German Enlightenment. In parallel, I want to mention some elements of the biographies of the three authors that might be relevant for understanding the person behind the thinker and how the thinker defined the person. To fulfill these two ambitious objectives, which could warrant a book on their own, I will build upon what I began in the introduction to Part I. Rather than focusing on three or six separate sections dedicated to each of the three authors, I will explore their similarities and differences. This exploration may involve contextual aspects and biographical elements – or, as is often the case, a blend of both.

An additional section will be dedicated to addressing the asymmetry among the three authors considered. Kant was indirectly influenced by Genovesi's ideas and directly by Smith's, while both Smith and Genovesi had no knowledge of each other's philosophies and they did not know Kant's thought given the chronological timeline. Thus, one section will examine the strength of these ties and their consequences on the aspect of Kant's moral philosophy that will be the focus of this study.

The third aim of this chapter is to showcase different interpretations of Smith's political economy, Genovesi's civil economy, and Kant's moral economy. I will provide an overview of the secondary literature for each author, highlighting key philosophical and economic contributions with a particular emphasis on the relationship between markets and morality. I do not purport to provide a systematic literature review; instead, I offer a curated selection that serves both to familiarize readers with some issues and controversies presented by these three authors and, concurrently, to position my interpretations, which will be elaborated upon in Chapter 3, within the broader literature. At the same time, I am not suggesting any relativistic approach to the history of ideas. I am convinced Kant's, Genovesi's, and Smith's thoughts have their intended meanings and that we, as interpreters, can approximate those. However, I also believe the curious situation is inescapable, and the only antidote we have is the pluralism of interpretations. By presenting many interpretations in this chapter, I will explicitly and implicitly show the readers the strengths and limits of my own interpretation of the three economic enlightenments. Borrowing Kant's honest and suggestive conclusion of the *Groundwork of the Metaphysics of Morals*, "this is all that can fairly be required of a philosophy that strives in its principles to the very boundary of human reason."[3]

2.2 Similarities

Kant, Genovesi, and Smith share numerous commonalities. First, they all served as university professors. In 1752, Smith became the chair of moral philosophy at the University of Glasgow. Genovesi held different positions at the Royal University of Naples: from 1741 to 1745, he was a professor of Metaphysics; from 1745 to 1753, he was the chair of Ethics and Moral Philosophy; and, finally, in 1754, he was appointed to the Chair of Commerce and Mechanics (Commercio e Meccanica).[4] The last passage is particularly significant as Genovesi occupied one of the first chairs of economic matters instituted in Europe,[5] and, using his own words, he transitioned from being a metaphysician to becoming a merchant, "*da metafisico a mercatante.*"[6] Kant took a long path to secure a chair at the university. From 1747 to 1755, he worked as a private tutor, visiting various homes to teach young students primarily about natural sciences. In 1755, he became a *Privatdozent* at the University of Königsberg, earning his salary not from the institution but directly from students through tuition fees. Additionally, starting in 1766, he served as the assistant librarian at the Royal Castle Library in Königsberg. His academic journey culminated in 1770 when he was appointed to the Chair of Logic and Metaphysics at the University of Königsberg.[7]

The three professors were also philosophers who dedicated some of their attention to economic matters. This is particularly clear in the case of Smith, often regarded as the "father" of economic science.[8] His work *An Inquiry into the Nature and Causes of Wealth of Nations*[9] is viewed as a foundational text for classical/political economy and neo-classical economics. Genovesi was forced by the course of events to devote his attention to economic matters. Upon becoming the Chair of Commerce and Mechanics, and before publishing his *Lezioni di Commercio o sia d'Economia Civile* (1765–1767),[10] he began studying numerous local and international texts related to the field. For instance, in 1757, he oversaw the Italian release of John Cary's (1649–1722) *An Essay on the State of England*, enhancing it with his own commentary and one chapter titled "Thought on Universal Commerce" ("Ragionamento Sul Commercio Universale").[11] Simultaneously, he engaged with Montesquieu's *The Spirit of Laws*, as testified by an Italian edition published after Genovesi's death (1777)[12] that included his annotations. Among the three philosophers, Kant seems to be the least interested in economic issues as he never dedicated a book to the topic. And yet, as I will show later, he frequently referred to economic topics in his works. One element that can testify to his interest was his close friendship with the English merchant Joseph Green (1727–1786) and his former student Christian Jakob Kraus (1753–1807), the latter being fundamental for Kant's knowledge of the topics explored in *The Wealth of Nations*. As Fleischaker documented:

A possible conduit of Smith's doctrines to Kant was the aforementioned Kraus, generally considered the most important expositor of Smith in Germany, and one of Kant's colleagues and best friends. ... returned to Königsberg as a professor of practical philosophy in 1781–2 He there became Kant's favourite lunch companion, so close a friend that for years people sent greetings to Kraus via Kant, the town of Königsberg is said to have marvelled at the sight of the two men always walking or sitting together.[13]

I will later demonstrate how significant economic concepts are in Kant's moral philosophy; for now, these two friendships illustrate how much the professor of Königsberg, whose love for knowledge had encyclopedic qualities, also valued economic issues.

As known, the eighteenth-century (political, civil, moral) economy was not a stand-alone science, or at least it had not reached the degree of autonomy and formalization that would emerge in later elaborations – above all, the rise of economics at the end of the nineteenth century. Genovesi, Kant, and particularly Smith played key roles in shaping the discipline. However, neither Kant nor Smith identified as economists, and Genovesi even humorously labeled himself a merchant instead of an economist. They were three philosophers whose interests ranged from metaphysics to astronomy, theology to natural sciences, morality to mechanics, and rhetoric to botany, among other fields. In their intellectual endeavors, they also considered economic topics as related to politics, law, morality, and other disciplines.

Another trait shared by Genovesi, Kant, and Smith concerns the economic reality of the countries in which they lived. Section 2.3 will demonstrate that the Scottish, Italian, and Prussian socio-political and economic contexts differed, but here, I show that they shared one common element beneath these distinctions. I'm referring to the First Industrial Revolution, a captivating period that the three philosophers witnessed at its onset. However, they did not observe its subsequent developments, which had significant implications regarding the economic issues that were the subject of their theoretical discussions. Smith stands out as the most obvious example. In the period from 1776, the year of Smith's *Wealth of Nations*, to 1817, the year in which David Ricardo (1772–1823) published his *On the Principles of Political Economy and Taxation*, England changed radically. During these years, the world faced two significant revolutions – the French and the American – alongside another equally vital one: the Industrial Revolution. When Smith spoke of the division of labor in the pin factory, he was describing a production environment with no more than ten workers. The Industrial Revolution transformed both the economic landscape and the organization of factories. Indeed, society transitioned from an agricultural system to an industrial one. The steam engine, invented by James Watt (1736–1819), symbolized the Industrial Revolution and significantly transformed the economic landscape. Previously, producing goods relied on human-, animal-, or waterpower. However, with the advent of the coal-fired steam engine, this limitation was surpassed, leading to the development of modern factories. By the late nineteenth century, these evolved into large manufacturing plants, marking a shift toward predominantly industrial capitalism. Neither Smith, Genovesi, nor Kant lived long enough to witness these epochal changes. We must remember this when evaluating their theories about economic agents' behaviors in the market, as we may mistakenly think they were already theorizing about contemporary market societies.

All three philosophers are recognized as Enlightenment thinkers. Among the trio, Kant authored a distinguished treatise regarding the concept of Enlightenment. In his own words:

Enlightenment is man's emergence from his self-incurred immaturity. Immaturity is the inability to use one's own understanding without the guidance of another. This immaturity is self-incurred if its cause is not lack of understanding, but lack of resolution and courage to use it without the guidance of another. The motto of enlightenment is therefore: Sapere aude! Have courage to use your own understanding.[14]

Reason and science constituted the two foundational pillars upon which the structure of the eighteenth-century European Enlightenment was erected. The Enlightenment thinkers engaged in a battle on two fronts. On the cultural-academic front, they needed to confront and overcome superstitions, prejudices, and uncritical adherence to traditions through a reasoned, critical perspective. Correspondingly, their goal was to challenge societies built on privileges and hierarchies – whether divinely or naturally imposed – and censorship. They aimed to transition, through reforms or revolutions, toward a society that was free, equal, and possibly fraternal, where individuals would be educated in the public application of reason:

For enlightenment of this kind, all that is needed is freedom. And the freedom in question is the most innocuous form of all-freedom to make public use of one's reason in all matters. But I hear on all sides the cry: Don't argue! The officer says: Don't argue, get on parade! The tax-official: Don't argue, pay! The clergyman: Don't argue, believe! (Only one ruler in the world says: Argue as much as you like and about whatever you like, but obey!) All this means restrictions on freedom everywhere.[15]

To argue and to do it in the public sphere was fundamentally the objective of the Enlightenment, which did not merely articulate the aspirations of a select few but encapsulated the *Weltanschauung* of an entire epoch. The history that should be transformed by philosophy had its own philosophy of history. The Enlightenment thinkers of the eighteenth century viewed the transition from the "dark ages" of the Middle Ages through Humanism and the Renaissance as a continual progression of humanity and its most defining aspect, reason. Genovesi, Kant, and Smith actively engaged with this intellectual milieu and contributed to its development. Genovesi's and Smith's theories highlight the economic impacts of the Enlightenment project: the emergence of a commercial society founded on free exchanges among individuals aimed to dismantle the feudal system's hierarchy, privileges, and rigid structure. The upcoming section will explore the specifics of the German, Italian-Neapolitan, and Scottish Enlightenments. Before that, we should concentrate on two interconnected factors that relate to the commitment of the three philosophers to the Enlightenment project.

Isaac Newton's (1643–1727) theory of universal gravitation, which contributed significantly to the dissemination of the concept of an ordered and rational universe, exerted a profound influence on Enlightenment thought. The impact of the natural sciences on the social sciences during the eighteenth century can be attributed to the considerable prestige attained by the former. The rising economic science made no exception.[16] In numerous respects, the contributions of Newton and the principles of Newtonian physics were pivotal to the theoretical frameworks established by Smith, Genovesi, and Kant. Genovesi's theory of reciprocity, viewed as the essential law governing human relationships, is influenced by a kind of moral Newtonianism that shaped his scientific perspective.[17] Ferdinando Galiani (1728–1787), a contemporary of his and probably the most famous Italian economist of that period, directly referenced Newtonian gravitational theory: just as planets stay in their orbits due to gravitational law in Newton's mechanics, a similar principle applies in economics transactions, where "love of money, namely the desire of living happy, is in the man exactly what gravity is to physics."[18] Galiani's methodology asserts that the love for money is just as precise and scientific as the law of gravity. Specifically, this love for money equates to a desire for happiness. Like Galiani, Genovesi articulated his ideas using Newtonian concepts. However, while Galiani claimed that the only fundamental force is the "love of money," Genovesi identified two driving forces behind human behavior: *forza concentriva* (self-love) and *forza diffusiva* (love for others).[19]

Newton's influence on Smith's ideas has been subject to scholarly inquiries.[20] Hetherington argues that Smith's *History of Astronomy* profoundly resembles Newton's argument, especially on the concept of natural law, and this also had consequences on the economic arguments exposed in *Wealth*.[21] Montes is critical of this juxtaposition and argues for a different connection between the two thinkers:

> this wrong image has given place to many interpretations that view Smith as an inheritor of Newton. His system of economics would be an image of Newton's system of the world. But as I have argued in this essay, Newton's methodology moves away from a positivistic reading, which is predominant in modern economics. Newton's methodology, and Smith's, as I have attempted to show, entail a notion of an open system, a permanent motivation for seeking truth and an emphasis on the method of resolution above composition. In sum, a distinctively Scottish Enlightenment's approach, that favours phenomena over abstractions.[22]

My book does not aim to evaluate these differences in the literature, but it is clear that Newton and Newtonian concepts served as reference points for Smith and the broader Scottish Enlightenment.

The significance of Newtonian concepts within Kant's philosophy transcends mere references or re-elaborations of particular natural laws or principles.[23] The Kant–Newton relationship necessitates a somewhat more detailed explanation than that provided by Smith and Genovesi cases. In a particular sense, Kant's philosophical endeavor, as elucidated in the *Critique of Pure Reason*, represents an effort to establish and substantiate, from a philosophical standpoint, the accomplishments that modern science had recently attained. He confronted two great authors and, to a certain extent, intellectual mentors who, from opposite sides, posed challenges to his project on providing an adequate philosophical foundation for modern science and, in particular, physics. I am referring to Christian Wolff (1679–1754), one of the most important authors of German Rationalism, and David Hume, a Scottish philosopher who was part of British empiricism. The conclusion of the *Critique of Pure Reason* goes as follows:

> Now as far as the observers of a scientific method are concerned, they have here the choice of proceeding either dogmatically or skeptically, but in either case they have the obligation of proceeding systematically. If I here name with regard to the former the famous Wolff, and with regard to the latter David Hume, then for my present purposes I can leave the others unnamed. The critical path alone is still open.[24]

Kant's philosophy is characterized by the notion of criticism, denoting an investigation into the limitations of a particular faculty and concurrently exploring its conditions of possibility and legitimacy. He opposed the dogmatism of Enlightenment philosophers, such as Wolff, who used reason to challenge tradition yet neglected to examine the boundaries and potential of reason itself. Differently from what Wolff believed, human beings cannot have access to the ultimate principles of reality – the *noumena*, things-in-themselves. This limit becomes the ground and condition of the possibility of the scientific knowledge of phenomena, things as they appear to an observer. Differently from what Hume argued, the laws through which reason organizes the materials coming from senses have the character of necessity and universality:

> Now such universal cognitions, which at the same time have the character of inner necessity, must be clear and certain for themselves, independently of experience; hence one calls them a priori cognitions: whereas that which is merely borrowed from experience is, as it is put, cognized only a posteriori, or empirically. Now what is especially remarkable is that even among our experiences cognitions are mixed in that must have their origin a priori and that perhaps serve only to establish connection among our representations of the senses.[25]

Hume argued that the perceived necessity of rational principles like causation arises from repeated subjective experiences and is thus an illusion. This is in line with his own interpretation of Newton: "It is clear, therefore, that Hume views all of Newton's laws of motion as inductively derived empirical propositions, which (deceptively) appear to be derived from reason simply because the constant and regular experience on which they are in fact based is so pervasive."[26] In contrast, Kant sought to preserve the necessity and universality of human knowledge of phenomena through his criticism and the concept of a priori. He acknowledged Hume's importance in awakening him from his "dogmatic slumber"[27] but, at the same time, he attempted to rescue science, and in particular Newtonian science, from the threat of Hume's skepticism. At the end of our brief detour in Kant's philosophy, we can fairly argue that, in a sense, Newton's ideas were more than central to his thinking.

The last point I want to explore, shared by Genovesi, Kant, and Smith, is perhaps one of the more intriguing aspects. All three Enlightenment philosophers had complicated relationships with both religious and, occasionally, political authorities. Genovesi was a Catholic priest. And yet, the freedom of thought with which he discussed pantheism, reason, and faith was considered too innovative for his time.[28] His interest in John Locke's (1632–1704) doctrine of the origin of ideas and empiricism was too far from the neo-scholasticism of the time endorsed by the Catholic Church.[29] In 1744, to avoid excommunication and heeding the counsel of Celestino Galiani (1681–1753) – who had helped him secure his first chair in metaphysics – Genovesi was compelled to include an appendix in his metaphysical work, which essentially served as a declaration of Catholic faith. Despite this addition, his theological-philosophical work faced fierce criticism from ecclesiastical circles. Consequently, his first metaphysics book was released without the approval of the archbishop of Naples, Cardinal Spinelli, as Genovesi declined to omit specific passages from the text. After losing his chair in metaphysics, Genovesi took on the newly established ethics chair in 1745, viewing it as a temporary fix that left him quite bitter. His contentious relationship with the ecclesiastical authorities persisted throughout his career, culminating in the inclusion of his *Lezioni di Commercio o sia d'Economia Civile* on the Index of Prohibited Books in 1817. In 1748, during a competition for a chair of theology, one of his competitors (the abbot Molinari) "presented to the Pope a list of 14 heretical propositions ... which he claimed had been extracted from the theological manuscripts of the Abbot Genovesi."[30] He was also harshly attacked and accused by a friar from Puglia, Father Maria T. Mamachio, in the book published in the year of Genovesi's death (1769), entitled *Del Diritto libero della Chiesa di acquista e di possesso beni temporali, sia movable che immobili*. Mamachio's charges are discussed in an appendix to Giuseppe Maria Galanti's (1743–1806) *Elogio storico* (1772), where Genovesi's student defends his teacher with extreme force and conviction from the accusations of heresy. Galanti wrote: "Mr. Genovesi was regarded as a monster, because he introduced freedom of thought into Italy; and because he cited the works of Galileo, Newton, Grotius. This is how the good and the true are always received by the students of error."[31] This marks a pivotal moment for both his academic journey and the Italian economic thought tradition. Genovesi, previously sidelined as a philosopher and theologian, reinvented himself from a metaphysician to a merchant, as he liked to say. The Royal University of Naples established an unprecedented chair in commerce and mechanics for him, one of the earliest known in Europe.[32]

Smith's relationship with the Presbyterian Kirk of Scotland was less eventful but not less problematic. In his hometown of Kirkaldy, the young Smith immersed himself in the devout Calvinist environment, where he forged a lasting friendship with the (future) Reverend John Drysdale (1718–1788), renowned for his "modified" approach to Calvinist theology. When appointed as a Professor at the University of Glasgow, Smith "signed the Calvinist Confession of Faith before the Presbytery of Glasgow"[33] and endorsed his mentor Francis Hutcheson's (1694–1746) responses to an archaic and oppressive interpretation of Calvinism, advocating for a more contemporary and tolerant approach. In the early eighteenth century, the Presbyterian Kirk of Scotland systematically suppressed all manifestations of dissent and heresy. A notable instance of this is the banishment of his esteemed colleague, Hume, from the Scottish academic milieu. Smith experienced Kirk's evolution toward a more moderate stance;[34] nevertheless, he remained profoundly circumspect in articulating his genuine theological convictions. Two signs illustrate his reluctance to discuss controversial theological issues. Firstly, Smith never released a treatise solely focused on theology, although it's unclear if he might have written one since he ordered half of his manuscript to be burned after his passing. More clearly, he hesitated to publish the *Dialogues Concerning Natural Religion*, authored by his close friend Hume. Hume tasked Smith with publishing his manuscript, but Smith was bewildered and ultimately backed out of his commitment to bring the *Dialogues* to print while Hume was dying. The cautious philosopher likely worried about being labeled a heretic or, at the very least, perceived as sympathetic to Hume's controversial views on theology. Overall, I agree with Kennedy when he writes that "Adam Smith's religiosity is enigmatic because of the circumstances in which he worked as a moral philosopher."[35] Furthermore, a cautious stance regarding the Presbyterian Kirk may also relate to Smith's concern for the most significant person in his life: "The main cause, I suggest, for his lifelong circumspection in religious matters was his deep love for his mother, Margaret Douglas Smith, and his respect for her religious beliefs. He chose not to provoke public controversy by anything he might write on religion that could come to her notice, as it surely would."[36]

Kant's conflicts with political-religious authorities are perhaps one of the most famous aspects of his life. From 1792 to 1794, he engaged in ongoing discussions with King Friedrich Wilhelm II's (1744–1797) cabinet and its censor about his religious writings on radical evil. To bypass theological censorship, he attempted to compile and publish his essays on this topic in a book (*Religion within the Bounds of Bare Reason*) through the approval of the University of Jena. Ultimately, this effort led to a reprimand, and Kant promised to stop writing on these subjects: "I find that, as Your Majesty's loyal subject, in order not to fall under suspicion, it will be the surest course for me to abstain entirely from all public lectures on religious topics, whether on natural or revealed religion, and not only from lectures but also from publications. I hereby promise this."[37] He honored his promise, at least until the monarch died in 1797.

I have shown that Genovesi, Kant, and Smith shared numerous commonalities. To further explore the profiles of these three authors and the historical contexts in which they lived, I shall now proceed to illustrate some differences.

2.3 Differences

Genovesi was a Catholic priest and abbot, whereas Kant and Smith were raised and lived in Protestant countries without holding any official religious positions. I do not wish to emphasize this difference in order to argue that Genovesi was more constrained and subject to censorship by religious authorities. I have previously shown that the Presbyterian Kirk of Scotland and the Prussian sovereigns exerted similar levels of control as the Catholic hierarchies. I am also not implying that Smith and Kant operated within a distinct "spirit of capitalism" as defined by Max Weber (1864–1920).[38] Weber indeed selected Benjamin Franklin (1706–1790) as the epitome of the "spirit of capitalism," and Smith even shared a meal with the Founding Father of America. It is also accurate to state that the counterreformation hindered the growth of commerce and trade in Italy, favoring an agricultural and feudal structure, and this marked a difference between northern and central Europe.[39] However, the fully developed manifestations of different spirits of capitalism[40] had yet to emerge during the times of our three philosophers, who could only witness the early stages of economic realities – the seeds of development rather than the mature fruits that would have come with the Industrial Revolution.

A further distinction relates to the academic books of the three philosophers. Genovesi and Smith focused on economic matters in two significant books, whereas Kant did not compose a similar treatise.

This indicates that understanding Kant's economic theories necessitates further research to find them in his moral, political, legal, and historical writings. For instance, my interpretation of his moral principle for economic agents will primarily draw from his 1785 work on moral philosophy and lecture notes from the ethics class recorded by his students in the same year.[41] In the secondary literature review, I will show that other authors have identified Kant's primary contributions to economic thought in different books or periods. The lack of a reference point, such as Genovesi's *Lezioni* or Smith's *Inquiry*, complicates the interpreters' task and somewhat diminishes clarity. This is why I needed to create the label "moral economy" to classify Kant's economic concepts, as civil economy and political economy are already common in the literature related to Genovesi and Smith.

The disparity in their academic contributions extends beyond their economic publications. A comparison of the number of books published during their lifetimes reveals a significant imbalance between Kant, Genovesi, and Smith. The former authors published numerous books on various subjects. Although Genovesi's works have yet to be translated into English, he wrote about metaphysics, logic, morality, commerce, political philosophy, and several academic letters discourses.[42] Kant was a notably prolific author, with his works categorized into three distinct periods: 1747–1760, focusing on natural sciences; 1760–1781, which marks a transition between British empiricism and critical philosophy; and after 1781, renowned for transcendental philosophy and historical-political writings. In contrast, Smith completed two major works during his lifetime: *The Theory of Moral Sentiments*[43] (1759; *Theory*, henceforth) and *The Wealth of Nations* (1776; *Wealth*, henceforth), along with some posthumous publications addressing a range of subjects, including ancient physics and the history of astronomy.[44] Does this suggest that Smith was a less systematic author compared to his Enlightenment colleagues? I believe this assessment is flawed for a couple of reasons. Firstly, as I previously stated, Smith wrote extensively beyond what he published, and he inexplicably sought to have some of his works destroyed. Secondly, and crucially, in the conclusion of his *Theory*, Smith alluded to another significant project he intended to undertake:

I shall in another discourse, endeavour to give an account of the general principles of law and government, and of the different revolutions they have undergone in the different ages and periods of society, not only in what concerns justice, but in what concerns police, revenue, and arms, and whatever else is the object of law. I shall not, therefore, at present enter into any further detail concerning the history of jurisprudence.[45]

Much like Genovesi and Kant, Smith was interested in various facets of reality, which is evident in the encyclopedic nature of his two main works that, although centered on moral and economic topics, delve into numerous areas of knowledge.

Key differences among the three authors lie in their relationships with the Enlightenment. Kant participated in the Enlightenment period and project while maintaining the requisite distance to engage with it critically. As I previously illustrated, his criticism begins with examining the limits and conditions that define the legitimacy of reason across different domains, including metaphysics, morality, and religion. Genovesi and Smith appear to be more reflective of their eras, although the Neapolitan philosopher formulated a unique critical approach that, as I will demonstrate in the following section, may have unintentionally influenced Kant. Nonetheless, this is neither the main nor the most significant difference between Kant, Genovesi, and Smith regarding the Enlightenment.

The title of this book clearly indicates that discussing the Enlightenment in singular terms is overly simplistic. In Europe, numerous manifestations of Enlightenment existed, each rooted in the shared principles outlined in the previous section, yet distinguished by their unique characteristics. Understanding these distinctions is vital for grasping the political and cultural contexts in which thinkers like Genovesi, Kant, and Smith operated. For instance, the German Enlightenment cannot be fully appreciated without considering the political, religious, and cultural conditions from which it arose. Unlike the French Enlightenment, the German *Aufklärung* did not represent a burgeoning bourgeois class seeking to carve out its social position while challenging the authority of an absolutist monarch. The German territory was fragmented into numerous small states controlled by local nobles and landlords, which hindered the emergence of the bourgeois class. Consequently, German Enlightenment thinkers were more moderate in their calls for political and religious reforms compared to their French or English counterparts. Additionally, they viewed Frederick II of Prussia, their Enlightened monarch, as a catalyst for social and cultural change. One example is his appointment of Pierre Louis

Moreau de Maupertius (1698–1759) as president of the Royal Prussian Academy of Sciences, which facilitated the exchange of ideas from the French and British Enlightenments. Kant's moral and political writings, along with his reformist and contractualist perspectives, can be contextualized within this framework.[46]

Kant's establishment of morality based on the principles of autonomy and freedom can also be traced within the German Enlightenment thinkers' emphasis on autonomy and self-determination in opposition to any form of dogmatism. Nevertheless, the German Enlightenment constituted a pluralistic movement. We can identify at least three distinct phases, with Kant serving as a significant figure and protagonist of the third phase. The first phase can be located at the end of the seventeenth century and the beginning of the eighteenth century and it is known as *Frühaufklärung* (early Enlightenment).[47] The main feature was an alliance between Christian Thomasius's (1655–1728) advocation for a philosophy that could serve as a means of civil progress and Pietism. Pietism was a religious movement that originated with German Lutherans in the seventeenth century. Its key characteristics focused on returning to the core message of Luther's teachings, including a strong emphasis on personal faith and individual religious renewal in opposition to traditional theology. It encouraged both private and public reading of the Scriptures in gatherings known as *collegia pietatis* and highlighted the practical outcomes of a vibrant faith, such as asceticism and legalism. Numerous educational institutions were established, and the young Kant, from 1732 to 1740, attended the Collegium Fridericiarum, which was directed by Pastor Franz Albert Schulz (1692–1763), a noted Pietist theologian and educator. The response to Pietism and Thomasius's practical methodology was rooted in Wolff's rationalism, which asserted a systematic, logical, and ontological explanation of reality grounded in reason. Philosophy transformed from being a tool for social change to the key for accessing the deepest structures of reality. According to Wolff, by beginning with clear and well-defined rational principles, like the principle of noncontradiction, and using a deductive method, a philosopher can explore every facet of reality. This second phase of Enlightenment was followed by the *Spätaufklärung* (late Enlightenment),[48] which shifted the focus back to practical issues, including anthropological, religious, and cultural matters. This period is characterized by Kant's criticism, which notably commenced with criticism of Wolff's dogmatic rationalism, coupled with a resurgence of the spirit inherent in Thomasius's philosophy as reinterpreted through Leibniz's philosophy and British empiricism.[49]

Smith was a key figure in the Scottish Enlightenment. Like their German[50] and Italian-Neapolitan[51] counterparts, Scottish Enlightenment thinkers believed in the advancement of humanity throughout history. As Paganelli summarized well:

> This large crowd of literati was closely bound together by family relations, teacher-student relations, and bonds of friendship. They would interact regularly not just in the three major universities of Scotland (Glasgow, Edinburgh, and Aberdeen), but also and especially in intellectual clubs and societies, such as the Rankenian Club, the Literary Society of Glasgow, the Aberdeen's Philosophical Society, the Select Society, the Poker Club, the Oyster Club, and the Philosophical Society of Edinburgh which eventually turned into the Royal Society of Edinburgh, among the most famous ones.[52]

Like the German Enlightenment, pinpointing the boundaries or main topics discussed in the Scottish Enlightenment is challenging, particularly given its mutual influences with what is referred to as the English Enlightenment – this has to be also traced to the political relationships between Scotland and England and the creation, via the Acts of Union of 1707 promoted under Queen Anne's (1665–1714) reign, of Great Britain. Some argue that the Scottish Enlightenment is just the product of Scottish thinkers like Hutcheson, Smith, Hume, and Thomas Reid (1710–1796), while others consider English thinkers like Shaftesbury as part of that tradition.[53] Moreover, there were many different positions and even oppositions in the same movement. The most famous example is Reid's philosophy of common sense, according to which we have a direct relation to things and not ideas, as a reaction to Hume's skepticism, which Reid saw as the culmination of Descartes's reflections on *res cognitans*, mediated by George Berkley's (1685–1753) and Locke's idealism.

For our purposes, it is noteworthy to emphasize a distinctive aspect of the Scottish Enlightenment compared to other European Enlightenments. This is captured by the title of Smith's book of moral philosophy published in 1759, *The Theory of Moral Sentiments*. Scottish Enlightenment thinkers place significant value on the role of reason; however, they also accord considerable importance to affects, feelings, and sentiments in shaping our moral conduct.[54] In Smith's moral and economic philosophy, emphasis on moral sentiments is complemented by two other significant characteristics of the Scottish Enlightenment, namely, the belief in a natural order of the universe and, as a consequence, supraindividual mechanisms that result in advantageous outcomes. More broadly, as I shall elaborate in the section devoted to Smith's interpreters, a recurring theme in Smith's *Theory* and *Wealth* is that nature or providence – however these concepts are to be interpreted – has endowed humanity with inherent sentiments that, through interpersonal interactions, tend to yield beneficial outcomes. Within the *Theory*, fundamental sentiments of sympathy and resentment give rise to codes of morality and justice. In *Wealth*, basic sentiments of self-love and the impulse to engage in trade, barter, and exchange, coupled with a sense of justice, contribute to the prosperity of nations. This phenomenon stems from the belief in natural religion, accompanied by an implicit assumption that the universe is, or operates as if it is, structured to foster positive outcomes through spontaneous processes – one of the distinctive, albeit not original, contributions of the Scottish Enlightenment.[55]

The Italian Enlightenment is often characterized as "late" compared to other European Enlightenments.[56] This observation is especially pertinent to the Neapolitan Enlightenment, where numerous factors impeded the assimilation of Enlightenment ideas and obstructed moral and civil progress. Specifically, I am referring to the ancien régime mentality of the Neapolitan agricultural and feudal society, which was upheld by foreign dominations such as the Spanish Aragon, the Austrian monarchy, and the Bourbon monarchs of France, as well as the Catholic Reformation of the seventeenth century. Many Neapolitan Enlightenment thinkers widely shared this feeling of cultural and civil underdevelopment. From Galanti's very colorful pages of Genovesi's biography, we can derive an accurate and heartfelt description of the Italian cultural panorama, where thinkers were too busy studying "antiquity ... ; while human reason and the sciences, which improve man and perfect government, were making marvelous progress elsewhere."[57] Something similar can be read in the pages of another biographer of Genovesi:

The city of Naples had no public libraries other than that of S. Angelo a Nilo ... [where] Genovesi did not find Spinosa's works, and was forced to work second-hand on his exhibits. The novelties were suspect; and the Holy Office took care that the suspect things were not only closed, but buried ... Few read; and they allowed little to be read.[58]

This is why Genovesi and his students, heirs of the great tradition of Giambattista Vico (1668–1744) and Pietro Giannone (1676–1748), conceived themselves as "reformers," that is, intellectuals with the aim of fostering social change. The market was seen as one of the places where the transition from a feudal, static, hierarchical society toward a free, equal, fraternal one could be realized.

The thirty years from 1750 to 1780 can be regarded as the golden age of Italian economic thought. During this time, it appears that the Enlightenment in Italy selected economic science as its key discipline. Genovesi's civil economy emphasizes that technology and scientific research must not be seen as goals on their own but rather as instruments for advancing civilization and enhancing the population's well-being. Remarkably, Genovesi chose to title his economic book *Lezioni* (Lessons) differently, for example, from Smith's *Inquiry*. The relationships he built with students were crucial for the Neapolitan thinker. This highlights the civic aspect of his contributions to economic science and its connection to the Neapolitan Enlightenment project.

One can observe another peculiar, although not exclusive, aspect of Neapolitan Enlightenment in the work of one of Genovesi's students, namely Giacinto Dragonetti (1738–1818). This pertains to the strong anti-feudal polemics and the advocacy for civil reforms to challenge privileges and rent-seeking behaviors. Genovesi and Dragonetti argued that the Kingdom of Naples was plagued by significant corruption and a decline in civic virtues. Most citizens prioritized their own interests, leading to a steady deterioration in attention toward the common good and the social and economic progress of society. Dragonetti, along with other figures of the Italian Enlightenment, strongly criticized this situation, yearning for a revival of splendor and prosperity in Naples. His criticism of feudalism, articulated in his work *Origine dei feudi nei regni di Napoli e Sicilia* (On the origin of feuds in the kingdoms of Naples and Sicily, 1788),[59] showcases this perspective. As his mentor Genovesi, Dragonetti believed that feudalism hindered civil development by incentivizing corrupt rewards and privileges while stifling genuinely virtuous actions. In contrast, a well-structured reward system that recognizes true virtue and promotes the collective good can help restore the connections among citizens and foster their civic virtues. For the Neapolitan reformers, philosophy's purpose is, or at least should be, to serve as the intellectual engine for civil progress. Genovesi contended that abstract theories and debates should be substituted with more tangible and practical insights. I will share a passage from his *Discorso sopra il vero fine delle lettere e delle scienze* (1753), which can be regarded as a manifesto of the Neapolitan Enlightenment:

> It cannot be said that reason is in a nation that has reached its maturity, where it still resides more in the abstract intellect than in the heart and hands. It is always beautiful, but where it is not operative it is still immature, which can, if you like, adorn men, but not be useful to them ... We still love to argue more than to act ... A certain vanity of genius still keeps us attached to things more specious than useful, we still believe ourselves greater when we are admired as incomprehensible than when we are considered useful.[60]

The Neapolitan Enlightenment embraced the theme of practical knowledge, which had long been cherished in the Italian tradition. Genovesi expresses his disappointment that neighboring nations have advanced in sciences while his own people remain backward. Nonetheless, in his view, the Kingdom of Naples possesses all the necessary advantages to showcase a modern culture: its fertile soil, favorable climate, strategic location suitable for trade (Genovesi emphasizes that trade could restore the kingdom's prosperity, which relies on well-understood laws that need to be disseminated), a large population, and an industrious workforce. However, he notes that this industry "is blind without the good knowledge that perfects the arts, and good knowledge is inseparable from the light of letters that increase and correct reason, it is manifest that it is a very difficult thing, not to say impossible, for a nation to be wisely industrious, and therefore rich, great and powerful, without such a beautiful light of human minds."[61]

After discussing the similarities and differences among the three Enlightenment thinkers, it is important to explore how Genovesi's and Smith's ideas may have influenced Kant's philosophy.

2.4 Visible and Invisible Ties

One clear aspect of Kant's relationships with Genovesi and Smith is that, throughout his life, the German philosopher never engaged with Genovesi's works. In contrast, he read the *Theory* and might have read the *Wealth*. Can we deduce from this that Smith had an impact on Kant's philosophy, unlike Genovesi? In the subsequent discourse, I shall endeavor to respond to this inquiry by first examining Genovesi's connection to Kant's criticism, followed by an exploration of the influence exerted by Smith's works on Kant's moral philosophy. Although the following exposition has only indirect consequences for the three moral principles of economic agents that I will present in Chapter 3, it is significant in enhancing the intellectual portrayals of the three authors from whom those principles originated.

Upon investigation, I found a few Italian authors asserting that Genovesi's works had a direct impact on Kant's ideas or, at the very least, exhibited similarities between them. Among them, as I will show, there are also famous names of Italian and European philosophy. I will begin with the last in chronological order, Giorgio Tonelli (1928–1978). In a 1974 paper titled "Kant's Critique of Pure Reason within the Tradition of Modern Logic,"[62] which was later published as a book in 1994,[63] Tonelli wrote:

> Around the middle of the century the correction and verification trend in logic was further developed abroad, under the name of *Art of Criticism*, with the Italian Genovesi (*Logica sive Ars critica*, 1745) and with the Portuguese Monteiro (*Logica seu Ars critica*, 1768): they both had an international reputation, and their interest for the "Critique" in this sense was accepted by several Catholic German philosophers. It is most probably under their influence that Kant adopted the term "Critique", in order to denote his methodology of verification and correction in metaphysics. Thus, the very title of Kant's work is, in its specific meaning, of logical extraction, or else we should assume that a very astonishing coincidence took place in that case.[64]

Tonelli proposes that Kant's criticism, which I previously noted as central to philosophical maturity and Enlightenment contributions, might stem from Genovesi's and others' reinterpretation of Logic as a critical art. Tonelli claimed that Kant did not engage directly with Genovesi but that the latter was fundamental for Alexander Baumgarten's (1706–1757) works in logic and aesthetics. Kant's biographies consistently mention that he used Baumgarten's *Metaphysica* as a handbook for his lectures on the subject, frequently annotating the text, so he was very well familiar with this author of the German philosophical scene. The link between Kant and Genovesi, mediated by Baumgarten, is intriguing but, for now, lacks supporting evidence.[65]

Tonelli was not alone in stressing a similarity between Kant's and Genovesi's philosophies. If not a direct link, Giovanni Gentile (1875–1944), one of the major exponents of Italian idealism and minister of public education during Mussolini's Fascist regime, emphasizes an anticipation of Kantian themes in Genovesi: "the conclusion, frankly critical, ... has not only a personal value; but also an absolute one, as a criticism of reason, or, as Genovesi says, of human capacity in general."[66] According to Gentile, Genovesi arrived at Kantian ideas through his interpretation of Locke's: "understanding Locke's reflection as it should be understood historically, that is, as the central nucleus of the human intellect, not as its content, but as its constitution, not as its product, but as its function, a true Kantian a-priori in embryo."[67] Gentile referenced these similarities in his exploration of the history of Italian philosophy, notably mentioning another Italian thinker, Francesco Fiorentino (1834–1884). Fiorentino, like Gentile, examined the history of Italian philosophy and highlighted the existence of Kantian concepts in Genovesi's work and commented, "one might say that a premonitory breath of Criticism was blowing in Naples at that time, and that Genovesi, under the double influence of Leibniz and Locke, had a distant presentiment of the problem that was tormenting the mind of Immanuel Kant at the same time."[68]

While Tonelli mentioned an indirect influence, and Gentile and Fiorentino stressed significant similarities, Antonio Rosmini (1797–1855) argued that Genovesi not only foresaw Kant's criticism but also critically assessed and dismissed Kantian solutions before their formulation by the German philosophers. In one of his long footnotes, typical of his writing styles, Rosmini argued that Genovesi refused Kant's version of innate forms according to which,

> there is in our soul a radical virtue of such a nature that on occasion of conceiving the beings which act on our senses, the soul emits from within itself the forms which had not existence before, and joins them with the *matter* furnished by sensible experience ... as this second way of interpreting the system of *innate forms*, I cannot refrain from quoting some remarks of Antonio Genovesi in a letter to Conti. From them we shall see that the system of Kant had in substance been thought of and refuted in Italy even before being imported into it from Germany.[69]

This chapter and book do not serve as venues for exploring Genovesi's insights on innate forms, the presence of Kantian ideas in his logic works, or Baumgarten's significance in this story. The intention of these Italian authors, apart from Rosmini – who held a negative view of Kant – was likely to align Genovesi with one of the key figures of the European Enlightenment.[70] Regardless, my more modest goal was to illustrate a quasi-invisible connection between two of the three authors of this book, which reveals itself through shared intellectual interests and themes. More visible and direct is the influence of Smith on Kant, to which I shall turn now.

That Kant knew Smith's works seems to be the most accredited hypothesis present in the secondary literature.[71] In his book *The Idea of Justice*, where both Kant's and Smith's philosophies hold an important place, Amartya Sen, a winner of the Nobel Prize in economics, wrote that

> Immanuel Kant too knew *The Theory of Moral Sentiments* (originally published in 1759), and commented on it in a letter to Markus Herz in 1771 (even though, alas, Herz referred to the proud Scotsman as "the Englishman Smith"). This was somewhat earlier than Kant's classic works, *Groundwork* (1785) and *Critique of Practical Reason* (1788), and it seems quite likely that Kant was influenced by Smith.[72]

Smith's *Theory* was translated into German by Christian Rautenberg (1728–1776) in 1770, one year before the aforementioned letter, while *The Wealth of Nations* was translated by Johann Friedrich Schiller (1737–1814) in 1776–1778 and then translated again by Christian Garve (1742–1798) in 1794. In addition to Sen, both the German translations of the *Theory* and of the *Wealth of Nations* can be traced back to before Kant's moral philosophy writings. Sen's quote is also important because, in his view, Kant and Smith exemplify two distinct aspects of Enlightenment political philosophy. Kant embodies transcendental institutionalism, which aims to theorize about ideally just social institutions, while Smith focuses on comparative approaches that emphasize social achievements and the gradual reduction of injustices. This leaves us with an intriguing question about what, if anything, the German philosopher might have taken from his Scottish colleague.

The literature discussing Smith's influence on Kant and the potential similarities between the two authors is extensive and has evolved over time.[73] One consistent point among scholars – aside from the varying nuances and objectives of each contribution – is that certain Smithian moral concepts, such as the impartial spectator, sympathy, respect, and moral actions, were either embraced or reinterpreted in Kant's moral philosophy. In his book *Adam Smith und Immanuel Kant*,[74] for example, the German economist August Oncken (1844–1911) argued that the concept of "general rules" in Smith corresponds to the concept of inner moral law in Kant's philosophy:

> It is well known that Kant's moral theory is rooted in the moral commandment of the so-called "categorical imperative". This derives from the innate moral law and reads: "Act in such a way that the maxim of your will can at all times be considered as the principle of a general legislation." The "general rules" have a completely similar meaning in Smith's ethics. They are the highest guiding stars for human behavior. However, they have no formulation; they are perhaps even more formally formulated than even Kant's imperative. But the comparison that Smith chooses to characterize them is completely consistent with the concept of a legislation intended for the general public ... The cultivation and awareness of this inner moral law constitutes the "dignity" of man and the drive to obey its commandments occurs again in both theories through the feeling of respect for the majesty of this moral law (reverentia in Kant, reverence in Smith).[75]

Although the interpretation of Oncken may be debated, it serves as a clear example of how Smith's impact on Kant's writing can be traced. To wrap up this section, I would like to highlight another approach: identifying Smithian terms and expressions within Kant's (moral) philosophy. This method would also effectively introduce the Kantian and Smithian themes that will be explored in the following sections, which focus on secondary literature.

In the *Groundwork*, which is the book on which I will base my interpretation of Kant's moral principle for economic agents, there are two key references to Smithian concepts. In the preface, Kant argued that "All trades, crafts, and arts have gained by the *division of labor*, namely when one person does not do everything but each limits himself to a certain task that differs markedly from others in the way it is to be handled, so as to be able to perform it most perfectly and with greater facility."[76] It is known that the concept of division of labor is at the center of Smith's *Wealth*. For Smith, the division of labor extends beyond specialization in production and increased productivity; it stems from humanity's inherent tendency to engage in trade and exchange. Additionally, Smith viewed the division of labor as a social organization system – not merely economic – that enabled the involvement of disadvantaged individuals in productive activities. Without this system, lesser-skilled workers – due to various factors such as education, physical capabilities, or cultural barriers – would face marginalization and exclusion, as was common in the *ancien régime* societies. This perspective is why Smith, the Scottish Enlightenment philosopher, regarded the commercial society founded on the division of labor as more civilized and ethical than earlier European societies.

Kant applied Smith's concept to his inquiry. Why is the division of labor important in moral philosophy? According to Kant, his predecessors created confusion by failing to separate the rational a priori investigation into the foundations of morality from the practical applications of moral principles. This is why he employs Smith's socioeconomic concept to state his methodological approach to his research object, namely, the "*supreme principle of morality.*"[77] The German term *Grundlegung* (groundwork) translates directly to "laying the ground." In the *Critique of Pure Reason*, Kant first examined how we come to know objects, then he shifted the focus to how we actively create them – actions are objects that we somehow bring to life. Our actions are always guided by certain principles. To clarify moral science, we need to identify the fundamental and highest moral principle. The *Groundwork* purpose is both descriptive, aiming to "identify,"[78] and prescriptive, intending to "corroborate."[79] But where do we locate the supreme moral principle? We cannot discover it through experience, as experience only pertains to the world as it is, while morality pertains to the world as it ought to be. As Kant recognized in his *Critique of Pure Reason*, successful foundational efforts must occur within the a priori or pure domain – whereas these terms refer to a domain that is free from any empirical determination.

At the start of section I, Kant mentioned another Smithian idea, this time originating from the *Theory*: "not to mention that an *impartial rational spectator* can take no delight in seeing the uninterrupted prosperity of a being graced with no feature of a pure and good will."[80] Kant began his philosophical exploration to identify the supreme principle of morality, asserting it cannot be derived from empirical factors, like human desires, passions, or inclinations, nor from the outcomes of actions. The true moral value lies in the good will of the rational beings carrying out an action, which, as the quote emphasizes, must be pure – free from any empirical influences. Later, he connected the good will to more famous concepts such as duty, moral law, categorical imperatives, autonomy, and freedom. And yet, it is significant that he immediately employed the Smithian concept of the impartial spectator. In Smith's moral philosophy, we are not the most suitable judges of the appropriateness of our actions, as we are evidently too involved in them. This is why we must consider a spectator: an individual who is relatively detached from our actions or proposals. Smith proposed three levels of impartial spectatorship. While others can observe our actions as spectators, their opinions may not represent the best moral viewpoint for evaluating our own morality, as they could be biased due to pre-existing connections or interests regarding the outcomes of our actions. The second level involves our conscience, which Smith described as an internal judge that observes and assesses our actions impartially. By sympathizing with this impartial spectator and their judgment of our behavior, we can gauge the moral appropriateness of our intentions. The third level pertains to God; however, I believe Kant primarily focused on the first two levels of impartial spectatorship.

What motivated Kant to incorporate the qualification of rationality for the impartial spectator? The more obvious explanation seems to be that, during his foundational exploration of the sources of morality, he sought to elucidate that a pure and good will may receive the endorsement not from any impartial observer, regardless of how detached this (imaginary or actual) observer may be from the action. As he clarified in his critique of Wolff's universal practical philosophy, "the metaphysics of morals has to examine the idea and the principles of a possible pure will and not the actions and conditions of human volition generally, which for the most part are drawn from psychology."[81] We are back to the concept of division of labor, which, along with the unbiased spectator characterized as "rational," highlights Kant's recognition of and critical assessment of Smith's ideas.

This chapter concludes the overview of Genovesi's, Kant's, and Smith's lives, historical contexts, and intellectual connections. I will now dedicate individual sections to each philosopher, discussing interpretations of their economic ideas, especially concerning moral issues, primarily drawn from secondary literature. As mentioned earlier, this groundwork will pave the way for the next chapter, where I will outline their three moral principles for economic agents.

2.5 Smith's Political Economy[82]

Thomas Robert Malthus (1766–1834), a key figure in the school of thought known as political economy, alongside Smith and David Ricardo (1722–1823), wrote:

The professed object of Dr Adam Smith's inquiry is the nature and causes of the wealth of nations. There is another inquiry however perhaps even more interesting, which he occasionally includes in his studies and that is the inquiry into the causes which affect the happiness of nations [...]. perhaps Dr Adam Smith has considered these two inquiries as still more nearly connected than they really are.[83]

Malthus's assertion is an excellent starting point for exploring the different interpretations of Smith's perspective on the link between markets and morality. Following Smith's death, a centennial debate on the "Adam Smith Problem" commenced.[84] At the heart of this dispute lies the connection between Smith's two key works: *Theory* and *Wealth*. In essence, it explores how Smith's role as a moral philosopher influenced his perspectives as a political economist. While *Theory* expresses the complexity of human nature, including inclinations, passions, moral sentiments, and more, *Wealth* seems to exclude many of these elements while describing economic agents, reducing them to their self-love or self-interest and a few virtues (self-command, prudence) attached to that. Malthus appears to support this idea by claiming that Smith, as a political economist, neglected the inquiry into happiness of nations and individuals. He did not, as he did in his *Theory*, account for the various factors that influence human happiness, leading him to assume that increased wealth would unavoidably lead to greater happiness for nations. Many scholars have disagreed with this interpretation. The debate did not start with Malthus, but rather in the German historical school of economic thought. Rather than recount the history of the Adam Smith Problem, I will outline three primary positions that reflect three interpretations of Smith's perspective on markets and morality.

The first position implicitly adopts Malthus's perspective. *Theory* and *Wealth* are distinct books that tackle separate issues and should be read independently. All the moral concepts presented in *Theory*, such as the aforementioned impartial spectator or sympathy, hold little to no significance concerning Smith's political economy. To grasp Smith's perspective on the market sphere, it suffices to combine a few concepts. The first is the human propensity to truck, barter, and exchange, which, for Smith, is connected to a natural desire we have to persuade each other:

If we should enquire into the principle in the human mind on which this disposition of trucking is founded, it is clearly the natural inclination everyone has to persuade. The offering of a shilling, which to us appears to have so plain and simple a meaning, is in reality offering an argument to persuade one to do so and so as it is for his interest.[85]

When it comes to a market exchange, persuasion becomes a means for being believed to obtain something. What is that which we know and want to be recognized as knowledgeable of when we exchange goods or services with one another? In *Wealth*, Smith explains that "whoever offers to another a bargain of any kind, proposes to do this. Give me that which I want, and you shall have this which you want."[86] I desire that you believe me when I tell you that this thing X is what you want, and I add that you want it so much that you should be disposed to give me Y, something I want, in return. This concept of self-love and self-interest, independent from moral considerations such as benevolence, friendship, or humanity, is sufficient to explain how the market operates. The market functions as a positive-sum game, meaning all participants gain by the end of the day. When individuals act according to their self-interest and natural tendencies – factors that also foster the division of labor – society reaps the rewards. This implies that economic agents inadvertently contribute to the prosperity of their countries. Smith describes this phenomenon as the invisible hand mechanism, which suggests that we boost national wealth more efficiently by pursuing our own interests in trade rather than merely considering it in our utility functions. Therefore, *Wealth* is a book that holds its own moral perspective[87] distinct from *Theory*.

The first interpretation is related, though not entirely or exclusively, to what is known as the "Chicago Smith."[88] The Chicago interpretation reflects Smith's concepts expressed by the Chicago school of economics, a neoclassical economic theory that emerged in the United States during the twentieth century. George Stigler (1911–1991), a distinguished figure in the field, remarked that Smith "put into the center of economics the systematic analysis of the behavior of individuals pursuing their self-interest under conditions of competition."[89] What *Wealth* shows, according to Stigler, is that "the immensely powerful force of self-interest guides resources to their most efficient uses ... in short, it orders and enriches the nation which gives it free reign. Indeed, if self-interest is given even a loose rein, it will perform prodigies."[90] Among these prodigies, there is a noticeable rise in states' wealth/gross domestic product that does not depend on moral sentiments, impartial observers, or sympathies.

The second interpretation counters the reductionism and separatism of the first. When *Theory* and *Wealth* are viewed as stand-alone and disconnected texts, it leads to a simplistic understanding of humans as mere economic agents driven by self-interest. At the start of *Theory*, the moral philosopher Smith clearly cautions against this outcome: "How selfish soever man may be supposed, there are evidently some principles in his nature, which interest him in the fortune of others, and render their happiness necessary to him, though he derives nothing from it, except the pleasure of seeing it."[91] The market should not be viewed as a distinct social realm where human moral feelings and benevolent emotions fade away. Smith offered a profound analysis of sociality rooted in the idea that benevolence, humanity, sympathy, and other moral sentiments are essential traits of human nature.[92] Aware of human beings' intricate nature and motivations, he naturally identified these psychological aspects as crucial for a functioning market. In this alternate perspective on the Adam Smith Problem, the market's value as a practice lies in the shared concern among the parties engaged in the exchange. You care about my well-being while I care about yours, and we are both mindful of our own interests. Thus, the market represents a vast network of intentional collaborations aimed at mutual benefit, highlighting the intersection of political economy and moral philosophy. This is the rationale behind the inability to read Smith's two books independently; they represent two manifestations of the same overarching project.

Famous scholars adopted this perspective. Recently, Sen explained that this interpretation does not imply an exclusion of self-interested motives for economic agents, but rather an enrichment of them with other features:

The butcher, the brewer, and the baker want to get our money in exchange for the meat, the beer, and the bread they make, and we – the consumers – want their meat, beer, and bread and are ready to pay for them with our money. The exchange benefits us all, and we do not have to be committed altruists to find reasons to seek such exchange. This is a fine point about the motivation for trade – interesting in itself – but it is not a claim about the adequacy of self-seeking for the success of a society or even of the market economy. In the rest of Smith's writings, there are extensive discussions of the constructive role of other motivations that influence human action and behavior. For example, in the Moral Sentiments, Smith argues that while "prudence" is "of all virtues that which is most helpful to the individual," "humanity, justice, generosity, and public spirit, are the qualities most useful to others." The working of society goes much beyond the motivation for seeking a trade, and even the successful operation of the market economy demands more than self-love.[93]

Frequently, authors supporting this perspective on the Adam Smith Problem tend to minimize the significance of the invisible hand within Smith's economic theory. A notable instance is Emma Rothschild, who argued that the term "invisible hand" appears only three times in Smith's writings, used as an "ironic and useful joke,"[94] and, crucially, that "the invisible hand is in conflict with other parts of Smith's work; that it is the sort of idea he would not have liked."[95]

In this perspective, the concept of persuasion related to the propensity to truck, barter, and exchange alters its significance. Rather than dominating your exchange partners by persuading them that you know what they want, you should try to establish communication with them by sympathy. The mutual exchange of pieces of information might bring both exchange partners to know better their reciprocal wants and needs, becoming both the persuaded and persuader at the same time. Numerous scholars demonstrate that persuasion can exist without deception,[96] and they apply this concept to analyze Smith's perspective on market exchange. All these scholars implicitly challenge the reductionist and separatist interpretations of the Adam Smith Problem. Lisa Herzog argues that Smith contrasted a view of deceiving persuasion with one based on sympathy and successful communication between equals. In her own words, "exchange among equals is akin to the attempt to persuade others by honest arguments ... in a growing commercial society ... the citizens can recognize each others as equals with whom mutually useful exchanges are possible and use the rhetoric appropriate for this purpose."[97] Leonidas Montes called this a sympathetic persuasion, which, in his view, Smith took for granted as the basis of market exchange so much not to mention sympathy in *The Wealth*. From a different angle, Michele Bee argues that persuasion is not necessarily aimed at receiving the approval of others but rather a deserved approval, which is the "pleasure of having persuaded the others that we really deserve their approval, and thus as the pleasure of having obtained their deserved esteem."[98] This concept can be translated into the market realm, where self-interest does not invariably imply the pursuit of personal gain at any expense. Instead, it accommodates the presence of moral sentiments, which compel me to consider the interests of the exchange partner as well.

There is a third solution to the Adam Smith Problem, which can be considered, in a certain respect, to occupy a position midway between the two preceding solutions. *Theory* and *Wealth* should not be interpreted as distinct intellectual pursuits; concurrently, they cannot be regarded as merely two aspects of the same issue. Rather, the two works ought to be viewed as complementary to one another. This interpretation is based on the coherence among Smith's works. Smith indicated in his *Theory* that social passions – such as benevolence, friendship, humanity, and generosity – are more commonly observed in close relationships, like those within families. Thus, it becomes evident that he prioritized self-interest in the impersonal market, where economic agents interact with strangers. This position is well explained in a paper by Luigino Bruni and Robert Sugden:

Significantly, when he describes the "social passions" (listed as "generosity, humanity, kindness, compassion, mutual friendship and esteem, all the social and benevolent affections"), his principal examples are of the family. To illustrate the social passions, he draws a rose-tinted picture of what, for him, is an ideal family, characterized by "cheerfulness, harmony and contentment," in contrast to a family in which the social virtues are absent (38–40) ... The suggestion is that the social passions are exercised in the softer and (we seem to be being told) optional domains of family and intimate friendship, and that these are separate from the harsher and more essential worlds of politics and economics.[99]

Bruni and Sugden articulate a gender dichotomy in Smith's viewpoint, wherein the family is emblematic of the feminine sphere linked to feminine passions and virtues, whereas the market is delineated by masculine inclinations such as self-interest and virtues, including prudence and self-command. This aligns with the context of Smith's era, where the term "businesspeople" coincided with "businessmen." Social equilibrium arises from the understanding that men can express feminine passions and virtues, provided they are demonstrated within the private realms of family and friendship. Therefore, *Theory* and *Wealth* should not be viewed as unrelated works or merely two chapters of the same text; instead, they are complementary pieces of a larger puzzle.

I will not delve further into this third position, as it aligns most closely with my interpretation of the Adam Smith Problem. In the next chapter, when I outline the moral principles for economic agents derived from Smith's political economy, I will base my analysis on this understanding of his key works and their interconnections. It is important to recognize the numerous topics connected to the Adam Smith Problem and, more broadly, to Smith's moral and economic ideas. These include state regulation,[100] international trade,[101] his stadial model of historic development,[102] his perspective on colonialism,[103] the impact of domination on human behavior,[104] his insights into vanity,[105] the theological influences on his philosophy,[106] and his views on religion.[107] And yet, for my purposes, it is sufficient to remember that the three proposed solutions to the Adam Smith Problem are all credible and can be supported with sound arguments. I have chosen the one that I believe most closely aligns with the fundamental principles of Smith's thought and could be beneficial for modern BE. However, as I stated at the outset, I do not claim to have uncovered the "true Smith."

2.6 Genovesi's Civil Economy

To date, there is no issue comparable to the Adam Smith Problem that has been identified as the "Antonio Genovesi Problem." While the works of the Neapolitan author have been translated into many languages, the lack of English translations of his main works, including the *Lezioni di Commercio o sia d'Economia Civile*, can explain why he received less attention from the literature. Furthermore, the harsh judgment of the highly influential Italian economist Francesco Ferrara (1810–1900) suggested that "the merits of the foundation of economics belong to the English Smith, or to the French Turgot, not to Genovesi, to Verri, to Beccaria,"[108] and this signaled a decline in interest in Genovesi's economic ideas. Joseph A. Schumpeter (1883–1950) recognized the role of Ferrara in the reception of Genovesi's ideas in his *History of Economic Analysis*: "It was I think F. Ferrara who set the example of speaking of Genovesi in derogatory terms, possibly because he never could see any merit in anyone who was not a thoroughgoing free-trader."[109] And yet, there are some divergent interpretations of Genovesi's civil economy, which, as we shall see, have had an international revival in the last few decades.

The initial author to consider is Rosmini. Rosmini notes that Genovesi's use of the adjective civil/civile in relation to economy reflects his Enlightenment concept of *incivilmento* (civilizing process).

This idea was pivotal in the thinking of another writer, Gian Domenico Romagnosi (1761–1835), who contended that the progress of societies and nations reflects a journey of advancing civilizations and enhancement of arts and customs. Hence, Genovesi conceived the market as an expression and means of overcoming a hierarchical, feudal, static world toward a society founded on the freedoms of the moderns, on the improvement of manners and customs, and on the overcoming of privileges and abuses. Rosmini viewed Genovesi as the pioneer of a philosophical lineage that Romagnosi and Melchiorre Gioia (1767–1829) would later follow.[110] Nonetheless, this perspective leads Rosmini to voice stern criticisms of Genovesi's thought, which he perceives as an embodiment of sensism. This viewpoint is seen as a limiting and flawed understanding of humanity, where will and reason are overshadowed by the overwhelming influence of the senses. Consequently, the anthropological issue evolves into a moral one when sensualist philosophers, according to Rosmini, assert that the pursuit of pleasurable sensations is the ultimate aim of human actions, representing the happiness that everyone seeks. At the end of a long footnote devoted to Genovesi, Rosmini wrote: "Genovesi's ideas would perhaps be correct if human beings were constrained by nature to withdraw with themselves. His teaching supposes that they are essentially egoists. It is, therefore, essentially sensistic because it sees in human beings only the senses and what is good for the senses, all of which perish with the body."[111]

Certain aspects of Genovesi's philosophy appear to support Rosmini's interpretation. According to Genovesi, "every man is born with the right to employ whatever lends to their conservation and happiness, that is to "the minimum of evils."[112] Instead of rejecting the concept of "utility," Genovesi clarified in another section of *La Diocesina*, his work on moral philosophy, that "the idea of useful is always a complex notion of true and false utility, composed by various relations and subject to many alterations, as far as our passions and the variety of our specific interests are concerned, and thus it may not be a constant and fixed rule."[113] Genovesi expertly navigated the philosophical currents of his era and earlier centuries. He recognized how a statement supporting "the minimum of evils" could be misinterpreted as a precursor to utilitarianism and sensism. Thus, in his *Lezioni*, he carefully distinguished between forms of evils, "[originating] from a natural sensation, from sympathetic or unpleasant energy and from reflection,"[114] explaining that the second form is the primary influence on human behaviors.

Recent literature has countered Rosmini's critique of the egoism present in Genovesi's anthropology and civil economy.[115] In the initial paragraphs of the *Lezioni*, Genovesi distinctly embraced the Aristotelian and Thomistic view on humanity's social nature. As I have shown elsewhere, Genovesi's *homo homini natura amicus* was not only opposed to Thomas Hobbes's (1588–1679) *homo homini lupus*, but also in line with Thomas Aquinas's (1224–1724) *naturaliter homo homini amicus est*.[116] For Genovesi, the market is not only the realm of self-interest; there is a form of sociality in the market, a "qualified" sociality, which is a constitutive part of commerce: "Man is a naturally sociable animal: goes the common saying. But not every man will believe there is no other sociable animal on earth ... How is man more sociable than other animals? ... [it is] in his reciprocal right to be assisted and consequently in his reciprocal obligation to help us in our needs."[117] In his view, focusing on common good and public trust (*fede pubblica*) is essential for virtuous market transactions. Genovesi argued that self-interest and concern for others are not inherently negative. He viewed the market as a reflection of the overarching law of civil society, which encompasses reciprocity or mutual assistance. As previously noted, Genovesi's concept of reciprocity – considered the foundational law of human interactions – stems from a moral form of Newtonianism that informs his scientific perspective. Thus, market exchanges among individuals are not merely a byproduct of their individual needs. In Genovesi's civil economy, participants in market transactions can intentionally pursue their own benefits while also considering the well-being of the person with whom they are exchanging. This approach reflects the inherently social nature of human beings.

Bruni and Stefano Zamagni assert that the key distinction between Smith's political economy and Genovesi's civil economy lies here.[118] The former, as noted by Malthus, primarily investigates the "wealth" of individuals and nations without directly addressing happiness or human flourishing. In contrast, the latter focuses on *pubblica felicità* (public happiness), emphasizing civic virtue and the common good. Thus, the term civil reflects both *incivilmento* and *civitas*, with the latter term highlighting the material and spiritual advancement of people, communities, and nations. In one of his letters, Genovesi summarized this aspect:

work for your own interest; no man could act otherwise than for his own happiness; he would be a man less of a man: but do not want to make others miserable; and if you can, and as much as you can, try to make others happy. The more one works for interest, the more, provided one is not crazy, one must be virtuous. It is a law of the universe that one cannot make our own happiness without making that of others.[119]

The common good possesses a material dimension, directly connecting it to the economic realm; however, it also encompasses a formal aspect that pertains to the relational flourishing of individuals within their social environments.

This perspective will serve as a foundation for the moral principle related to economic agents in the following chapter. However, recent literature provides at least one additional interpretation of Genovesi's civil economy. As one of this chapter's goals is to present a broader view of secondary sources, I will emphasize certain authors' alternative viewpoints concerning Genovesi's economic ideas. In a sense, this small branch of literature moved from a critique to Bruni and Zamagni's perspective. They believe that the essence of Genovesi's civil economy lies not in the mutual assistance depicted in the reciprocal relationships between individuals. In contrast, Genovesi was an Enlightenment author who emphasized the importance of politics, especially through the sovereign, in fostering public happiness. Federico D'Onofrio[120] contented to Bruni that when Genovesi referred to *pubblica felicità* he was referring to the goal and duty of an absolute monarch toward his people. A comparable argument has been posited by Adrian Pabst, who perceives Genovesi's civil economy first and foremost as a theory of government. However, differently from D'Onofrio, Pabst aimed to discover Genovesi's theory of the complex relationships between individuals, civil society, and the monarch that constitute the political bodies of the polity: "The human capacity for virtue is a significant ordering device of the polity, and Genovesi roots civil life (*vita civile*) in the mutual exchange of different natural faculties and virtues. In terms of his political and economic thought, this means that virtue is central to the division of labour and the right proportions between different activities, including production and trade."[121] From a different locus of analysis, that is, Genovesi's translation and engagement with Cary's *An Essay on the State of England*, Sophus Reinert concurred on the fact that for Genovesi reforms could only be implemented by an absolute monarch (the Enlightened absolutism of Russia and Prussia monarchs).[122] Reinert, however, contested the prior literature by suggesting that Genovesi's civil economy does not possess any distinctive elements to establish it as an independent tradition from the political economy. Instead, it should be viewed as one of the many versions of political economy developed in eighteenth-century Europe.

Like the Adam Smith Problem, I believe a definitive interpretation cannot be established. In my opinion, each interpretation has influenced the development of the thoughts and projects of its proponents. Rosmini critiques Genovesi within his broader condemnation of sensism, a philosophy criticized for neglecting the spiritual complexity of human beings. Bruni and Zamagni have revitalized the civil economy tradition to comprehend both the historical and contemporary Italian approaches to market economy, aiming to inspire new research and practices. Pabst, along with Scazzieri, utilizes Genovesi's perspective on polity and political entities to challenge the reductionist and dualistic tendencies in modern economics and political science.[123] They argue that these frameworks for observing social life are fundamentally flawed as they disregard the interconnectedness of economic structures and political actions and vice versa. In their view, the failure of this dualism is evident in policies that cannot effectively promote the systemic interests of society's foundational structure. In my instance, as stated, I will embrace the interpretation from the Italian school of civil economy of Bruni and Zamagni. I believe this perspective aligns closely with the essence of Genovesi's ideas and is beneficial for extracting moral principles for economic agents relevant to BE.

2.7 Kant's Moral Economy[124]

In the realm of BE, Kant's moral philosophy is frequently categorized as deontology.[125] This classification highlights Kant's anti-consequentialist focus on the ethics of rights and duties, which has been leveraged to support various issues, such as "meaningful work for employees, a democratic workplace, non-deceptive advertising, and a non-coercive relationship with suppliers," among many others.[126] For instance, research on Kantian leadership occupies an important place in ethical leadership literature. The Kantian leadership approach emphasizes respecting individual autonomy and dignity while promoting equal relationships between leaders and their followers.[127] Another example involves utilizing Kant's differentiation between perfect and imperfect duties to clarify the responsibilities of managerial teams toward stakeholders[128] or the obligations of commercial agents to their partners and society at large.[129] Since my analysis in the upcoming chapter primarily draws from the concepts presented in Kant's *Groundwork*, I will now present two specific and narrow areas of literature that share this focus: moral purism and its critiques and the moral limits of the market authors.

In BE, some critics refer to a stance known as moral purism.[130] This viewpoint, associated with Kant, argues that markets are inherently morally deficient due to self-interest and instrumental relationships. According to Kant, morality diminishes in the presence of any self-interest, a concept known among moral purists as the exclusion thesis. Proponents of moral purism emphasize the importance of pure intentions or motives, leading Kant to deem all actions involved with any degree of self-interest or instrumentality as immoral. Those authors usually rely on Kant's *Groundwork* and, alongside the overall critical attitude Kant expresses throughout the work toward self-interest actions, on the second formula of the categorical imperative, the formula of humanity, that goes as follows: "so act that you use humanity, in your own person as well as in the person of any other, always at the same time as an end, never merely as a means."[131] In addition, moral purists might refer to Kant's famous concept of the kingdom of ends. When individuals abstract from any material goals, eliminating all empirical determinations, and view themselves as rational, thus free and autonomous, they conceptualize themselves in relation to other rational beings governed by self-imposed rules. In doing so, they enter the realm of the kingdom of ends. This space should not be understood as a physical location; rather, it represents an ideal accessible to all rational beings. What moral laws would be established in the kingdom of ends? Does the market fall within this kingdom? In the moral purist view, the key passage is the one in which Kant states that in the kingdom of ends "everything has either a price, or a dignity."[132]

Dubbink and Van Liedekerke effectively argue how much moral purism stems from Kant's moral philosophy. In their own words, "There are good reasons why Kant is an ideal candidate for a rebuttal of moral purism."[133] I believe they present a central argument along with three supporting ones – all of which are valid interpretations of Kant's thought beyond moral purism. Starting with the latter three, Dubbink and Van Liedekerke contend that Kant was acutely aware of the risks associated with moral purism due to his Pietist upbringing.

Additionally, they suggest that Kant recognized the danger of interpreting every good action as rooted in self-interest, which could lead to a transformation of morality into mere moralism (an interesting blend of morality and purism). This viewpoint would foster skepticism about moral exemplars, as they, too, would be subject to suspicion. For Kant, although moral exemplars do not form the basis of morality, they are crucial in how individuals first engage with moral concepts. Consequently, the notion of moral purism could undermine moral practice itself.

Dubbink and Van Liedekerke's core argument against moral purism is the distinction in Kant's philosophy between the formal meaning of a concept and its representation: "The formal meaning refers to what we mean to say with these concepts; the representation refers to how we can get hold of the concept in daily, empirical life."[134] The fault of moral purists is to

> confuse the formal meaning and the representation. They see no need to transpose the formal meaning into a representation, holding empirical elements. As a consequence, the criterion becomes impossible to meet in empirical life. Hence, they conclude that there never is morally worthy conduct in practice. They fail to see that the real problem is their misuse of a merely formal concept as an empirical criterion.[135]

Dubbink and Van Liedekerke argue that certain empirical criteria can be identified that relate to the rational and pure understanding of morality. Three specific criteria highlighted are self-discipline, sacrifice, and moral pride.

While I concur with the critique of moral purism, my stance differs significantly from that of Dubbink and Van Liedekerke. We each advocate for distinct methods of integrating Kant's perspective into BE. My focus is on identifying Kant's moral principle for economic agents, which I believe to be primarily a formal concept. Importantly, I am not seeking empirical evidence for this moral principle; at the same time, I am careful to avoid the pitfalls of moral purism, particularly the confusion between Kant's distinction between moral science and ethics. This understanding arises from engaging with another set of authors who frequently reference Kant's *Groundwork*, particularly those discussing the moral limits of the market.

Elizabeth Anderson referenced Kant to clarify her distinction between intrinsic and extrinsic goods. Humans act to achieve various ends: An intrinsic good is an end valued for its own sake, while an extrinsic good is valued only because it relates to another valued end. Additionally, not all extrinsic goods qualify as instrumental goods. Instrumental goods are those valued for their ability to help us attain a preferred goal. Nonetheless, extrinsic goods can exist without being instrumental, as exemplified by hanging a poorly made painting in my home solely because it was a gift from my best friend; in this case, the painting's value is derived from our friendship. Where does Kant fit into the distinction between extrinsic and intrinsic goods?

Kant's famous imperative to regard humanity as an end in itself expresses something similar to the first sense of "end" I have in mind when I say that intrinsic goods are the ends for the sake of which we act. Taking humanity as one's end is to act for the sake of or with due regard for the persons affected by one's actions. Such action involves not only promoting their welfare but can also include such activities as participating in projects important to them or taking their opinions seriously in discussion.[136]

The importance of this passage is revealed in chapter 7 of her book, where Anderson deals with "The Ethical Limitations of the Market."[137] Kant is never explicitly mentioned. However, the lexicon employed leaves little room for doubt about Kant's presence: "We understand the nature of economic goods by investigating the ways we value commodities. ... I call the mode of valuation appropriate to pure commodities 'use'. Use is a *lower*, impersonal, and exclusive mode of valuation. It is contrasted with higher modes of valuation, such as respect."[138] Anderson then presents five norms governing the production and consumption of economic goods: use is impersonal, egoistic, exclusive, want-regarding, and oriented to "exit." In chapter 1 of her book, Anderson describes how we value goods differently and how different goods elicit different evaluative responses from us. The quote on price-dignity from Kant's *Groundwork* is mentioned to distinguish goods with relative worth from goods with intrinsic worth. Evaluations are revealed in actions: People evaluate goods of relative worth by *using* them and the goods of intrinsic worth by *respecting* them. Anderson then comments, "Kant's ideal of human rationality grounded his distinction between the way we should value persons and the way we should value things."[139]

In my view, the key message of Anderson's reading of Kant is twofold. The first aspect addresses the moral limits of the market.

Certain items should not be classified as "economic goods" because economic reasoning is not the appropriate lens through which to evaluate them. Aspects like health, friendship, humanity, freedom, rights, animal rights, and others should not be treated as commodities. When these goods enter the market, they are devalued – reflected in Anderson's earlier quote where "lower" implies diminished worth – by inappropriate valuation methods. Thus, economic logic should not infiltrate social spheres; it ought to remain limited to commodity exchanges, ensuring that noneconomic goods stay true to their nature and aren't commodified. A comparable argument is presented by Debra Satz, who explicitly discusses this issue Kant:

In the nature of our concepts of honor, divine grace, and true love ... these things have no market price. At the very least, using the market to distribute these goods would represent a change in the way people understand these goods; our current usages *would be undermined*. Someone who offers to buy my friendship does not really understand what it means (in our culture) to be or to have a friend. There are also some goods that people regard as simply irreplaceable, without any equivalent. As Kant said about human beings, they have a dignity and not a price.[140]

I have no further comments or adjustments regarding this thesis. I align with Anderson's and Satz's concerns about the commodification of certain "irreplaceable" goods, and I believe the reference to Kant's ideas is appropriate My concern arises from Anderson's second argument presented in chapter 7. In this instance, it appears that Anderson suggests that, within a Kantian framework, the market operates as an immoral space. Economic goods fall under the category of use, suggesting that those who manage them may be seen as less "moral" compared to individuals handling goods that command respect. In the marketplace, only instrumental goods are traded. Yet, it's essential to recognize that all instrumental goods are extrinsic; there is nothing intrinsic in market transactions. The feature of impersonality, the first of the five norms characterizing economic goods, is again explained through Kantian concepts: "Each party to a market transaction views his relation to the other as merely a means to the satisfaction of ends."[141] This reflects Kant's second formulation of the categorical imperative, which states that humanity must never be treated "merely as a means" (*bloß als mittel*). Blinded and driven by my wants, I egoistically use the other party in the market exchange as a mere means of obtaining what I want.

One might challenge my interpretation of Anderson's thesis by arguing that she does not classify markets as immoral zones. In fact, markets are better described as amoral, suggesting that morality is not the appropriate measure for economic logic. In this context, markets can be likened to competitive sports; while competition might not possess inherent moral goodness, it also does not entail a moral failing. Rather, morality exists as an external category to economic realms. In addition, I may have misunderstood the moral limits of the market literature's primary message as presented by Anderson. The essence of her argument is that the growth of markets and their evaluative logic replaces alternative evaluative frameworks, thereby reducing human autonomy.

My response is that the distinction between amoral and immoral hinges on our interpretation of Anderson's use of the adjective "lower" and, as a matter of fact, also Satz's use of the verb "undermined." These terms suggest a moral standard that the market deviates from more than other areas of social life. Does this imply that the market is morally deficient? While this might not hold in absolute terms, like categorizing markets as "evils," it seems accurate in comparative terms, akin to stating that the morality of the market is inferior to that of other social realms. Even if the core stance of the moral limits of the market authors is that markets are amoral, their interpretation of Kant appears to align more closely with an immoral (or perhaps low-moral) perspective than an amoral one.

Concerning the autonomy issue, Anderson contends that Kant's differentiation between use and respect is flawed. He believes this simplifies a range of evaluative modes (use, respect, love, compassion) applicable to various goods (human beings, animals, environment) into just two categories. I believe Anderson's interpretation in this context is problematic. When Anderson recalls Kant's quote, she deals with the concept of the kingdom of end. In the preface of the *Groundwork*, Kant made it clear that he was dealing not with the empirical but with the rational part of the discipline, more specifically that the "pure part of philosophy ... limited to determinate objects of understanding."[142] When applied to ethics, this would be the *metaphysics of morals* (metaphysik der sitten). The scheme Kant presents is as follows:

Ethics (*Ethik*) = Moral Science (*Moral*) + Practical Anthropology (*praktische Anthropologie*)

Consequently, the various evaluative approaches Anderson believes are missing in Kant's moral framework are evident in his overarching perspective on ethics. Kant frequently indicates in *Groundwork* that his exploration pertains to what is good "without limitation" (ohne einschränkung), specifically the moral law. However, this understanding of good does not encompass all that is commendable and worthy. By incorporating additional empirical factors, such as the pursuit of happiness and human passions, one uncovers in Kant the variety of evaluations and goods that Anderson seeks: perhaps not directly tied to moral value, yet still deserving of praise. Thus, interpreting Kantian moral philosophy in a way that dismisses its relevance to the autonomy thesis is misguided.

I have illustrated Kant's moral philosophy as presented by the moral limits of the market and moral purism literature. Simultaneously, I have engaged critically with these areas of literature. Once again, I do not claim to have uncovered the "true Kant." More cautiously, the discussion in which I have begun to express my interpretation of Kant's moral economy serves as a foundation for what is to come in the following chapter, where I will outline Kant's moral principle for economic agents.

Notes

1. Santori, P. (2024). The curious case of the three Adam Smiths: Women and the Nobel Prize in Economics. *Journal of Contextual Economics–Schmollers Jahrbuch*, 1–16.
2. The paradox, evidently, can be intricately complicated by numerous factors. I shall highlight two such factors: one stemming from my personal experiences at various conferences I have attended, and the other derived from the history of philosophy. The former pertains to the political motivations that underlie the interpretation of an author. At times, scholars promote interpretations that serve to position an author within a particular tradition of thought that they endorse or support. This phenomenon is clearly observable in the case of Adam Smith, whose ideas have, for centuries, been categorized under various political and economic labels (such as the champion of free-market economy rather than an advocate for political intervention in the market, proto-socialist, post-liberal, among others). I must admit that I harbored no agenda when attending these meetings; however, this did not render me immune to the paradox. On a deeper

philosophical plane, the hermeneutic tradition, particularly the work of Hans-Georg Gadamer, illustrates that the community to which we belong (including our socio-cultural contexts) significantly shapes the trajectory of our pre-comprehension and subsequent interpretation of a text. Consequently, the tensions inherent in the paradox – merely representing subjectivity in search of objectivity – are both inescapable and generative as they sustain ongoing dialogue and heighten attention to these classical authors.

3. Kant, *Groundwork*, 72.
4. See Guasti, N. (2006). Antonio Genovesi's Diceosina: Source of the Neapolitan Enlightenment. *History of European Ideas*, *32*(4), 385–405; Dal Degan, Antonio Genovesi and Italian Economic Thought.
5. Some argue that Genovesi held the first chair of economics in Europe. See Bruni, L. (2007). The "technology of happiness" and the tradition of economic science. In Bruni, L., & Porta, P. L. (eds.), *Handbook of Economics of Happiness*. Cheltenham, Edward Elgar, 24–52; Zamagni, S. (2020). On the birth of economic science during the Italian-Scottish Enlightenment: Two paradigms compared. *Roczniki Nauk Społecznych*, *48*(2), 5–28. However, as demonstrated by other researchers, there was at least one antecedent in Uppsala, Sweden, namely, the chair of "jurisprudentiae, oeconomiae et commercium" established in 1741. See Magnusson, L. (1992). Economics and the public interest: The emergence of economics as an academic subject during the 18th century. *The Scandinavian Journal of Economics*, 94, 249–257.
6. See Bellamy R. (1987). "Da metafisico a mercatante": Antonio Genovesi and the development of a new language of commerce in eighteenth-century Naples. In Pagden A. (ed.), *The Languages of Political Theory in Early-Modern Europe*. Cambridge, Cambridge University Press, 277–300; Stapelbroek, K. (2006). Preserving the Neapolitan state: Antonio Genovesi and Ferdinando Galiani on commercial society and planning economic growth. *History of European Ideas*, *32*(4), 406–429.
7. See Cassirer, E. ([1865] 1981). *Kant's Life and Thought*. New Haven, Yale University Press.
8. See Norman, J. (2018). *Adam Smith: Father of Economics*. New York, Basic Books.
9. Smith, A. ([1776] 1976). *An Inquiry into the Nature and Causes of the Wealth of Nations*. In Campbell, R. H., Sranner A. S., & Todd, B. (eds.), *The Glasgow Edition of the Works and Correspondence of Adam Smith*, vol. 2. Indianapolis, Liberty Fund.
10. Genovesi, A. ([1765–1767] 1824–1825). *Lezioni di commercio o sia d'economia civile con un ragionamento sull'agricoltura e un*

     altro sul commercio in universale di Antonio Genovesi. Milan, Società Tipografica dei Classici Italiani. In this book, all quotations from *Lezioni* have been translated from Italian.
11. Genovesi, A. (1757). Ragionamento sul commercio universale. In Cary, J., *Storia del commercio della Gran Brettagna scritta da John Cary mercatante di Bristol, tradotta in nostra volgar lingua da Pietro Genovesi giureconsulto napoletano. Con un Ragionamento sul commercio in universale, e alcune annotazioni riguardanti l'economia del nostro regno, di Antonio Genovesi*. Naples, Benedetto Gessari, vii–cviii.
12. Genovesi, A. ([1777] 1838a) *Lo spirito delle leggi di Carlo Secondat Barone di Montesquieu con le annotazioni dell'abate Antonio Genovesi. Tomo Primo*. Milan, Giovanni Silvestri; Genovesi, A. ([1777] 1838b) *Lo spirito delle leggi di Carlo Secondat Barone di Montesquieu con le annotazioni dell'abate Antonio Genovesi. Tomo Secondo*. Milan, Giovanni Silvestri.
13. Fleischacker, S. (1996). Values behind the market: Kant's response to the "Wealth of Nations." *History of Political Thought*, 17(3), 380.
14. Kant, What is Enlightenment?, 54.
15. Kant, What is Enlightenment?, 55.
16. See Schabas, M., & De Marchi, N. (2003). Introduction to oeconomies in the age of Newton. *History of Political Economy*, 35(5), 1–13.
17. In a paper with Luigino Bruni, we demonstrate how Genovesi used the Newtonian lexicon to argue that the invisible hand's operations are not the fundamental economic force driving the common good of society. See Bruni & Santori, The other invisible hand.
18. Galiani, F. ([1750] 1803). *Della Moneta, Collezione Custodi di Scrittori Classici di Economia Politica. Parte Moderna*. Milan, De Stefanis, 91.
19. In the upcoming chapter, I will thoroughly explore the significance of Genovesi's work anthropology.
20. For a critical literature review, see Knell, M. (2025). Isaac Newton, Robert Simson and Adam Smith. *Homo Oeconomicus*, 41(1), 1–16.
21. See Hetherington, N. S. (1983). Isaac Newton's influence on Adam Smith's natural laws in economics. *Journal of the History of Ideas*, 44(3), 497–505. See also Raphael, D. D. (1988). Newton and Adam Smith. In Sweet-Stayer, M. (ed.), *Newton's Dream*. Montreal, Queen's Quarterly, 36–49.
22. Montes, L. (2008). Newton's real influence on Adam Smith and its context. *Cambridge Journal of Economics*, 32(4), 572.
23. One example is the relationship between Kant's Second Law of Mechanics and Newton's law of inertia. For an extensive discussion

and a literature review, see Watkins, E., & Stan, M. (2023). Kant's philosophy of science. *The Stanford Encyclopedia of Philosophy*. https://plato.stanford.edu/archives/fall2023/entries/kant-science/. Last accessed Dec. 2, 2025.
24. Kant., I. ([1781] 1998). *Critique of Pure Reason*. Cambridge, Cambridge University Press, 704.
25. Kant, *Critique of Pure Reason*, 128.
26. De Pierris, G., & Friedman, M. (2024). Kant and Hume on causality. *The Stanford Encyclopedia of Philosophy*. https://plato.stanford.edu/archives/fall2024/entries/kant-hume-causality/. Last accessed Dec. 2, 2025.
27. Kant, I. ([1783] 2004). *Prolegomena to Any Future Metaphysics*. Cambridge, Cambridge University Press, 10.
28. The following discussion of Genovesi's history is derived from a chapter I co-authored with Luigino Bruni and Stefano Zamagni in a collaborative book. See Bruni, L., Santori, P., & Zamagni, S. (2021). *Lezioni di Storia del Pensiero Economico. Dall'Antichità al Novecento*. Rome, Città Nuova.
29. See Zambelli, P. (1972). *La formazione filosofica di Antonio Genovesi*. Naples, Morano.
30. Galanti A. M. (1772). *Elogio storico dell'abate Antonio Genovesi*. Naples, Androsio, 49. My translation.
31. Ibid., 30. My translation.
32. This initiative was supported and funded by Bartolomeo Intieri, a Tuscan who managed the estates of Tuscan families in Campania and supported and funded this initiative.
33. Ross, I. S. (2010). *The Life of Adam Smith*. Oxford, Oxford University Press, 109.
34. See Herman, A. (2003). *The Scottish Enlightenment: The Scots' Invention of the Modern World*. London, Fourth Estate.
35. Kennedy, G. (2011). The hidden Adam Smith in his alleged theology. *Journal of the History of Economic Thought*, 33(3), 400.
36. Kennedy, G., The hidden Adam Smith, 388.
37. Draft of a letter of October 12, 1794. In Sorensen, R., & Proops, I. (2024). Kant and the king: Lying promises, conventional implicature, and hypocrisy. *Ratio*, 37(1), 51–52.
38. Weber, M. (2005). *Protestant Ethic and the Spirit of Capitalism*. London, Routledge Classics.
39. See Bruni, L. (2024). *Capitalismo meridiano: alle radici dello spirito mercantile tra religione e profitto*. Bologna, Il Mulino.
40. I discussed the difference between the Mediterranean-Catholic spirit of capitalism and the Weberian one in my first monograph: Santori, P.

(2021). *Thomas Aquinas and the Civil Economy Tradition: The Mediterranean Spirit of Capitalism*. London, Routledge.
41. Kant, *Groundwork of the Metaphysics of Morals*; Kant, I. (2016). Natural right course lecture notes by Feyerabend. In Rauscher, F. (ed.), *Lectures and Drafts on Political Philosophy*. Cambridge, Cambridge University Press.
42. For a complete list, see Villari, L. (1959). *Il pensiero economico di Antonio Genovesi*. Florence, Le monnier.
43. Smith, A. ([1759] 2012). *The Theory of Moral Sentiments*. New York, Dover Publication.
44. I am not referring to the *Lectures on Jurisprudence* that were notes taken by his students during the lectures.
45. Smith, *Theory of Moral Sentiments*, 512–513.
46. See Rawls, J. (2000). *Lectures on the History of Moral Philosophy*. Cambridge, MA, Harvard University Press.
47. See Mulsow, M. (2015). *Enlightenment Underground: Radical Germany, 1680–1720*. Charlottesville, University of Virginia Press.
48. See Niekerk, C. (2003). "Spätaufklärung": Rethinking the late eighteenth century in German literary history. *The Journal of English and Germanic Philology, 102*(3), 317–335.
49. A central figure regarding the relationship between Enlightenment and established religion is Gotthold Ephraim Lessing. Lessing's objective, upon closer examination, was not to denigrate the concept of mystery when confronted with human reason; rather, he sought to illustrate how faith in such mystery is rendered inappropriate in a historical context where humanity has developed the requisite tools to tackle religious questions through a methodology more aligned with the attained rational maturity. Consequently, Lessing did not aim to exploit the irrationality inherent in mysteries and dogmas but rather to engage our rational capacities in relation to them. Firmly believing that humanity as a collective had, by his era, progressed to a stage where it was finally equipped to comprehend the philosophical essence of mystery, Lessing adopted this endeavor as his primary goal, thereby transforming the now unacceptable and outdated elements of mysteries and dogmas to align with the newly arrived rationality of humankind.
50. See Reill, P. H. (1975). *The German Enlightenment and the Rise of Historicism*. Berkeley, University of California Press.
51. See Rao, A. M. (2005). Enlightenment and reform: An overview of culture and politics in Enlightenment Italy. *Journal of Modern Italian Studies, 10*(2), 142–167.
52. Paganelli, M. P. (2015). Recent engagements with Adam Smith and the Scottish enlightenment. *History of Political Economy, 47*(3), 366–367.

53. See Herman, *The Scottish Enlightenment*; Broadie, A. (2012). *The Scottish Enlightenment*. Edinburgh, Birlinn.
54. This can be exemplified through Shaftesbury's reflections on second-order affections and Hutcheson's speculations regarding a moral sense.
55. See Hamowy, R. (1987). *The Scottish Enlightenment and the Theory of Spontaneous Order*. Carbondale, Southern Illinois University Press. Viner, J. (2015). *The Role of Providence in the Social Order: An Essay in Intellectual History*. Princeton, Princeton University Press.
56. See Venturi, F. (1962) *Riformatori napoletani*. Milan, Ricciardi. For parallels between Neapolitan and Scottish Enlightenment, refer to Robertson, J. (1997). The Enlightenment above national context: Political economy in eighteenth-century Scotland and Naples. *The Historical Journal*, 40 (3), 667–697.
57. G. M. Galanti, *Elogio Storico*, 13. My translation.
58. Racioppi, G. (1871). *Antonio Genovesi*. Naples, Morano, 82. My translation.
59. Dragonetti, G. (1788). *Origine dei feudi nei regni di Napoli e Sicilia*. Naples, Nella Stamperia Regale.
60. Genovesi, A. ([1753] 1984). *Discorso sopra il vero fine delle lettere e delle scienze*. Naples, Istituto Italiano per gli Studi Filosofici, 24. My translation.
61. Ibid., 47. My translation.
62. Tonelli, G. (1974). Kant's *Critique of Pure Reason* within the tradition of modern logic. In Funke, G. (eds.), *Akten des 4. Internationalen Kant-Kongresses: Mainz, 6.–10. April 1974, Teil 3: Vorträge*. Berlin, De Gruyter.
63. Tonelli, G. (1994). *Kant's Critique of Pure Reason Within the Tradition of Modern Logic*, ed. by Chandler, D. H. Zürich, Georg Olms.
64. Tonelli, Kant's *Critique of Pure Reason*, 190.
65. See Pozzo, R. (2016). Review of J. Colin McQuillan, *Immanuel Kant: The Very Idea of a Critique of Pure Reason*, Notre Dame Philosophical Reviews, 17, 1–3.
66. Gentile, G. ([1903] 2003). *Storia della filosofia italiana. Dal Genovesi al Galluppi*. Florence, Le Lettere, 4. My translation.
67. Ibid., 12. My translation.
68. Fiorentino, F. (1887) *Manuale di Storia della Filosofia a Uso dei Licei, Diviso in Tre* Parti. *Seconda Edizione*. Naples, Morano, 606. My translation.
69. Rosmini, A. (1883). *The Origin of Ideas by Antonio Rosmini Serbati. Translated from Fifth Italian Edition of the Nuovo Saggio sull'Origine delle Idee*. London, Kegan Paul, 368–369.

70. I cannot affirm this with certainty and I will explore the issue further in future works.
71. For a literature review, see Fleischacker, S. (1991). Philosophy in moral practice: Kant and Adam Smith. *Kant-Studien, 82*(3), 249–269.
72. Sen, *The Idea of Justice*, 124. As reported by Fleischacker, indirect sources tell us that Kant defined Smith as his "Liebling" among the contemporary writers on moral sense and passions. See Fleischacker, Philosophy in moral practice, 250.
73. In addition to Fleischacker, see Meld Shell, S. (1980). *The Rights of Reason*. Toronto, University of Toronto Press; Oz-Salzberger, F. (1995). *Translating the Enlightenment. Scottish Civic Discourse in Eighteenth-Century Germany*. Oxford, Oxford University Press; Haakonssen, K. (1996). *Natural Law and Moral Philosophy: From Grotius to the Scottish Enlightenment*. Cambridge, Cambridge University Press; Tribe, K. (2016). The German reception of Adam Smith. In Mizuta, H. (ed.), *A Critical Bibliography of Adam Smith*. London, Routledge.
74. Oncken, A. (1877). *Adam Smith und Immanuel Kant*. Leipzig, Duncker & Humblot.
75. Ibid., 90–91. My translation. On the notion of respect between Smith and Kant, see also Walschots, M. (2022). Achtung in Kant and Smith. *Kant-Studien, 113*(2), 238–268.
76. Kant, *Groundwork*, 2. My italics.
77. Ibid., 7.
78. Ibid.
79. Ibid.
80. Ibid., 9. My italics.
81. Ibid., 6.
82. This section draws on Santori, "The curious case of the three Adam Smiths."
83. Malthus, T. R. ([1798] 1966). *An Essay on the Principle of Population*. London, Macmillan, 303–304.
84. For an overview of the main positions in literature, see Montes, The Adam Smith Problem.
85. Smith, A. ([1896] 1982). *Lectures on Jurisprudence*. In Meek, R. L., Raphael, D. D., & P. G. Stein (eds.), *The Glasgow Edition of the Works and Correspondence of Adam Smith*. Indianapolis, Liberty Fund, 295.
86. Smith, *Wealth of Nations*, 26.
87. I will expose the virtues related to self-interest such as prudence and self-command in the next chapter.
88. Evensky, J. (2005). "Chicago Smith" versus "Kirkaldy Smith." *History of Political Economy, 37*(2), 197–203.

89. Stigler, G. J. (1976). The successes and failures of Professor Smith. *Journal of Political Economy, 84*(6), 1201.
90. Stigler, G. J. (1971). Smith's Travels on the Ship of State. *History of Political Economy, 3*(2), 265.
91. Smith, *The Theory of Moral Sentiments*, 10.
92. Heath, E. (1995). The commerce of sympathy: Adam Smith on the emergence of morals. *Journal of the History of Philosophy, 33*(3), 447–466.
93. Sen, A. (2011b). Uses and abuses of Adam Smith. *History of Political Economy, 43*(2), 257.
94. Rothschild, E. (1994). Adam Smith and the invisible hand. *The American Economic Review, 84*(2), 319.
95. Ibid.
96. See Herzog, L. (2013). The community of commerce: Smith's rhetoric of sympathy in the opening of the *Wealth of Nations*. *Philosophy & Rhetoric, 46*(1), 65–87; Montes, L. (2019). Adam Smith's foundational idea of sympathetic persuasion. *Cambridge Journal of Economics, 43*(1), 1–15; Bee, M. (2021). The pleasure of exchange: Adam Smith's third kind of self-love. *Journal of the History of Economic Thought, 43*(1), 118–140.
97. Herzog, The community of commerce, 74.
98. Bee, The pleasure of exchange, 119.
99. Bruni, L., & Sugden, R. (2008). Fraternity: Why the market need not be a morally free zone. *Economics & Philosophy, 24*(1), 45.
100. See Reisman, D. A. (1998). Adam Smith on market and state. *Journal of Institutional and Theoretical Economics (JITE), 154*(2), 357–383.
101. See Myint, H. (1977). Adam Smith's theory of international trade in the perspective of economic development. *Economica, 44*(175), 231–248.
102. See Paganelli, M. P. (2022). Adam Smith and economic development in theory and practice: A rejection of the stadial model? *Journal of the History of Economic Thought, 44*(1), 95–104.
103. See Williams, D. (2014). Adam Smith and colonialism. *Journal of International Political Theory, 10*(3), 283–301.
104. See Luban, D. (2012). Adam Smith on vanity, domination, and history. *Modern Intellectual History, 9*(2), 275–302.
105. See Slegers, R. (2024). Vanity and social media: Adam Smith reassures us that we are not all narcissists. *Journal of Contextual Economics–Schmollers Jahrbuch*, 1–14.
106. See Santori, P. (2022). Idleness and the very sparing hand of God: The invisible tie between Hume's dialogues concerning natural religion and Smith's *Wealth of Nations*. *Journal of the History of Economic Thought, 44*(2), 246–267.

107. Iannaccone, L. R. (1991). The consequences of religious market structure: Adam Smith and the economics of religion. *Rationality and Society*, 3(2), 156–177.
108. Ferrara, F. (1852). Preface. In *Biblioteca dell'Economista*, vol. 3. Turin, Cugini Pomba ed Editori Librai, xxxvi.
109. Schumpeter, J. A. ([1954] 1986). *History of Economic Analysis*. Taylor & Francis e-library, 172.
110. See Santori, P. (2019). The foundation of the right of property: Rosmini as Genovesi's interpreter. *International Review of Economics*, 66(4), 353–367.
111. Rosmini A ([1865] 1993) *The Philosophy of Right. The Essence of Right*, vol. 1. Durham, Rosmini House, 346.
112. Genovesi A ([1766] 1973). *Della diceosina o sia della filosofia del giusto e dell'onesto*. Milan, Marzorati, 161.
113. Genovesi, *Della diceosina*, 60. My translation.
114. Genovesi, *Lezioni di Commercio*, 31.
115. I am referring to the contemporary Italian school of civil economy, which includes Italian authors such as Luigino Bruni, Stefano Zamagni, Pier Luigi Porta, and more modestly the author of this book, and international scholars as Robert Sugden.
116. See Santori, *Thomas Aquinas and the Civil Economy Tradition*, chap. 5.
117. Genovesi, *Lezioni di Commercio*, 13.
118. See Bruni & Zamagni, *Civil Economy*.
119. Genovesi, A. (1962). *Autobiografia e altri scritti*. Milan, Feltrinelli, 449. My translation.
120. D'Onofrio, F. (2015). On the concept of "felicitas publica" in eighteenth-century political economy. *Journal of the History of Economic Thought*, 37(3), 449–471. See also Bruni's response in Bruni, L. (2017). On the concept of economia civile and "Felicitas Publica": A comment on Federico D'Onofrio. *Journal of the History of Economic Thought*, 39(2), 273–279.
121. Pabst, A. (2018). Political economy of virtue: Civil economy, happiness and public trust in the thought of Antonio Genovesi. *The European Journal of the History of Economic Thought*, 25(4), 583. See also Pabst & Scazzieri, Virtue, production, and the politics of commerce.
122. See Reinert, S. A. (2011). *Translating Empire: Emulation and the Origins of Political Economy*. Cambridge, MA, Harvard University Press, chap. 4.
123. Pabst, A. & Scazzieri, R. (2023). *The Constitution of Political Economy*. Cambridge, Cambridge University Press.
124. This section is based on Santori, The market in the kingdom of ends.

125. See Micewski, E. R., & Troy, C. (2007). Business ethics – deontologically revisited. *Journal of Business Ethics*, 72(1), 17–25; Arnold, D. G., & Harris, J. D. (eds.). (2012). *Kantian Business Ethics: Critical Perspectives*. Cheltenham, Edward Elgar Publishing; Bowie, N. (2017). *Business Ethics: A Kantian Perspective*. Cambridge, Cambridge University Press.
126. Bowie, N. (2002). A Kantian approach to business ethics. In Donaldson, T., Werhane, P. H., & Cording, M. (eds.), *Ethical Issues in Business: A Philosophical Approach*. New Jersey, Prentice Hall, 62.
127. See Bowie, N. (2000). A Kantian theory of leadership. *Leadership & Organization Development Journal*, 21(4), 185–193.
128. See Robinson, R. M. (2022). *Business Ethics: Kant, Virtue, and the Nexus of Duty – Foundations and Case Studies*. Cham, Springer Nature.
129. Dubbink, W., & Van Liedekerke, L. (2014). Grounding positive duties in commercial life. *Journal of Business Ethics*, 120, 527–539. For a parallel between Kant and Smith based on the former concept of imperfect duties, see White, M. D. (2010). Adam Smith and Immanuel Kant: On markets, duties, and moral sentiments. *Forum for Social Economics*, 39, 53–60.
130. See Bowie, *Business Ethics*; Dubbink & Van Liedekerke, Rethinking the purity of moral motives; Santori, The market in the kingdom of ends.
131. Kant, *Groundwork*, 41.
132. Ibid., 46.
133. Dubbink & Van Liedekerke, Rethinking the purity of moral motives, 383.
134. Ibid., 388.
135. Ibid., 389.
136. Anderson, E. (1995). *Value in Ethics and Economics*. Cambridge, MA, Harvard University Press, 19–20.
137. Ibid., chap. 7
138. Ibid., 144. My italics.
139. Ibid., 9.
140. Satz, D. (2010). *Why Some Things Should Not Be for Sale: The Moral Limits of Markets*. Oxford, Oxford University Press, 80. My italics.
141. Anderson, *Value in Ethics and Economics*, 145.
142. Kant, *Groundwork*, 4.

3 The Three Economic Enlightenments

3.1 From History to Theory

Research into the history of ideas is a precious ally for BE.[1] In the joint venture of the two for providing valuable insights to address contemporary issues, they arrive at a moment in which the complexities of interpreting past authors and schools of thought give way to clear and precise rules of conduct. This is what happens in this chapter. Does this mean that the insights gained in Chapter 2 on Genovesi, Kant, and Smith are now irrelevant? Should we put aside the historical, cultural, and social backgrounds in which these authors elaborated their theories? Furthermore, what about the *ex post* interpretations of their views? Should they be reduced to cherry-picking the most convenient? Obviously, the answers to all these questions are "no, no, no, no"; however, these answers need to be qualified by some preliminary remarks.

First, presenting moral principles elaborated by ancient authors without referencing their anthropological views, that is, their views of human beings, would be impossible. Kant's concept of duty can be fully comprehended only if we presuppose that rational (reason) and empirical (desire, emotions, inclination) parts in humans interact and they are often opposed to one another. Genovesi viewed things differently, building his moral view of the markets on a virtue ethics framework. According to Genovesi, human actions are related to character traits that express each person's excellence on his or her journey to human flourishing. Smith seemed to be closer to Genovesi than Kant, although his economic and moral analysis emphasized the role of supra-individual mechanisms (the invisible hand and the interplay of moral sentiments in producing codes of morality and justice). The next section describes some common elements of these three moral views based on the previous chapter's analysis as a background.

Second, the three philosophers lived during the Enlightenment. Not just arising from intellectual curiosity, the ideas of the Enlightenment are the basis of modern Western societies, and they still have visible effects.[2] The ideas of freedom, equality, and the priority of reason and science over tradition and superstition (to mention a few) are also part of our liberal democracies because they were advocated during the Enlightenment in the eighteenth century.[3] Needless to say, these ideas have major differences when applied to nowadays. For example, one such difference that is indirectly relevant to this analysis is that, currently, we live in postmodern societies in which the ideals of the Enlightenment have been put into serious discussion.[4] In contrast, one such difference that is directly relevant to this analysis is that the current extension and configuration of the markets differ from those of the eighteenth century.[5] Yet, our societies and those of Genovesi, Kant, and Smith are not entirely different with some similarities; rather, they are similar with some differences.[6] Such an awareness is essential for any analysis that applies ancient ideas to contemporary issues.

Third, a stylistic reason to place the historical analysis in the chapter before the theoretical one exists. If I continuously interrupt the presentation of the moral principles elaborated by these three authors to account for the complexities of their own thoughts and those mentioned by their posthumous interpreters, the text would be much harder to read. However, this book aims to provide conceptual tools to people interested in BE, not necessarily in the history of ideas. To find a balance between complexity and clarity, I have tried to depict the intricacies related to the interpretations of these authors' ideas in Chapter 2 so that I can fully devote Chapter 3 to presenting their three models in the clearest and most accessible way possible.

Fourth, the field of analysis is too vast to be within the scope of this text; hence, I had to limit it. Genovesi, Kant, and Smith wrote about many economic issues, from economic policy to monetary issues and from international commerce to fiscal issues. In this book, I am specifically interested in what they said about the behavior of free economic agents during a market exchange. All three of them were interested in the descriptive aspect – how people usually behave in such situations – and (mostly) in the prescriptive aspect – how people should behave. Some interpreters argue that, for each author, one or two principles can be used to understand all their reflections on economic issues or, in general, their theories. I am quite prudent as each of these authors has his own contradictions, and each of these theories has its internal tension. By limiting the analysis field, I think I can present a coherent view of each of them in a limited range of situations, that is, the market exchange between free individuals.

Finally, the issue of cherry-picking exists. I would not refuse this label as attached to my analysis, although I have to characterize it. My choices between (or beyond) the many readings elaborated in secondary literature are not connected to my tastes but to the utility of each theory. Paraphrasing Sen's famous lecture (*Equality of What?*[7]), one might ask: Utility of what? Here, my interpretations of each author are useful in depicting three moral principles that, in turn, can constitute three moral rules for the economic agents involved in market exchange. At the beginning of Chapter 4, I will explain how these moral principles can be applied to concrete situations and how they relate to moral reasons and motivations. For now, stating the aim of this chapter as presenting the reader with three different moral perspectives, each attached to one of the authors considered (Genovesi, Kant, and Smith), would suffice. The book is devoted to bringing pluralism to BE by adding more perspectives to triad of consequentialism, deontology, and virtue ethics. The subsequent discussion is a precise attempt to reach that goal.

The chapter is structured as follows. In Section 3.2, I present the concepts of inclination and reason. These anthropological elements are common and play an important role in the views of Genovesi, Kant, and Smith. The following three sections (3.3, 3.4, 3.5) will depict the three moral principles of economic agents. For each of them, I will provide the premises on which the three philosophers elaborated on their moral rules, some corollaries, and explanations. In Section 3.6, I will discuss the similarities and differences between the three moral principles of economic enlightenments.

3.2 Inclination and Reason

Genovesi, Kant, and Smith adopted anthropological essentialism.[8] The three of them believed that human beings have some natural and immutable characteristics in their nature, which constitute their essence. We are born with the same natural features that external factors, such as education, culture, society, and so on, might eventually modify. While the three philosophers advanced three different anthropologies, they used similar, if not identical, terminology to indicate the essential features of human beings. An analysis of their essence remains necessary to understand what prompts humans to act.

In this section, I will explicate two of the features that remained implicit in the historical analysis of the previous chapter. While they disagreed on how these two features relate or have to relate to bringing humans toward moral actions, Genovesi, Kant, and Smith agreed that inclination[9] and reason constitute two essential characteristics to understanding why we act and how we should act. They correspond to two stages, pre-reflective (inclinations) and reflective (reasons) stages, from which we can elaborate on moral principles.

In a pre-reflective stage, inclinations are forces that drive human beings to action. In everyday life, we feel impulses, desires, and passions that spontaneously drive us toward certain choices or behaviors. As human beings, we are naturally inclined toward certain patterns of actions, even before we stop and reflect on how right or wrong those actions are. Think about people we deem to be naturally generous. They donate and help others without the need for a reward, incentive, or obligation. Generosity can be an example of an inclination, and the same is valid for its opposite – selfishness. In common language, we say that people are born with these tendencies, and Genovesi, Kant, and Smith called them inclinations.

In *Groundwork*, Kant recurrently mentioned inclinations as drivers of human decisions and actions. He mentioned four kinds of actions to describe the scope of morality, which, as we will see in detail later, coincide with duty. There are actions contrary to duty, actions "in conformity with duty but to which human beings have no inclination immediately,"[10] actions that are in conformity with duty for which the person has "an immediate inclination,"[11] and actions done from duty. When Kant put the adjective "immediate" close to inclination, he also expressed the pre-reflective nature of inclination. To be inclined toward something is to desire something before any thoughts or reflection on it. Kant pushes his argument even further to say that happiness is the sum of all human inclinations: "All people have already, of themselves, the strongest and deepest inclination to happiness because it is just in this idea that all inclinations unite in one sum."[12]

Inclinations were also central to Smith's moral philosophy and political economy. In the *Theory*, Smith used propensity and inclination interchangeably: "The obvious observation, therefore, which it naturally falls in our way to make, is that our propensity to sympathize with sorrow must be very strong, and our inclination to sympathize with joy very weak."[13] Sympathy or fellow feeling is a crucial concept for Smith's moral philosophy, and it involves both pre-reflective and reflective dimensions. In the pre-reflective stage, the inclination is equal to propensity, whose etymology – from the Latin *propensus*, past participle of *propendere*, *pro-* "forward, down" + *pendere* "hang" – reveals something natural to who we are, something we experience spontaneously. In *Wealth*, the propensity to "truck, barter, and exchange" and the inclination toward our own good are said to be the main drivers of the modern market economy. While Smith did not associate the terms self-love and inclination directly, their closeness can be inferred from the analysis of his text. Right before explaining how, in a civilized society, people in need of cooperation from others should elicit their self-love. Smith described how the other alternative, that is, expecting help from others (benevolence), is a flaw and an impractical endeavor: "Man sometimes uses the same arts with his brethren, and when he has no other means of engaging them *to act according to his inclinations*, endeavours by every servile and fawning attention to obtain their good will. He has no time, however, to do this upon every occasion."[14] Here, man's inclinations coincide with his self-interest (or self-love), that is, what the man wants to obtain from others. Similar to sympathy, self-love also has a reflective part. However, when associated with inclinations, self-love means something that naturally and spontaneously drives human beings toward the objects of their desires.

Genovesi devoted a chapter of his *Istituzioni di Metafisica per Principianti*[15] (Metaphysical institutions for beginners) to describing the inclinations of human beings. In Genovesi's thoughts, we clearly see the essentialist perspective: "This is why those inclinations that are found in all men, and always, and united with nature itself, are called natural."[16] Genovesi mentions the love of existence and the desire to avoid pains and difficulties, as much as possible, among the basic inclinations. This theme recurs in his *Ragionamento sull'Agricoltura* (Reasoning about agriculture), where he writes that "each man, by force of nature, loves before anything else to exist, and to exist without discomfort and hardship ... these two natural inclinations."[17] For Genovesi, these two natural inclinations, among others, are pre-reflective drivers of human actions. We could be born in different countries, receive different educations, have different means of subsistence, and so on; and yet, we are said to be human insofar as we share the same basic inclinations that prompt us toward certain actions and decisions before any reflection or reasoning.

So far, I have shown that Genovesi, Kant, and Smith used inclinations to describe the pre-reflective drivers of human actions. However, I have not focused on the inclinations that they believe are relevant to driving our economic actions, specifically during a market exchange. I will do that in the forthcoming sections that are devoted to each of their moral principles for economic agents. Before that, I will explain the reflective moment.

The three philosophers were the protagonists of the Enlightenment period. This means that they all agreed on the importance of reason in determining human actions. Reason constitutes the reflective moment, that is, the moment in which we think about the kind of decisions and actions toward which our inclinations are directing us. Genovesi, Kant, and Smith argued that humans are rational, as they can find reasons for their actions. For them, essentialism does not mean determinism. Without a reflective moment, our decisions and actions result exclusively from our inclinations and external circumstances. While our inclinations determine our actions, we are free to choose the kind of action we want to take, that is, the reasons that motivate our actions. If we ask ourselves whether our inclinations are directing us toward the right thing to do, we are looking for moral reasons. Moral principles are not necessarily separated by inclinations. Conversely, they result from the interplay between reason and inclinations, pre-reflective and reflective stages. Even in Kant's moral philosophy, where the distinction between the rational (reason) and empirical (inclinations) parts is accentuated, and morality is said to be just in the rational nature of human beings, inclinations play a crucial role. As Barbara Herman argued, "The key to understanding Kant is in the idea that moral worth does not turn on the presence or absence of inclination supporting the action, but on its inclusion in the agent's maxim *as* a determining ground of action."[18] The first and second stages are hierarchically ordered.[19] The reflective moment is essential to determine moral principles as well as the rules of conduct. This is valid in the thoughts of Kant, Smith, and Genovesi; however, as I will describe in the final section, significant differences and nuances exist about the kind of hierarchy involved. Be as it may, inclinations cannot and should not be eliminated from morality, because doing so would mean ignoring an essential part of human beings.

The next three sections show how the interplay of inclinations and reasons led the three philosophers to advance three moral principles for economic agents involved in market exchange. In particular, I will show how these moral principles can be inferred from the theories of the three philosophers. The results will involve the principle of self-interest and non-tuism for Smith, the principle of mutual assistance for Genovesi, and the duty of honoring the spirit of mutually beneficial contracts for Kant. I will apply these moral principles to case studies related to incomplete contracts in Part II of the book.

Before moving to the exposition, one final note is required. Genovesi, Kant, and Smith knew that human beings are more complex than their inclinations and reason. Hence, what determines us to act in a certain way or decide on a course of action is the result of many elements, such as spiritual life, external influences (education, culture), circumstances, or how we formulate or are presented with a moral problem. At the same time, this awareness does not diminish the value of referring to moral principles in everyday life. The three moral principles of economic enlightenments are a treasure we should preserve *ceteris paribus*, that is, while considering all the other elements.

3.3 Smith's Political Economy: Self-Interest and Non-Tuism

In the *Theory*, Smith described a variety of drives of human actions: inclinations, passions, virtues,[20] and sentiments.[21] Smith provided a rich analysis of sociality based on the hypothesis that benevolence, sympathy, and a capacity to understand how fellows feel are fundamental properties of human nature. Similar to all major moral philosophers of his time, Smith understood the richness and complexity of human nature and motivations quite well. However, in terms of the economic sphere, two main inclinations play an important role: benevolence and self-love. The former is scarce, whereas the latter is dominant. One of the most famous passages from *Wealth* proves this: "But man has almost constant occasion for the help of his brethren, and it is in vain for him to expect it from their benevolence only. He will be likelier to prevail if he can interest their self-love in his favor and shew them that it is for their own advantage to do for him what he requires of them."[22] For Smith, cooperation is a crucial element of society, without which human beings cannot live together. We can obtain the help of others to accomplish our aims primarily in two ways. First, we can appeal to their goodwill, that is, benevolence, and hope that they will help us without expecting a return. However, because each person trades with many others in a commercial society, market relations cannot generally be based on humanity, benevolence, or friendship. Second, Smith envisages appealing to others' self-interest:

> It is not the benevolence of the butcher, the brewer, or the baker, that we expect our dinner, but from their regard to their own interest. We address ourselves, not to their humanity, but to their self-love, and never talk to them of our own necessities, but of their advantages. Nobody but a beggar chooses to depend chiefly upon the benevolence of his fellow citizens.[23]

Being the realm of mutual advantage, the market derives from cooperation between free individuals. All economic agents involved in a market exchange have their own individual benefit in mind. They do not think about the good of the parties with whom they are exchanging, as long as it is not related to their own good. It comes naturally as a pre-reflective inclination, as the merchants show: "I have never known much good done by those affected to trade for the public good. It is an affectation, indeed, not very common among merchants, and very few words need be employed in dissuading them from it."[24]

The inclination toward self-love or self-interest does not mean the uncontrolled pursuit of one's goals. For the market to work, its participants must respect the principles of justice, and they might do so for different reasons, such as an innate sense of justice,[25] a concern for their reputation,[26] or the fear of legal punishment.[27] However, the impersonal principles of justice differ from those governing intimate sociality or benevolence:

> Society may subsist among different men, as among different merchants, from a sense of its utility, without any mutual love or affection ... Beneficence, therefore, is less essential to the existence of society than justice. Society may subsist, though not in the most comfortable state, without beneficence; but the prevalence of injustice must utterly destroy it.[28]

The reflective moment brings reason into the picture. Assuming that self-love is central to the working of the market sphere and benevolence and humanity are too little to explain the cooperation we see every day in the markets, we can ask the following question: Is this a good thing?

Smith had clear ideas about it. He not only described the functioning of the market based on self-love but also prescribed it. First, mutual advantage is achieved by cooperation based on self-love.[29] At the end of the day, the butcher, brewer, and baker get what they want (money to save or spend on other goods), and we obtain what we want (meat, beer, bread). Mutual benefit is good for the parties involved in the exchange. Yet, if we conceive of the market as a network of mutually beneficial transactions between free individuals, society as a whole benefits from it. This is the well-known idea of the invisible hand, that is, the fact that the public good results from unintentional actions, that is, actions whose motivation was not to promote the public good. Let us recall what Smith wrote about merchants, whom he did not see doing great things when they traded to promote the public good. The merchant "intends only his own gain, and he is in this, as in many other cases, led by an invisible hand to promote an end which was no part of his intention ... By pursuing his own interest he frequently promotes that of the society more effectually than when he really intends to promote it."[30]

Reason directly concerns the Enlightenment project. If we are free to pursue our self-love, we are not subject to constrictions by other people (as in feudal society). Moreover, we do not need to beg for what we want. Smith told us that the market allows us to satisfy our economic needs without dependency, and this corresponds to equality, dignity, and self-respect. The market gives each person the (negative and positive) freedom to act in his or her interest, subject to the constraints he or she imposes on himself or herself when others act on his or her freedom. Market relations are free horizontal relations among equals: The tradespersons and their customers are symmetrically positioned concerning a mutually beneficial transaction, in contrast to the asymmetric/hierarchical relationship of inferior and superior, as the beggar and the person from whom he or she begs. Through this property, the market supports the virtues of independence, moral equality, and even fraternity.[31]

Taking stock, we found that reason helps us discover that good reasons exist to follow our inclinations when involved in a market exchange. The right thing to do is follow self-love. However, before arriving to state the moral principle emerging from Smith's view, an important nuance must be stressed. Without reducing Smith's view to neoclassical interpretations (see Chapter 2), an element caught by a later reader might be of interest. I am referring to the concept of non-tuism elaborated by nineteenth-century economist Philip Henry Wicksteed (1844–1927). Wicksteed wanted to demonstrate to Smith and political economists that limiting human motivations for undertaking an economic exchange to self-interest was reductive. Someone may want to start a market transaction for altruism or other interests that are not strictly theirs. Wicksteed admitted a wide range of motivations as determinants of economic action except, and here is the point, for one. When we care about the good of the party with whom we are exchanging and when their identity emerges and interests us, then the action cannot be said to be an economic one:

> The things and doings with which economic investigation is concerned will therefore be found to include everything which enters into the circle of exchange – that is to say, everything with which men can supply each other, or which men can do for each other, in what we may call an *impersonal capacity*; or, in other words, the things a man can give to or do for another *independently of any personal and individualised sympathy* with him or with his motives or reasons.[32]

From this understanding, Wicksteed elaborated the principle of non-tuism as something between egoistic (self-love) and altruistic (benevolence) motivations:

> Once more, then, if *ego* and *tu* are engaged in any transaction, whether egoism or altruism furnishes my inspiring motive, or whether my thoughts at the moment are wholly impersonal, the economic nature of the action on my side remains undisturbed. It is only when tuism to some degree, actuates my conduct that it ceases to be wholly economic. It is idle, therefore, to consider "egoism" as a characteristic mark of economic life.[33]

The consideration of the good of the other with whom I am exchanging, *disjointed by my own interest*, should not be part of any market transactions.

While Wicksteed's non-tuism went beyond Smith's text, I argue that it remains faithful to the spirit of Smith's thought. In Smith's view of market transactions based on self-interest, no place is left for concern for the good of the exchange partner.[34] As counterfactual proof, in *Wealth*, Smith listed the virtues of economic actors, among which, prudence and self-command are the most important. As Smith understood, both virtues are related to self-interest and advise the economic actors not to blindly follow their self-interest but to moderate it when necessary. Importantly, these virtues do not ask economic actors to care about other's good or that of society. The correct functioning of the market – grounded in self-interest, invisible hand, prudence, and self-command – allows human beings to fully express other inclinations and virtues directed to other's good (humanity, generosity, compassion) in other spheres of their lives.

From the pre-reflective and reflective moments of Smith's theory, the moral principle of self-interest and non-tuism emerges: When you are involved in a market transaction that you have freely joined, you should care about your own interest. The interest of the exchange partner should concern you insofar as it promotes your own (no more than that).

An important corollary to this principle is related to the consequences of not adopting it. What would happen if we cared about the interest of the exchange partner independently of how they promoted our own? In Smith's political economy, two main problems exist: economic inefficiency and uncertain genuine sociality. The former has been extensively investigated in mainstream economics literature under the label of market inefficiencies or failure.[35] The latter directly concerns Smith's theory of sociality. Let us assume that we go along with the view of caring about others in the market exchange and seeking authentic friendship in the market sphere. How sincere can a friendship be when money is in the picture? This is a matter of conventional wisdom and has a long history in Western philosophy. Aristotle perfectly knew that friendship based on utility "is for the commercially minded" and, therefore, holds a qualitatively inferior rank compared to true friendship based on virtue.[36] In Smithian terms, you need to have a certain independence to have a real friendship. You are not dependent on someone; you can choose that person as your friend (elective friendship).[37]

Moreover, the independence of your friends assures you against the risk that they are interested in you, not in your money. According to Smith, the market is the means through which you gain independence; therefore, you can have authentic and genuine relations in spheres of social life other than the market. If the market functions well when self-interest is the rule and not the exception, we risk inefficiency when elements such as humanity, benevolence, and sympathy are introduced. That inefficiency, in turn, can cause the loss of our independence, leading to problems in other spheres of social life (family, groups, and friendship).

3.4 Genovesi's Civil Economy: Mutual Assistance

Genovesi explicitly mentioned the natural inclination to exist with the least amount of pain and discomfort. However, adopting Newtonian lexicon, something very common during the Italian Enlightenment, he spoke about two basic forces/inclinations determining human actions: concentric force (*forza concentrativa o concentriva*) and diffusive force (*forza diffusiva o espansiva*).[38] The first corresponds to Smith's notion of self-love, while the latter refers to an inclination to care for and promote others without expecting any return. One central element to understanding Genovesi's anthropology is that he describes these two forces as both basic and primitive.[39] He criticized some of his illustrious predecessors for having recognized these two forces in the pre-reflective moment but, at the same time, argued that one is more basic than the others.

On the one hand, Genovesi opposed Mandeville's and Hobbes's egoistic conceptions of man: "Hobbes founds all on *forza concentrativa*, and the *forza diffusiva* springs only from a higher degree of the *concentrativa*, that is fear."[40] Genovesi refused the idea that we are naturally inclined to care about others just because, in our deep essence, that care is connected to our own good. On the other hand, there are authors who committed the opposite mistake: "On the contrary, Plato, Cicero, Grotius, Cumberland, Puffendorf, and all those who followed them made a mistake. They are based only on the *forza espansiva*, from which they give rise to the *concentriva* by reverberation. Philosophy that can seduce warm fantasies but does not satisfy nature."[41] These anthropological accounts depict a naïve view of human beings as if we always care about each other without having any interest in seeking a return.

Genovesi's anthropology recognized two basic inclinations/forces that always determine us regardless of the domain of social life we are involved in, for example, family, politics, association, markets, and so forth. As human beings, we always feel the influence of these two forces. But there is more to it. According to Genovesi, the effect of these two forces is not identical but varies according to the social sphere of the situation in which we are involved. For example, in our family, we are driven more by the *forza diffusiva* than by the *forza concentriva*. In contrast, in the market sphere, where we often interact with strangers, we are more driven by the *forza concentriva* over the *forza diffusiva*. Yet, human beings must find harmony, or equilibrium, between these two basic forces.[42] Anyone can easily understand this anthropological thesis. If we forget to care about our own good in our family life and always prioritize the good of another family member over our own good, we suffer in the medium or long run. The same goes for the market sphere. If we follow Smith's moral principle and ignore the presence of *forza diffusiva* during market transactions, we deny part of our nature. As we saw in Chapter 2, Genovesi adopted the Aristotelian and Thomistic understanding of human beings as social animals, that is, as people who can flourish and reach happiness only through genuine and authentic social relationships.[43]

How can harmony and equilibrium between the two basic forces be found? This happens in the reflective moment, that is, through reason. Through self-reflection and reasoning, we can understand the importance of harmonizing the two forces and the ways to do so. Genovesi furnished an important hint. When he used the term equilibrium, he referred to Aristotle's notion of proportionality.[44] Equilibrium does not mean perfect equality, as if the two basic forces have always been equally important in determining our actions. Genovesi's anthropology aimed to understand the role of the two forces in various domains of social life to see which one is more influential and to "not to forget" about the presence and importance of others. He did not argue to be altruistic in the market or egoistic in the family but to find a different equilibrium for each sphere.

Genovesi's idea of market transactions originated from his anthropological vision.[45] During the market transaction between free individuals, other's good can be pursued intentionally alongside one's individual good. Genovesi calls mutual assistance (*mutua assistenza*) the mutual concern of both parties during a market exchange. In a commercial society based on exchanges between free individuals, equilibrium can be found and maintained as the two forces converge toward a common end: mutual benefit. A free market is a place where, through the medium of price mechanisms, human beings are mutually useful and thus assist one another in meeting their respective needs. In this framework, the common good is neither an unintentional consequence (like the invisible hand) nor a by-product of self-interest. This marks a significant difference between the thoughts of Smith and Genovesi. Using Smith's example but reversing his main thesis, we could argue that for Genovesi, the butcher, the baker, and the brewer can intentionally promote the interests of buyers and society without renouncing their gains from trade or creating inefficiencies. The competitive and cooperative nature of market exchange is not a naïve interpretation of market society. This is how Genovesi, theoretically and empirically, saw commercial society as a large-scale cooperation effort for mutual benefit, whereas other-regarded motivations remain as basic as self-interested ones.

This economic aspect of mutual assistance aligns with the general mutual assistance characterizing social life: "Friendship and reciprocal trust between citizens foster mutual assistance in life's troubles."[46] The market itself is conceived as an expression of the general civil society law, that is, reciprocity. The common good is part of everyone's intentions, alongside their self-interest. For civil economy humanism, no common good exists without intentionally seeking it, meaning that the market is not a space extraneous to other places of social life, a realm of greed to be contained, if not banished, within the city (*civitas*), while elsewhere (family, civil society, politics), the common good is pursued. On the contrary, the fundamental law of the market is intentional mutual benefit, that is, mutual assistance.

To sum up, the outcome of the interaction between the pre-reflective (two basic forces) and reflective (reason) moments is the moral principle of mutual assistance: When you are involved in a market transaction that you freely join, you should care about your own interest and, beyond your own interest, to a certain extent, about the interest of your exchange partner.

Some corollaries are attached to Genovesi's moral principle. For example, mutual assistance does not imply that people get involved in market exchanges because they care about the good of their exchange partners. Imagine a situation in which you have to choose between two of your friends, where one owns a bar with an overpriced cup of expresso and another owns a bar with an espresso of the same quality that is sold for a reasonable price. In such a case, Genovesi would argue that someone is free to choose. If you want to go to the second bar because you cannot afford to pay a high price for everyday coffee, you are not doing something immoral. The moral principle of mutual assistance applies to different situations. For example, you might know nothing about computers and need one. You go to the shop and ask the seller (whom you do not know) that you require a medium-performance laptop, probably not an expensive one. You also admit your ignorance about computers. It is the end of the day, and the seller has two computers left, one high-performance priced at 10,000 euros and one medium-performance priced at 2,000 euros. What should the seller do? It would not be unlawful if she had proposed an expensive computer to you, taking advantage of your scarce knowledge. In this case, the seller exclusively follows her *forza concentriva*, seeking maximum gain. However, according to the principle of mutual assistance, the seller should sell you the 2,000 euros computer. She must consider your interests while not forgetting about hers. The *forza diffusiva* does not mean altruism. The principle of mutual assistance does not require the seller to give you the computer for free. In contrast, it requires the seller to consider her and your own benefits simultaneously. At the end of the day, if she sells you the 2,000 euros computer, both of you will be satisfied.[47]

To better grasp Genovesi's view, we can use the terminology recently elaborated in behavioral economics. The principle of mutual assistance requires exchange partners to adopt "we rationality" or "team reasoning." Instead of seeing the exchange as a zero-sum game, where one benefits from another's loss, they should consider it a positive sum exchange, in which both benefit. Instead of two different "I"-seeking goals, they should conceive of themselves as a "we" – a team pursuing a common goal: mutual advantage. From the "we" or "team" perspectives, it emerges that in some situations, individuals are asked to help their team members more. According to Genovesi, we can naturally adopt the "we" perspective in our intimate and nonintimate relationships. You do not need to consider the exchange partners as your friends or relatives. The principle of mutual assistance, as opposed to non-tuism, requires you to recognize them beyond what they can do for you and require them to do the same in the spirit of reciprocity. The extent of the "beyond" may vary depending on a reflection on the equilibrium between the two forces.

3.5 Kant's Moral Economy: Honoring the Spirit of Mutually Beneficial Contracts

For Kant, morality is about principles. The pre-reflective empirical part of inclinations can be a starting point, but we still need to rely exclusively on our rationale to find general moral reasons that can constitute the principles for our actions. Christine Korsgaard rightly summarized, "If there are any moral requirements, then there must be a metaphysics of morals, a body of synthetic a priori judgments concerning what we ought to do."[48] As Kant had already realized in his *Critique of Pure Reason*, any foundational attempt can succeed in an a priori/pure realm. Pure and a priori, not always synonymous in Kantian philosophy, here yield the same meaning: "Now morality is the only lawfulness of actions which can be derived entirely a priori from principles. Hence, the metaphysics of morals is really the pure morality, which is not grounded on any anthropology (no empirical condition)."[49] The two key concepts to understand Kant's moral philosophy are duty and categorical imperative.

Morality concerns what we ought to do rather than what we want to do; it is about duty. Duty *"is the necessity of an action from respect for the law."*[50] We perceive moral law as a necessity because our inclinations, such as self-love, often naturally bring us to do something different from what duty prescribes. For an exclusively rational person, duty may not make any sense. As human beings are both rational and empirical beings, duty expresses the idea that the principles of actions in the form of moral laws are determined exclusively by our reflective/rational capacity. This allows us to arrive at universal and objective (valid for all rational beings) moral principles. The categorical imperative is the formula in which we express the command that these objective principles have on us. According to Kant, by employing the formulas of the categorical imperative, human beings can understand whether their subjective principles of action can be considered objective and, consequently, be classified as duties.

The first formulation of the categorical imperative goes as follows: *"act only according to that maxim through which you can at the same time will that it become a universal law."*[51] The maxim is the subjective principle of action, that is, how we formulate reasons determined by our inclinations for our actions. Many interpreters have conceived this formula as a test.[52] If your maxim can be universalized, it can be conceived as a categorical imperative corresponding to a duty. To "universalize" a maxim, we need to imagine a society in which every rational being follows the maxim as the principle of their conduct in the same situation. If that society does not generate any form of contradiction, then it passes the universalization test.

Given these premises, I will now consider whether Smith's and Genovesi's moral principles for economic agents, which can be considered universalized maxims, pass or fail Kant's test. The moral principle of self-interest and non-tuism was considered by Kant himself, although the German philosopher was not referring specifically to the market sphere:

Yet a fourth, who is prospering while he sees that others have to struggle with great hardships (whom he could just as well help), thinks: What's it to me? May everyone be as happy as heaven wills, or as he can make himself, I shall take nothing away from him, not even envy him; I just do not feel like contributing anything to his well-being or his assistance in need.[53]

Following are the questions to ask: Can we conceive of a society like this? Would we want to live in such a society? Kant answered the first question positively. Society can subsist if everyone is disinterested in others' interests and needs. We can certainly imagine a market sphere in which everyone follows his or her personal interests and promotes others' interests as long as those are instrumental in reaching his or her own interests. In the technical terms employed by Kantian scholars, there is no contradiction in conception, that is, there is no logical contradiction. It remains the second question. For Kant, the absence of a contradiction in conception is not enough to establish that a maxim can be an objective principle of morality:

Even though it is possible that a universal law of nature could very well subsist according to that maxim, it is still impossible to will that such a principle hold everywhere as a law of nature.... One must *be able to will* that a maxim of our action become a universal law: this is as such the canon of judging morality.[54]

If there is a contradiction in will, morality is absent. This is the case for Kant, who used this example to theorize our imperfect duty to help each other reciprocally. This is not much because of the consequences – I might need help in the future, even if, in the present, I do not think so – but because our rational nature requires us to promote, to a certain extent, the ends of other people. Each of us has an absolute value as a human being. Kant expresses this concept through the second formula of the categorical imperative: "So act that you use humanity, in your own person as well as in the person of any other, always at the same time as an end, never merely as a means."[55] We cannot will that everyone, in the market, follows the principle of self-interest and non-tuism. Therefore, Smith's moral principle does not enter the Kantian realm of morality.

Things stand differently for Genovesi's principle of mutual assistance. Not only does not fail the universalization test, generating no contradictions, but it also aligns to the formula of humanity. A confirmation of my interpretation comes from Kant's *Lectures on Natural Right* (1784), namely, the lessons he gave to Königsberg University students while writing and publishing *Groundwork*. Kant explained the second formula of the categorical imperative with two examples that significantly originate from the market sphere: "Man is never merely a means; rather, he is at the same time an end. For example, if a mason serves me as a means of building a house, I serve him, in turn, as a means of acquiring money."[56] Reciprocal or mutual assistance is at the core of this understanding of markets and morality. The second example is even more significant:

If I arrange with my servant to give him 20 reichsthalers per year but it later turns out to be more expensive to live so that he cannot make do with that money, I do him no wrong if I continue to give him no more than 20 reichsthalers even though he asks for more, for I act in accordance with his [earlier] expressed attitudes. I have nonetheless not act[ed] equitably because he had thought that he would be satisfied with the 20 reichsthalers only as long as the relatively inexpensive times would allow it. I would be able to assume his intention ... "Equitable" can also be called "ethically just."[57]

This understanding of morality closely resembles that of Genovesi. However, we are discussing Kant's moral philosophy. Therefore, we are looking for a duty that expresses moral principles. I will advance the following formulation of Kant's moral principles for economic agents: When you have freely signed a mutually beneficial contract, you have the imperfect duty to care about your interest and, beyond your interest, to a certain extent, about the interest of your exchange partner.[58]

This is the duty to honor the spirit of mutually beneficial contracts of Kant's moral economy and, as with the other two moral principles, has its corollaries. First, we must characterize the adjective "imperfect" attached to duty. Kant distinguished between perfect and imperfect duties. The perfect duties comprise those that are narrow in their scope of application (do not lie, do not commit suicide) and whose principle must always be prioritized with respect to other determinants of our actions. However, the imperfect or meritorious duties have a wide scope of obligation (help others in need, cultivate your talents) and, sometimes, we might choose not to prioritize – as it happens in the case of conflicting duties.[59] Kant describes at length the imperfect duties we have toward others; however, the moral principles for economic agents present some differences. We owe the former to everyone, while the latter exclusively to our exchange partner. Kant implies that, when we enter into contracts, we acquire a duty to honor not only the explicit terms of the contract but also the mutually beneficial spirit in which the contract was made and the intentions behind the agreement. In the servant's case, the duty was to provide more to the servant because he agreed to work in exchange for enough money to live on, and he thought the amount they agreed on would be enough. Hence, if Kant gives him twenty Reichsthalers, he is honoring the explicit agreement but not the mutually beneficial intentions/spirit behind the agreement. My interpretation may explain why we owe something more to the servant than just the general imperfect duty of assistance we owe to all. The duty here is not one of assistance but honoring agreements.

Another corollary is related to the notion of "interest" in Kant's duty to honor the spirit of mutually beneficial contracts. Two kinds of interests can be distinguished: the interest a party signing a contract set for herself or the interest she effectively realizes, thanks to that market transaction. In the case of Kant and his mason, the latter aimed to get money that was proportionate to the work performed. Due to inflation, the mason's interest while signing the contract diverges from what he was actually able to achieve. Inflation was not Kant's responsibility; it was simply a change in circumstances. Yet Kant stated that promoting the mason's interest by raising his salary would be moral for him. Be careful here: Kant is not saying that any transaction in which the parties do not promote their respective interests in their effective realization is immoral. He simply states that for the time span covered by the contract, morality requires an imperfect duty from the parties involved in a market exchange in realizing their respective interests. Among the many meanings that Kant gave to imperfect duty, there is the idea that these are duties of wide obligation in which some parties can do more and others less without infringing on what duty requires.

In addition, a conflict of duties may occur. Suppose that after Kant increased the mason's salary, inflation continues to the point when

Kant feels its effect. Should Kant raise his mason's salary again? Should he prioritize the duty of honoring the spirit of mutually beneficial contracts over the duty he owes to himself? For these conflicting cases of duties, no unique answer exists. Perhaps new mutually beneficial contracts can be made to cover these situations, or the circumstances may change again. Be as it may, what remains immutable – as it happens in the a priori realm of the metaphysics of morals – is our imperfect duty of honoring the spirit of mutually beneficial contracts.

At this point, the reader might wonder why I have distinguished Genovesi's and Kant's moral principles for economic agents. Although slightly differently formulated, they share the same content. However, the overlap is only apparent. The two moral principles express two very different views of morality, and both constitute fruitful alternatives for people facing moral problems in market exchanges. The next section will be devoted to investigating this difference and other differences and similarities among the three moral principles of economic enlightenment.

3.6 Similarities and Contrasts

The moral principles described in the previous three sections have some common elements. First, they presuppose that people *can* and *want* to act morally in the market. Genovesi, Kant, and Smith believed that everyone is interested in morality, in knowing what is the right thing to do and why. In this respect, they refused the paradigm of the *homo oeconomicus*, an agent interested in maximizing utility and indifferent to moral problems.[60] While *homo oeconomicus* can exist in the pre-reflective moment, critical thinking transforms that *homo* into individuals interested in the rightness or wrongness of their actions. The message of the three economic enlightenments is simple: You can be a *homo oeconomicus* as long as you are aware of, and not indifferent to, the moral reasons behind your choice. Morality is not an optional element.

The second common element is that the three moral principles rely on inclination and reason. This emerges clearly in the thoughts of Smith and Genovesi. Even Kant's principle, expressed as a duty, starts with human inclinations. Without desires or maxims, no test of the categorical imperative could exist, and consequently, no useful duties to guide everyday actions would be pursued. For Kant, morality establishes a perimeter of morally permissible actions, within which inclinations (from desires to happiness) are important sources of motivation. However, in morally problematic situations, the motive of duty must have precedence.

The third common element applies specifically to the object of moral principles, that is, market transactions between free individuals. The freedom of economic agents and a certain equality between them are already presupposed. This is not a minor point. For example, Marx's critique of political economy focused mostly on the fact that authors such as Smith fought inequalities between landlords and servants but forgot that inequalities exist even in free market economies, in which exchanges do not always happen between peers; think about the classes of the capitalists and the proletariat.[61] I will say more about this in Chapter 7. For now, it is important to state that, through the label "free," I have deliberatively narrowed the scope of inquiry, taking freedom and a reasonable degree of inequality for granted. I defend my choice, once more, based on its utility. As they are, the three moral principles are adequate to address the moral problems emerging in many market situations. Part II will focus on case studies of incomplete contracts, in which the interesting elements would not pertain to what happens before but what happens during a market exchange. The three principles of economic enlightenment are tailor-made to provide alternatives to these kinds of problems, not to all the moral problems emerging in the economic sphere.

The differences emerge by comparing the three moral principles. Choosing different angles of observation, we can see that, in one sense, Genovesi and Kant are opposed to Smith, while, in another sense, Genovesi and Smith are opposed to Kant. The first opposition is related to the content of moral principles. Genovesi and Kant both agreed that economic agents, to a certain extent, should care for and promote the interests of exchange partners. This is opposed to Smith's view of self-interest when it is read through the lens of non-tuism. For Smith, economic agents should care about their own interests. The exchange partners' identities, needs, and desires are indifferent to a person who is starting a market transaction. The others are simply a means to an end; in a specular fashion, we are means to their ends. Our exchange partners' interests can be promoted as far as they are useful in achieving our aims. Genovesi and Kant opposed this view, saying that promoting the other person's interest beyond its utility for our interest does not mean being altruistic. Their moral principles entail that we can further our goals and aims while promoting others. Kant explicitly affirmed that there is a way to consider another person a means and an end simultaneously. Genovesi recognized that we flourish as human beings when we foster genuine and authentic relationships, which is also possible in the market sphere.

We return to the problem we encountered at the end of the previous section. Kant's and Genovesi's moral principles for economic agents seem identical. Yet they could not be more distant from one another. For Genovesi, continuity exists between pre-reflective and reflective moments. The moral principle elaborated by reason is in accordance with basic human inclinations, namely, the account of the two forces (*concentriva e diffusiva*). In this respect, Genovesi is much closer to Smith than to Kant. As explained in Chapter 2, Genovesi and Smith were two virtuous ethicists. For them, the moral principles that we use to develop our virtues are in continuity with our natural inclinations. Virtues express the excellence of human beings, which is obtained by acquiring character traits that result from the development of our natural inclinations. While Genovesi and Smith disagreed on the natural inclinations of economic agents, they agreed that moral principles are based on our natural inclinations mediated by reason.

However, Kant explicitly criticized those ethical systems that seek continuity between the empirical and the rational, the pre-reflective and reflective moments. In his view, these theories created nothing but confusion because they failed to provide a universal and unconditional foundation for morality. Morality is a priori; it is grounded in reason. Inclinations such as self-love say nothing about the morality of an action or the validity of a moral principle. Some people can be naturally selfish, while others can be naturally generous. As morality needs to be universal and valid for all, inclinations cannot provide solid ground. Reason can succeed, as we are all rational beings despite our empirical differences. In a nutshell, inclinations divide human beings while reason unites them.

Taking stock, the difference between Genovesi's and Kant's thoughts emerges when we move from the content of the moral principle to its role as a moral reason and motivation. Regarding moral reason, the principle of mutual assistance and the duty of honoring the spirit of a mutually beneficial contract emerge from dissimilar reflections on inclinations. The former seeks continuity with natural inclinations, while the latter takes natural inclinations as a starting point to be abandoned in favor of a rational principle. This difference has deep implications when considering moral reasons as motivations. Genovesi's and Kant's moral principles for economic agents prescribe similar, if not identical, patterns of action. However, the reasons for following these general rules of conduct are very different. For Kant, your natural inclination to assist your exchange pattern is not a valid motivation to follow your imperfect duty to honor the spirit of mutually beneficial contracts. The same goes if you are naturally selfish and you think it is a valid reason to ignore your duty. Despite your natural inclinations, you must do as duty requires because you are a rational being endowed with reason. Conversely, Genovesi's principle of mutual assistance sees your natural inclinations, corroborated by the reflective moment of reason, as valid motivations to act morally.

The difference between Genovesi (and Smith) and Kant's thoughts brought the discussion around the topic of moral principles, moral reasons, and motivations. As the theoretical aspect by itself might be misleading or vague, it is better to consider these ideas "in action," that is, as applied to concrete case studies. Therefore, I now turn to Part II of the book, "Application." The first section of Chapter 4 will resume the discussion from where we have left it, that is, the relation between principles, reasons, and motivations in market morality.

Notes

1. See Bird, F. (2009). Why the responsible practice of business ethics calls for a due regard for history. *Journal of Business Ethics*, 89, 203–220.
2. See Fukuyama, F. ([1992] 2006). *The End of History and the Last Man*. New York, Simon and Schuster; Pinker, S. (2018). *Enlightenment Now: The Case for Reason, Science, Humanism, and Progress*. London, Penguin. On the other side, Gray saw the ideas of the enlightenment as self-defeating in modernity: Gray, J. (2007). *Enlightenment's Wake: Politics and Culture at the Close of the Modern Age*. London, Routledge.
3. Much more could be said about enlightenment ideas that are still impactful. For a detail analysis, see Wahba, M. (1990). Ideals of the enlightenment for today. *Social Philosophy Today*, 3, 13–20; Zafirovski, M. (2010). *The Enlightenment and Its Effects on Modern Society*. New York, Springer; Pagden, A. (2013). *The Enlightenment: And Why It Still Matters*. Oxford, Oxford University Press.

4. On the relation between enlightenment and postmodernism, see Liedman, S. E. (ed.). (1997). *The Postmodernist Critique of the Project of Enlightenment*, vol. 58. Amsterdam, Rodopi; Israel, Enlightenment! Which enlightenment?; a milestone in this field of study is the book by Baker and Reill (Baker, K. M., & Reill, P. H. (2001). *What's Left of Enlightenment? A Postmodern Question*. Stanford, Stanford University Press), in which the relation between enlightenment and postmodernism is discussed and problematized.
5. For the evolution of the market exchange face to face between individuals, see Stobart, J., & Van Damme, I. (2016). Introduction: Markets in modernization – Transformations in urban market space and practice, c. 1800–c. 1970. *Urban History*, 43(3), 358–371. For the evolution of the "spirit of capitalism," see Boltanski, L., & E. Chiapello (2018). *The New Spirit of Capitalism*. London, Verso Books.
6. This methodological remark is essential. Scholars trying to apply ideas from ancient past, such as Aristotle's virtue ethics, or very different socio-cultural background, such as Confucius, to business ethics in western societies often overlook the fact that those societies were very different from the current ones. For example, Aristotle lived in a society in which the role of work was marginalized, and the views of "good life" were not as many as we have in contemporary pluralistic societies. Therefore, when someone applies Aristotle's idea of virtue to business ethics, Aristotelian virtue ethics is often wrongfully decontextualized to make it serve to contemporary problems. Having chosen three authors from the enlightenment, and having accounted for the socio-cultural context in which they lived, I have tried to avoid this dangerous form of anachronism.
7. Sen, A. (1980). "Equality of what?" In *Tanner Lectures on Human Values*, vol. 1. Cambridge, Cambridge University Press.
8. See Pihlström, S. (2003). On the concept of philosophical anthropology. *Journal of Philosophical Research*, 28, 259–286.
9. See Schapiro, T. (2009). The nature of inclination. *Ethics*, 119(2), 229–256.
10. Kant, *Groundwork*, 10.
11. Ibid., 11.
12. Ibid., 12.
13. Smith. *The Theory of Moral Sentiments*, 42.
14. Smith, *The Wealth of Nations*, 26. My italics.
15. Genovesi, A. (1775). *Istituzioni di metafisica per li principianti del signor abbate Antonio Genovesi. Ad uso delle scuole pubbliche di Venezia*. Venice, Tommaso Bettinelli Editore.

16. Ibid., 102. My translation.
17. Genovesi, *Lezioni di commercio*, 366–367.
18. Herman, B. (1993). *The Practice of Moral Judgment*. Cambridge, MA, Harvard University Press, 11.
19. Hierarchy of importance does not mean a temporal relation, such as first perceiving the inclinations and then, through reason, arriving at moral principles. This can happen in everyday life as well as in the moral analysis of philosophers. However, most of the times, the two things exist simultaneously and influence each other.
20. McCloskey, D. (2008). Adam Smith, the last of the former virtue ethicists. *History of Political Economy*, 40(1), 43–71.
21. Throop, C. J. (2012). Moral sentiments. In Fassin, D. (ed.) *A Companion to Moral Anthropology*. Chichester, Wiley-Blackwell, 150–168.
22. Smith, *The Wealth of Nations*, 26.
23. Ibid., 26–27.
24. Ibid., 456.
25. For Smith, justice is both simultaneously, a characteristic of institutions and a virtue of individuals. See Herzog, L. (2014). Adam Smith on markets and justice. *Philosophy Compass*, 9(12), 864–875.
26. See Bonica, M. J., & Klein, D. B. (2021). Adam Smith on reputation, commutative justice, and defamation laws. *Journal of Economic Behavior & Organization*, 184, 788–803.
27. For deepening the connection between moral sentiments and punishments, see Paganelli, M. P., & Simon, F. (2022). Crime and punishment: "Adam Smith's theory of sentimental law and economics." *Journal of the History of Economic Thought*, 44(2), 268–287.
28. Smith, *The Theory of Moral Sentiments*, 86.
29. This view was recently elaborated by economist Robert Sugden who provides a Smithian moral defense of the market. See Sugden, R. (2018). *The Community of Advantage: A Behavioural Economist's Defence of the Market*. Oxford, Oxford University Press.
30. Smith, *The Wealth of Nations*, 456.
31. See Bruni & Sugden, Fraternity.
32. Wicksteed, P. H. ([1910] 1933). *The Common Sense of Political Economy*. London, Routledge, 27.
33. Ibid., 180.
34. In several works, I have defended and substantiated this interpretation. See Santori, P. (2022). Is relationality always other-oriented? Adam Smith, catholic social teaching, and civil economy. *Philosophy of Management*, 21(1), 49–68; Bruni, L., & Santori, P. (2022a). The Adam Smith Problem theologically reconsidered. In Ballor, J. (ed.),

Theology, Morality and Adam Smith. London, Routledge, 258–275; Santori, Idleness and the very sparing hand of god; Santori, The curious tale of the three Adam Smiths.
35. There is no need to quote sources. It suffices to open (roughly) 90 percent books of microeconomics and see what their anthropological assumptions are and how they connect to market failures.
36. Aristotle (1984). *Complete Works of Aristotle: The Revised Oxford Translation*, vol. 2, ed. by J. Barnes. Princeton, Princeton University Press, 183.
37. See Bruni & Sugden, Fraternity.
38. See Zambelli, P. (1978). Antonio Genovesi and eighteenth-century empiricism in Italy. *Journal of the History of Philosophy*, 16(2), 195–208.
39. The two forces account fits with Genovesi's virtue ethics that I described in Chapter 2. When he spoke about the equilibrium between two forces, he was thinking about how to elicit virtuous behavior.
40. Genovesi, A. (1835). *Logica e Metafisica di Antonio Genovesi*. Milan, Società Tipografica dei Classici Italiani, 261. My translation.
41. Ibid., 262.
42. For a more extensive exploration of Genovesi's account of the two forces, see Porta, P. L. (2018). From economia civile to kameralwissenschaften. The line of descent from Genovesi to Beccaria in pre-Smithian Europe. *The European Journal of the History of Economic Thought*, 25(4), 531–561.
43. It might be objected that Genovesi's view should not result in a moral principle, rather in a list of virtues for economic agents. To this, I respond that while Genovesi gave crucial role to the notion of civic virtues, public happiness (common good), and public trust, the reference to a principle of action was not disjointed by virtuous. It was precisely to develop some character traits that we need moral principles to apply to in different circumstances, so to make the moral reasoning similar to a second nature and develop virtues and virtuous behavior.
44. I discuss Genovesi's understanding of Aristotle as mediated by Aquinas in Santori, P. (2020). Donum, exchange and common good in Aquinas: The dawn of civil economy. *The European Journal of the History of Economic Thought*, 27(2), 276–297.
45. What follows is based on my joint research with Luigino Bruni. See Bruni, L., & Santori, P. (2018). The plural roots of rewards: Awards and incentives in Aquinas and Genovesi. *The European Journal of the History of Economic Thought*, 25(4), 637–657; Bruni & Santori, The other invisible hand.

46. Genovesi, *Lezioni di Commercio*, 113. My translation.
47. I have detailed this example in the introduction of my book on Aquinas and civil economy. See Santori, *Thomas Aquinas and the Civil Economy Tradition*.
48. Kant, *Groundwork*, xii; see also Korsgaard, C. M. (1996). *Creating the Kingdom of Ends*. Cambridge, Cambridge University Press.
49. Kant, *Critique of Pure Reason*.
50. Kant, *Groundwork*, 16.
51. Ibid., 34.
52. See O'Neill, O. (1975). *Acting on Principle: An Essay on Kantian Ethics*. Cambridge, Cambridge University Press; Korsgaard, M. (1985). Kant's formula of universal law. *Pacific Philosophical Quarterly*, 66(1–2), 24–47; J. Rawls, *Lectures on the History of Moral Philosophy*; Kleingeld, P. (2017). Contradiction and Kant's formula of universal law. *Kant-Studien*, 108(1), 89–115.
53. Kant, *Groundwork*, 36.
54. Ibid.
55. Ibid., 41.
56. Kant, *Lectures on Natural Right*, 81.
57. Ibid., 92–93. The relationship between Kant and his servant falls within the scope of incomplete contracts. In Part II of the book, where I will apply the three moral principles of the three economic enlightenments, I will propose three case studies of incomplete contracts. Here, I revealed that my source of inspiration was Kant's text.
58. As I will explain in Chapter 4 devoted to incomplete contracts, this expression corresponds to mutually beneficial exchange between individuals.
59. See Dubbink, W. (2018). The bystander in commercial life: Obliged by beneficence or rescue? *Journal of Business Ethics*, 149, 1–13.
60. See Kirchgässner, G. (2000). *Homo oeconomicus*. Tübingen, Mohr Siebeck; Bee, M., & Desmarais-Tremblay, M. (2023). The birth of homo œconomicus: The methodological debate on the economic agent from J. S. Mill to V. Pareto. *Journal of the History of Economic Thought*, 45(1), 1–26.
61. See Marx, K. (2005). *Grundrisse: Foundations of the Critique of Political Economy*. London, Penguin.

PART II

Application

Business ethics is an interdisciplinary field of study. There, it is rare to find a theory that is not devoted to practice. This book is no exception. After having explored the historical and theoretical issues in Part I, I will turn to the application. However, "application" in BE can have many different meanings. Some scholars focus on particular business practices to assess their morality, whereas others look for best practices to orient specific economic sectors.[1] Application may also concern studies advising particular business figures, from managers and CEOs to people working in HR or ethical committees.[2] Other scholars propose their theoretical (sometimes historical) analyses to offer conceptual tools to people facing moral problems in everyday life.[3] This last stream of literature does not aim to provide tailor-made ethical solutions but rather to offer perspectives and alternative points of view to people (or independent observers) for framing moral problems related to business. In what follows, I will follow this pattern.

Political economy, civil economy, and moral economy, which I call the three economic enlightenments, are three perspectives from which a person facing a moral problem, an external observer of a controversial business situation, or a scholar reflecting on moral issues related to business can analyze the problem and eventually opt for a course of action (or evaluation) based on an ethical theory. As mentioned in Chapter 1, this is not a taste-based choice (Who do I prefer most? Genovesi, Kant, or Smith?). It is not even about an absolute preference ranking (i.e., Kant > Smith > Genovesi). Instead, it is the chance to have an ethical toolkit that goes beyond the triad utilitarianism–deontology–virtue ethics to frame and sometimes successfully address moral problems in business.

The three case studies I have chosen to illustrate how the three economic enlightenments can be applied are meant to represent only some of the moral problems that we face in everyday business life. I will focus on those that can emerge from the issue of incomplete contracts, that is, cases in which the terms of a mutually beneficial written agreement do not cover all the possible (and unforeseen) circumstances that can change the benefit for one or more of the parties involved. While any contract can be argued to be incomplete, the representativity of these case studies should be thought of differently.

The case studies I chose are based on real-life situations that I have been told by the people who have experienced them. I have added fictional elements to make the moral problems emerge more vividly. Choosing fictional rather than real case studies may be argued to be a disadvantage in terms of the applicability and representativity of the conceptual tools I developed in Part I. Things, however, stand precisely in the opposite way. First, the stories I will tell are not real but plausible. This means that they are connected to reality and, therefore, an excellent way to apply theory to practice. As far as representativity is concerned, the fact that the readers can easily imagine themselves as the protagonist of those situations makes my three case studies highly representative.[4] Everyone can wear the shoes of the contractor or house owners of Chapter 4, the researcher and participants of Chapter 5, or the bank's managers and customer of Chapter 6. The questions they asked themselves about the right conduct and motivation while facing moral problems in incomplete contract situations can be asked by anyone when facing similar circumstances. The same goes for the narratives through which they framed their own behaviors and conditions.[5]

There are two ways to achieve representativity with case studies. On the one hand, all circumstances and details should be removed to make the story genuinely universal. This strategy resembles Rawls's *A Theory of Justice*[6] and his concept of original position. This is a situation in which the parties who have to sign the social contract on behalf of the citizens are exposed to the veil of ignorance. This artificial device ensures they will not know what social position, level of wealth, state of health, and conception of a good life will characterize the citizens they represent. The veil of ignorance, for Rawls, meant that the conditions of justice and equality were met. This also means that universality and representativity are guaranteed by renouncing particularity. The problem with this methodology in BE is that the cases become so general that they are rarely helpful in assessing everyday moral issues.

Another notion of representativity that I adopt in this book is similar to what happens in literature – the characters and their stories are narrated in-depth, sometimes even within the complexity of spiritual life (think about the novels by Proust or Dostoevsky). Yet, these stories bring universal significance because everyone can relate to them. In other words, the trade-off between universality and particularity in literature is overcome: Characters and stories represent everyone insofar as everyone can relate to them. Aware of the growing interest in the nexus between BE and literature, I aim to achieve the same results by telling three case studies as three stories.[7]

Notes

1. See Joyner, B. E., & Payne, D. (2002). Evolution and implementation: A study of values, business ethics and corporate social responsibility. *Journal of Business Ethics*, 41, 297–311. See also Fatima, T., & Elbanna, S. (2023). Corporate social responsibility (CSR) implementation: A review and a research agenda towards an integrative framework. *Journal of Business Ethics*, 183(1), 105–121.
2. For example, there is a growing body of literature that intersects business ethics and leadership studies. See Ciulla, J. B. (2020). *The Search for Ethics in Leadership, Business, and Beyond*. Cham, Springer Nature. On business ethics and HR, see Vickers, M. R. (2005). Business ethics and the HR role: Past, present, and future. *Human Resource Planning*, 28(1), 26–33.
3. See Lurie, Y., & Albin, R. (2007). Moral dilemmas in business ethics: From decision procedures to edifying perspectives. *Journal of Business Ethics*, 71, 195–207.
4. The relation between moral imagination and business ethics has been extensively inquired in business ethics literature. See Werhane, P. H. (1999). *Moral Imagination and Management Decision-Making*. New York, Oxford University Press.
5. See Dubbink, W., & Slegers, R. (2022). The trolley dilemma and the art of making judgments on concrete situations. *Ethical Perspectives*, 29(3), 313–334.
6. Rawls, J. (1971). *A Theory of Justice*. Cambridge, MA, Harvard University Press.
7. See Michaelson, C. (2005). Dealing with swindlers and devils: Literature and business ethics. *Journal of Business Ethics*, 58, 359–373; Koehn, D. (2023). Narrative business ethics versus narratives within business ethics: Problems and possibilities from an Aristotelian virtue ethics perspective. *Journal of Business Ethics*, 189(4), 1–17.

4 | A Contractor under the Rain

4.1 Motivations before Actions

Human beings are interested in morality. When we feel spontaneously or naturally inclined to act in a certain way and ask if that is the right course of action, we move from the pre-reflective moment of instinct to the reflective moment of reason: "Reflection means consciously considering the reasons we have for making decisions."[1] The moral principles of the three economic enlightenments can be considered moral reasons insofar as they result from rational reflections on inclinations. They express not only general rules of conduct but also the reasons why we should endorse those rules. From Genovesi's and Smith's perspectives, one can provide reasons for following the inclinations; in parallel, one can find good reasons to rely exclusively on reason, as in Kant's moral philosophy. Another set of reasons regards the good of society. Smith believed that its moral principle would cause economic agents to unintentionally promote the public good, while Genovesi emphasizes intentionality in mutual assistance for public happiness (*pubblica felicità*).[2] Kant's moral principle prioritizes what is right to what is good (even the common good). That does not mean that the German philosopher ignored the topic of one's and society's happiness. For him, acting from duty and duty only will not necessarily make us or others happy but, more importantly, "worthy of happiness."[3] This is another moral reason to corroborate Kant's principle.

In the three economic enlightenments, moral principles can be followed and, more importantly, justified. They outline general rules of conduct and explain why some courses of action are the right ones. But moral reasons do not necessarily correspond to motivations: "Reasons are different from motivations in this important sense: reasons do not concern what people *actually* prompted to act, but they are about what *should* prompt them to act."[4] I can be motivated by traditions, habits, commands, laws, inclinations, principles, unconscious mechanisms, and so on. I can also have reasons to act that do not refer to morality, for example, when I am deciding if it is better to cook two similar vegan meals or what is the better way to change a lamp without breaking the electricity system. However, this book focuses on another kind of situation, that is, moral problems that might emerge within market transactions. Therefore, I focus on moral reasons for economic agents as expressed by moral principles.

The passage from moral reasons to moral motivation is also important. My motivation for acting becomes a moral motivation if it is aligned, at least, with a moral reason. But for this to happen, people should be presented with moral reasons and moral principles to adopt and reflect upon. This is what I offer to the readers of this book. Each of the three moral principles elaborated by Genovesi, Kant, and Smith is tied to a view of human beings, their inclinations, and their role in society. When faced with moral problems in market exchanges, people can use these three principles to frame their own situation and to look for different kinds of moral reasons for different rules of conduct and courses of actions. Ultimately, it will be the agents' own decision which moral reason (if any) will become its moral motivation and how that will be connected to their actions. The aim of this book is to offer alternatives, not to provide ready-made recipes for solving moral issues.

This chapter resembles almost entirely the structure of the next two ones. The only difference lies in this section and the next one on incomplete contracts. They aim to introduce the reader to the three case studies and specify the lexicon (moral principles, moral reasons, moral motivations) that will be employed. After that, I will adopt a threefold structure. First, I will describe the moral problem emerging from an incomplete contract by telling the story of economic agents involved in a market exchange. Then, I will consider how the three moral principles of Genovesi, Kant, and Smith furnish three rules of conduct and courses of actions to approach the problem. I will do that by adopting the viewpoints of all agents involved in the market exchange. This chapter, for example, will describe the three moral principles available to contractors and house owners. Finally, I will provide a comparative discussion of the moral reasons that the economic agents might adopt. The aim is not to answer the question "What is the right motivation?" but to evaluate the three possible answers coming from the three economic enlightenments.

4.2 Complete and Incomplete Contracts

One of the myths of contemporary economics is that a human beings is a *homo oeconomicus*.[5] The idea that we are perfectly rational and fully informed and that our decisions result exclusively from these two features has been debunked by many studies.[6] Even if *homo oeconomicus* is still the protagonist of economics textbooks, he is now presented as a useful fiction. Another myth is the one of complete contracts. Those are "contracts where everything that can happen is written into the contract. There may be some incentive constraints arising from moral hazard or asymmetric information, but there are no unanticipated contingencies."[7] The complete contract matches with the perfect rationality of the *homo oeconomicus*. However, it is evident that no contract can anticipate all the contingencies. If that were even the case, with an AI system able to foresee all possible future scenarios, we would end up with long and complicated contracts that no one would even think to sign. As Oliver Hart, winner of the Nobel Prize in economics in 2016 for his studies on contract theory, wrote, "Actual contracts are not like this [complete], as lawyers have realized for a long time. They are poorly worded, ambiguous, and leave out important things."[8] The same idea was reaffirmed by another Nobel Prize-winner in economics (2014), Jean Tirole: "Almost every economist would agree that actual contracts are or appear quite incomplete. Many contracts are vague or silent on a number of key features."[9] In real life, when we sign a contract that represents and structures a mutually advantageous exchange with someone else, we are almost always opting for an incomplete contract.

Incomplete contracts are central to economic life and, therefore, economic science. In Tirole's words, "incomplete contracting arguably underlies some of the most important questions in economics and other social sciences, and unquestionably has been left largely unexplored and poorly understood."[10] Today, many issues related to incomplete contracts have been inquired about and addressed. However, problems might still arise due to the "incompleteness" of contracts, that is, the impossibility of foreseeing all future situations. Among these are moral problems for the economic agents involved in a market exchange based on incomplete contracts. If two parties sign a contract at the moment X, imagining that the circumstances Y will be immutable for the duration of the contract, and then in the moment X1, independently from the will of the economic agents, the circumstances change and become Y1, a problem arises. One of the options is for the two parties to decide to renegotiate the contract.[11] This moment of renegotiation, which will be present in all the three stories I will tell in this book, can give rise to many problems and often it ends in a court of law. Another example might be a contract where the circumstances Y are immutable. Still, the contract stipulated at the moment X is not specific enough about the requirements of the behavior of one of the involved parties. Therefore, the result is one party's complaint against the other, a proposal of renegotiation that probably will be deemed unfair by one of the parties, and an appeal to a court of law. The incompleteness of contracts often brings parties to conflicts and disputes.

This book focuses on the moral problems emerging from incomplete contracts. More specifically, the three economic enlightenments apply to the moment the parties are thinking about how to renegotiate an incomplete contract. The three moral principles offer three alternative rules of conduct and the moral reasons for adopting one of those principles. It goes without saying that some things are taken for granted. One key feature of contracts is that they mutually benefit the parties who sign them. This is valid both in economics and political philosophy. Social contract theorists, from Hobbes and Jean-Jacques Rousseau (1712–1778) to, more recently, Rawls, David Gauthier, and Philip Petit, saw the political institutions of a society based on an agreement between individuals. I live in a society with certain institutions because they benefit me and the other people who live in that society. In a similar wake, I started a market exchange based on a contract because I saw a benefit attached to it. The moral principles of economic enlightenments apply to this kind of situation. Therefore, they presuppose that at the moment of signing the contract, the parties are (a) free to sign or not sign, (b) adequately informed about the nature of the market exchange, (c) in a condition of relative equality with each other so that no one has the power to set unilaterally the contract terms, and (d) protected by a system of rights and laws that guarantees the mutual respect of the contract terms. These conditions are not always met, but even when they are fully met, moral and nonmoral problems can arise from the incompleteness of the contract signed. Nonmoral problems can concern technicalities or practical issues emerging from unforeseen circumstances. For example, if two agents signed a contract for producing a certain product in a certain region, and later a military conflict affects that region, blocking or shutting down businesses, the cost and procedures for relocating the activities elsewhere is a nonmoral problem. Moral problems are related to the parties' behavior during renegotiation. They can take the form of the following questions: How should the costs be distributed? Is it right for one agent to ask the other to take the burden of the costs? Is it right for the other agent to refuse? The answers concern the contract stipulated, the unforeseen circumstances, and, not less importantly, the moral principles adopted by the agents and the moral reasons behind them.

Business ethics can provide aid to solve moral problems arising from incomplete contracts by furnishing moral principles for economic agents in the moment of renegotiation. This book offers alternative moral reasoning for people involved in a market exchange. It might not always be the case that the court of law could be avoided, but as we will see in the three case studies, moral reasoning can make an incomplete contract less incomplete. Morality, conceived as the consideration of what is right and what the reasons of others are, can compensate for the lack of information or the impossibility of unforeseen futures. This is not to say that morality is just instrumentally valuable. Furnishing moral principles to economic agents has value in itself, although it can facilitate market transactions. As Plato (428–348 BCE) would argue, morality is an instrumental and intrinsic good simultaneously. Although this book will focus on the former, they can help solve moral and nonmoral problems. It is time to prove it by applying the three moral principles of economic enlightenments to the first case study.

4.3 Case Study

4.3.1 *The Story*[12]

A married couple decided to renovate their house's façade. They have no big savings, and their joint income would not allow them to renovate the house while still paying the monthly mortgage. However, the national government had just introduced a super bonus scheme that allows them to have back 90 percent of the cost of making their house more energy efficient via tax credits. Therefore, they took the opportunity to start renovation works while incurring small costs. After consulting an architect and developing a project, they hired a contractor in charge of coordinating and directing a crew of four workers. As it happens in these cases, the couple and the contractor signed a mutually beneficial contract. The terms of the contract were clear. The works would have started on November 1, and the expected delivery date, that is, the date of the end of works, is December 22. The dates were convenient for two reasons. First, the house owners would have had their house back before Christmas vacation, while, for the duration of the works, they would have to live in the house of the mom of one of the partners. Second, the super bonus scheme, which was very expensive for public finances, was expected to end on January 1 by a new government led by a political coalition opposite to the one that initiated it. As can be easily imagined, those were months of high demand for work for contractors, as many people decided to start renovating their houses while incurring little or no costs. The couple was able to find an available contractor via informal channels in a time of shortage of contractors. The contractor, in fact, was the son of a close friend of one of the members of the couple. He accepted the job, knowing that his crew was already busy with other similar jobs.

The contract was explicit in the start and end dates for the works on the façade. However, among the few provisions attached to it, there was one peculiar to that kind of work: "Work on the façade cannot be run on rainy days, as the rain will damage the materials employed for renovation. Therefore, the contractor can modify the work schedule accordingly." This clause might appear common sense, but it generated problems typical of incomplete contracts. Before exposing the details of what actually happened, a few things can be noticed beforehand. First, the provision is unclear about the relation between modification of the work schedule and the end date of the works. There are at least two possible interpretations. On the one hand, the contractor might modify the work schedule so that the delivery date will be necessarily extended. On the other hand, it can be argued that the contractor will organize his crew so that even modifications in the work schedule will not affect the delivery date. But there is something else. The "accordingly" can also be interpreted in several ways. Does it refer to days where it effectively rained, or is it related to the weather forecast? While the weather forecast measurement is becoming increasingly accurate, it cannot accurately predict the duration of rains throughout the day. It gets even more unclear when weather forecasts refer not to the next day but to the following days or even weeks. Moreover, there are many sources through which one can access weather forecasts. To see this point, readers of this book can simply type the weather and the name of their city in an online search engine and see the many, and sometimes contradictory, results. All of these elements show how the contract was incomplete, as typical of those extending to a future span of time.

The course of events went as follows. At the beginning of December, many (not all) weather forecasts predict a rainy week. The contractor told the couple that he would have blocked the works that week, which might affect the renovated façade's delivery date. The couple was, at least, perplexed. After having consulted multiple weather forecasts, which predict some rainy days and some others not, they thought that the best solution would have been to decide on a day-to-day basis. They texted back the contractor with this counterproposal. They did not want to question the contractor's authority in directing the renovation works, but as the delivery date might be affected, they thought they were entitled to have a say on the matter. The contractor disagreed, mentioning the contract clause, which explicitly states that, on those issues, it is his opinion that matters. As often happens in real life, the incompleteness of the contract, expressed by the vagueness of the clause, created conflicts and tensions between exchange partners. To solve the situation, they agreed to organize a meeting in the presence also of the architect. This is the moment of renegotiation of an incomplete contract, and it is at this stage that the moral problem emerges.

4.3.2 The Moral Problem

The meeting between the house owners and contractors seems apparently unrelated to morality. After all, the matter of discussion regards practical and technical issues, like the reliability of weather forecasts and the rescheduling of the works. However, these practical issues become moral if we focus on the motivations of the people involved in the meeting of renegotiation. As I mentioned at the beginning of this chapter, we presuppose that both parties are interested in doing the right thing and not taking advantage of the exchange partner. Applying it to the case study, we can say that the contractor and house owners are interested in fairly relating one with the other. They wonder how they should approach the meeting and what moral principles should guide their conduct. What they will say to each other in the meeting will depend on the moral principle adopted and the reasons why it has been adopted.

At this stage, the important thing to notice is that there is no unique course of action, principles, moral reasons, and motivation. There are many at the disposal of the exchange partners. The moral principles of the three economic enlightenments might be useful not only for external observers (like us) analyzing the situation. I believe them to be very important for the economic agents to understand their role in the market exchange and the moral reasons driving their actions. To see how we can add a fictional element to the case study. Imagine the house owner's daughter has just graduated in economics. Among her third-year mandatory courses was a course on economic ethics. She attended the lecture on the moral principles of the three economic enlightenments. At dinner, the day before the renegotiation meeting, she addressed her parents, explaining each of those principles. Something similar happens to the contractor whose best friend graduated in international business administration. In that bachelor's, one of the courses was on "The Morality of Commercial Life," and one of the lectures devoted to the three economic enlightenments. The contractor calls his friend for advice, and he gets an explanation of the three moral principles in return. Despite the initial skepticism of the house owners and contractors about the utility of ideas coming from eighteenth-century philosophers such as Genovesi, Kant, and Smith, they listen attentively and find those moral principles and the reasons behind them as useful conceptual tools for their pre-renegotiation reflections. In the next section, I will show how the contractor and house owners could use the three economic enlightenments to frame their basic moral understanding and decide how to approach the renegotiation meeting.

4.4 Applying the Three Economic Enlightenments

The contractor and the house owners learned about the three economic enlightenments from different sources. The content is the same, and it corresponds to the three moral principles coming from Genovesi's, Kant's, and Smith's thought:

Principle of self-interest and non-tuism: When you are involved in a market transaction that you have freely joined, you should care about your own interest. The interest of the exchange partner should concern you insofar as it promotes your own (no more than that).

Principle of mutual assistance: When you are involved in a market transaction that you have freely joined, you should care about your own interest and, beyond your own interest, to a certain extent, about the interest of your exchange partner.

Principle of honoring the spirit of mutually beneficial contracts: When you have freely signed a mutually beneficial contract, you have the imperfect duty to care about your interest and, beyond your interest, to a certain extent, about the interest of your exchange partner.

Each of these principles entails an assumption about the pre-reflective inclinations and, in turn, moral reasons why it should be the guiding rule of conduct of one's behavior. In what follows, I will present the possible courses of moral reasoning of the contractor and the house owners that might bring them to adopt one of the three principles. In this process, moral reasons can become moral motivations.

4.4.1 Contractor

The moral principle of self-interest and non-tuism indicate a possible course of action for the contractor. During the renegotiation meeting, he needs to focus on his own interests. This would mean to insist on the fact that he is not violating the terms of the contract signed with the house owners. As the weather forecast predicts rain, he wants to better employ the working crew in other construction sites located in other cities. He might acknowledge and understand the disappointment of the house owners, but he is not responsible for fostering their interest beyond the mutually beneficial agreed terms. Not only should he refuse the accusation of being unfair but he also wants to avoid any moral blame. After all, the work will be (probably) delayed, not permanently interrupted. The contractor does not cause the reason for the delay; this happens because of external circumstances. There is no personal problem with the house owners. They are clients, and he would have behaved in the exact same way with other clients. For him, the friendship between his father and one of the house owners cannot and should not count as a reason to act differently. If the house owners do not acknowledge the rightness of his reasons, the contractor, following the principle of self-interest and non-tuism, might even be willing to go to court to settle the dispute.

Genovesi's and Kant's moral principles would suggest a different course of action. The contractor should approach the renegotiation meeting focusing on his interest but also on the interest of the exchange partner. If he decides to follow one of these two principles, he might want to think beforehand about possible middle-way solutions. For example, he can go there, making the promise that he will still interrupt the work, but he will try to speed it up as long as weather conditions allow it. In this way, the deadline would be respected. Please notice that while how the contractor can adjust the work to meet the deadline is a practical or technical problem, his willingness to do so is a moral issue. Another course of action, in the wake of Kant's example with his mason, would be to go to the meeting with the willingness to renegotiate the price. If the works are delayed up to the point that the exchange partners might incur costs associated with the stop of the super bonus, then they might decide to slightly lower their fee so that the house owners will not incur an unexpected loss that is too big. These possible courses of action entail the fact that the contractor cares about the interests of the exchange partner while still promoting his own.

At this point, the interesting question to ask is: Why should the contractor opt for one moral principle over the others? The moral reasons might be many. The contractor might opt for Smith's principle because he feels that it is in accordance with his first, spontaneous, pre-reflective reaction to the moral problem. He does not need to analyze human nature and its basic motivations to arrive at that conclusion. When the house owners contested his decision to postpone the work, the contractor's first reaction was disappointment and anger. He was simply caring about his business and, through that, his interest. Finding a moral principle aligned with his pre-reflective inclinations could be a good moral reason to pursue them. The same would apply if the contractor spontaneously felt interested in the reasons of the house owners. This happens many times in real life. One does not need to be benevolent or altruistic to care about the exchange partner's interests. Genovesi would argue that it is in our nature: As human beings, we have one force that drives us to our good and the other that drives us toward others' good. This can be a valid moral reason to follow the principle of mutual assistance.

Regarding Kant's moral principle for economic agents, the appeal to pre-reflective inclination is irrelevant. It does not matter what the contractor's first reaction to the moral problem was, what he naturally felt inclined to do. He is a rational being. As such, he is morally obligated to do the right thing according to the motive of duty. The contractor might be the most selfish or altruistic person in the world. None of this concerns morality, whose principle has to be found a priori. The duty of honoring the spirit of mutually beneficial contracts applies to the contractor: He should follow it even if he would not be spontaneously driven to do that.

There is another order of moral reasons at the disposal of the contractor. He thinks of himself as a citizen, and, among other things, this means that through his works, he contributes to the good of society. In this respect, the principle of mutual assistance offers him a moral reason why he should also care about the exchange partners' interests. In doing so, in fact, he is contributing to both his personal flourishing as a human being and to the common good. In Genovesi's view, the common good of society is made mostly of ties of genuine and authentic relationships between citizens. Mutual support and mutual care in economic activity are part of this common good. The contractor might think of himself as taking part in an intentional cooperation scheme for his good and the good of society. The personal relationship between one of the house owners and the contractor's father might be inserted in this perspective, but it is not diriment.

Another principle that the contractor might find suitable is Smith's one. He might think that he is simply opting for the most efficient solution by relocating his crew when they can work better. In the long run, he, his workers, and his clients will all benefit if he conducts business caring exclusively about his own interests. The contractor contributes to the good of society not by including it in the motivation for his actions but rather as a valuable by-product (a positive externality) of his economic self-interested activity. This awareness might give him moral reasons to follow the pattern of conduct of the principle of self-interest and non-tuism.

The reference to the good of society is less emphasized in the moral reasons surrounding Kant's moral principle. There, doing what is right for the right reasons is what counts most. Among these reasons, one's own good or the good of others (or society) can have a role if, and only if, they are considered from a rational perspective. The contractor knows that, as a rational being, he has duties toward himself and others. For Kant, acting morally is necessary to become a free and autonomous individual. If the contractor is interested in his moral and personal development, then he might find good moral reasons to follow the duty of honoring the spirit of a mutually beneficial contract.

It must be stated that this level of moral reasons surrounding Kant's moral principle might be less intuitive for a person not interested in philosophy or ethics. Doing what is right just because it is right: This is something everyone can understand. But the appeal to one's own good and society's good might reveal itself as something closer to individual everyday life experience and understanding.

4.4.2 House Owners

The house owners are presented with three moral principles that guide their conduct in the renegotiation moment. The principle of mutual assistance suggests approaching the meeting considering the contractor's interest. Immediately, this would mean excluding possible hidden motivations of the exchange partner, for example, the assumption that the contractor is using the weather forecast to take advantage of the situation. As they see him as a team partner, adopting that "we" perspective, they might genuinely be disposed to meet his request halfway. They might choose not to focus on the issue of reliability of weather forecasts. They should join the renegotiation meeting by proposing alternative solutions (renegotiation of the price, speed up work), with the willingness to find a solution that accommodates both partners' interests while keeping a spirit of cooperation and mutual help. This approach would also fit with Kant's moral principle.

Smith's moral principle advises a different approach. Leaving aside possible hidden self-interested reasons of the exchange partner, the house owners would care exclusively about their own interests. They signed a contract where the delivery date was fixed on December 22. If the contractor is not able to respect the delivery date because of external circumstances, it is not their problem. They might request that the contractor adopt a day-based approach even if this means that, on some days, the working crew could not be employed elsewhere. The contractor's eventual losses are not the house owners' problems. Even if this can cause problems in the relationship with the contractor's father (a family friend), they are willing to appeal to a court of justice to defend their legitimate interests. After all, business is business. In this respect, the moral principle might even suggest they inquire about relevant legal precedents where similar situations went to the court of justice and were solved in favor of the clients.

The moral reasons for adopting one of these principles resemble the one at the contractor's disposal. The reflections on one's own spontaneous reactions as a representation of pre-reflective inclinations, the concern about human flourishing, the common good, and moral development; all of these constitute valid moral reasons. The additional element might be related to how the house owners conduct their own business or behave in their work. If they act in a certain way in their economic activity, that might affect the moral reasons why they choose a moral principle rather than another in the contract related to the house façade. In other words, the moral principles they adopted and the reasons why they chose them, for example, in conducting their own business, might generate a standard of morality that they apply to the exchange partner. It goes without saying that the same can happen from the contractor's side.

Contracts are never signed in a void space. The individuals who signed them have their own history and way of seeing themselves and society, and all these elements can count as moral reasons for choosing one moral principle over the other. The purpose of this chapter, and, broadly speaking, of this book, was to propose new moral principles and reasons to employ while thinking about moral problems emerging in market exchange. We need now to see what can be made of these reflections by the contractor and house owners.

4.5 Discussion

Throughout the book, I have justified the moral principles of economic enlightenments based on their utility. The question that I need to answer is then the following: How are they useful to the house owners and the contractor of the case study exposed in this chapter? One could reply that the moral reflections of exchange partners can prevent the appeal to the court of justice and all the burdensome of transforming an economic dispute into a legal one. And yet, we saw that at least one of those moral principles, namely the principle of self-interest and non-tuism, might bring both parties to the conclusion that the renegotiation might rightly end in a court of justice. Therefore, the idea that moral reflection avoids legal problems cannot count as a utility motive for referring to economic enlightenment. While it is true that, in some cases, some moral principles can avoid the fact that incompleteness of contracts generates legal disputes, this does not count as a reason for economic agents to adopt them. More precisely, this reason would move the moral reflection from the moral principles to consideration of the consequences of one's rule of conduct and course of action. Therefore, it would fit into the consequentialist approach, which, while valuable in itself, is of little help for the exchange partners in cases like incomplete contracts. In a renegotiation process, where the interaction can take many forms and evolve in many different directions, the capacity to predict the consequences of one's action is severely undermined.

Deontology and virtue ethics approaches also seem to be of little usefulness in solving these moral problems. Imagine saying to the house owners and contractors that the right thing to do has to be based on their reciprocal rights and duties, regardless of the consequences. Both will appeal to the contract terms that, as we saw, were the main cause of the quarrel. Neither would benefit them to know that they have to act according to the virtues of justice and honesty, presenting those in an Aristotelian fashion as the middle ground of two opposite vices. In that respect, the contractor and house owners might both revendicate they are acting virtuously, which can exacerbate the quarrel rather than mitigate it. Am I implying that the three economic enlightenments might be more useful than the triad of virtue ethics, deontology, and consequentialism in this kind of situation? I am, although I still need to explain the reasons why that answer is true.

The moral principles for economic agents emerging from Genovesi's, Kant's, and Smith's theories help the contractor and house owners *to frame* the situation in which they are involved, their role in that situation, and, in general, the moral problem they are facing. On top of those elements, they furnish some rules of conduct and moral reasons that justify them. The utility of the three economic enlightenments is not to provide ready-made solutions to a moral problem but rather *to offer* alternative moral points of view for stimulating the exchange partners' reflections. To see the relevance of this consideration, we can consider a counterfactual. Imagine the contractor and house owners thinking about what they should do in the renegotiation meeting without having at their disposal the economic enlightenments perspectives. At the very least, their reflections would be *impoverished* by the lack of conceptual, moral tools to face the situation. It is also possible to imagine that the lack of valuable alternatives might diminish their genuine interest in morality, that is, doing the right thing in the renegotiation moment. Blending again Gauthier's lexicon, they might think of that situation as a "morally free zone," as a space where moral considerations might not be available and, therefore, be irrelevant.[13] I am pushing the counterfactual to an extreme not to show that there is no morality in the market without the three economic enlightenments but rather that they are precious allies for fostering moral reflections in economic agents.

Granted that the three moral principles are useful for framing moral problems faced by economic agents, do they also provide elements that indicate which of the three principles should be adopted? In other words, do the contractor and house owners have ultimate and irrefutable reasons for choosing Kant's principle rather than Genovesi's and Smith's, or another possible combination among the three? These questions can be answered on two different levels. First, there is the issue of understanding if one or more moral reasons might prevail over the other. If that is the case, then moral reasons can become a moral motivation to decide based on the chosen principle. Once that is decided, the exchange partners should understand how that moral principle can be applied to concrete situations, that is, how the moral principle will inform their decisions and actions.

The way in which moral reasons might be compared and weighted among each other depends on the exchange partners' reflection. For example, the contractor might attach great importance to his prereflective moral inclination. In everyday life discourse, this goes under the formula of "trust your instinct." Therefore, if the contractor spontaneously reacted from his self-interest, he might decide that this is more valuable than, for example, considering his moral development as a rational agent. The other way round is also possible. While recognizing the force of self-interest, the contractor might think that his duties as a rational being have more value. There are numerous possible combinations in the comparison of moral reasons. An important thing to notice is that, to adopt one of the three moral principles, the economic agent does not need to fully endorse all the moral reasons attached to it. What is absolutely relevant is that the exchange partners are presented with clear moral principles that express clear rules of conduct and the reasons why these should be adopted. As external observers, we might speculate about the possible reflection patterns of the house owners and the contractors, but, in the end, it is their choice. Once more, the utility of the three economic enlightenments is to provide valuable alternatives to ensure the choice is as free and informed as possible.

The second level concerns the transition from moral principles to decisions and actions. Even if moral reasons become moral motivations, many elements are still at stake in establishing how to apply a general principle to a specific situation. One of them is reputation. Imagine that the contractor has the (merited or unmerited) reputation of a self-interested and even greedy person. The house owners know this from more or less reliable stories that go around in their circles of friends. While the house owners have chosen the moral principle they want to adopt, this additional element might affect how they will apply it. If they decide to adopt Genovesi's or Kant's moral principles, they might approach the meeting hiding the fact that they are willing to find a halfway solution because of the fear that the contractor will take advantage. This relates to another element that lies between moral principles and decisions and actions. I am referring to the expectations about others' behaviors. Hundreds of studies in behavioral economics and ethics show how people decide what is the right thing to do based on what they expect other people will do. More than a moral reason for adopting one of the three moral principles, this element concerns the way in which moral principles will be applied to the concrete situation. The mutual expectations can come from reputation but also from the history of the exchange partner. Suppose that the contractor had already done reparation works for the house owners (and this was the case in the real-life scenario on which the case study is based). If the contractor showed, for example, to be willing to cooperate in the spirit of team reasoning, then the house owners, once they opted for Kant's or Genovesi's moral principles, can decide to approach the renegotiation meeting by showing willingness to cooperate as well. Considerations like this might seem nuances applied to a theoretical case study. However, in real life, they determine most of the interaction outcomes between exchange partners.

It is beyond the scope of this book to consider all the other elements that are in between moral principles and decisions or actions, such as cultural norms, political preferences, socioeconomic status, and so on. The aim of this chapter, and of the two following, is to show how the moral principles for economic agents elaborated by Genovesi, Kant, and Smith in the eighteenth century are still relevant for contemporary moral problems.

Notes

1. Van der Deijl, W. (2023). Moral reasons. In Dubbink, W., & van der Deijl, W. (eds.), *Business Ethics: A Philosophical Introduction*, Cham, Springer, 68.
2. For Genovesi, public happiness and common good can be considered synonyms. See Chapter 2.
3. Kant, I. (1996). *The Cambridge Edition of the Works of Immanuel Kant*, ed. by M. J. Gregor, Cambridge, Cambridge University Press, 244.
4. van der Deijl, Moral reasons, 69.
5. See Schwartz, T. (1972). Rationality and the myth of the maximum. *Noûs*, 6(4), 97–117.
6. Among many, see the classic Sen, A. K. (1977). Rational fools: A critique of the behavioral foundations of economic theory. *Philosophy & Public Affairs*, 317–344.
7. Hart, O. (2017). Incomplete contracts and control. *American Economic Review*, 107(7), 1732.
8. Ibid.
9. Tirole, J. (1999). Incomplete contracts: Where do we stand? *Econometrica*, 67(4), 741.
10. Ibid.
11. See Hart, O., & Moore, J. (1988). Incomplete contracts and renegotiation. *Econometrica: Journal of the Econometric Society*, 56 (4), 755–785.
12. As anticipated in the Chapter 1 and Part II, this is a real-life story that I am adapting to make it a good case study that analyzes the role of the moral principles of economic enlightenments.
13. Gaughier, *Morals by Agreement*, 90.

5 Unreliable Questionnaires

5.1 Research Approaches

This chapter focuses on a qualitative study carried out among the employees of a multinational corporation. Those in BE are well acquainted with the qualitative research method, which is particularly prevalent in disciplines such as sociology, management, and social psychology – to mention a few examples. Nonetheless, I will provide a short overview of the qualitative research approach. This is essential to set the stage for the story I will tell, which addresses a particular moral problem (incomplete contracts) that must be differentiated from other issues associated with qualitative research methodology.

The starting point is the distinction between qualitative and quantitative research approaches: "Often the distinction between qualitative research and quantitative research is framed in terms of using words (qualitative) rather than numbers (quantitative), or better yet, using closed-ended questions and responses (quantitative hypotheses) or open-ended questions and responses (qualitative interview questions)."[1] These methods are empirical, aiming to observe and analyze aspects of reality. Quantitative approaches concentrate on the relationships among variables through numeric data collection and statistical analysis. In contrast, qualitative approaches focus on understanding people's perspectives and lived experiences by asking open-ended questions. Despite their differences, these two methods are not mutually exclusive, as researchers frequently integrate both qualitative and quantitative findings.

An illustration of quantitative research is found in happiness studies within economics, where data are gathered to connect individual income levels with their happiness. A notable figure in this field, Richard Easterlin (1926–2024), merged two databases to assess self-reported happiness: (1) a Gallup pool-type survey, where people were asked, "In general, how happy would you say that you are – very happy, fairly happy or not very happy?"; (2) research made by the humanist psychologist Hadley Cantril in fourteen countries, where people were asked to classify their own satisfaction on a scale from 0 to 10.[2] In contrast, qualitative research aims to grasp the meanings individuals associate with happiness and its link to their personal experiences. This can be accomplished via participant interviews or by employing open-ended questions in surveys.[3] The idea is that qualitative methods provide a deeper understanding of social issues by directly engaging with the complexities of how individuals perceive and experience those issues, while quantitative methods, although more superficial, provide robust results by applying rigorous statistical analysis.

Both research methods encounter various challenges. These include representativity issues, insufficient resources or data, difficulties with data collection, environmental factors, control issues, and implicit and explicit biases in questionnaires, among others. An intriguing matter pertains to the feasibility and desirability of providing rewards or payments to individuals who are interviewed in a qualitative study.[4] The issue can be divided into two questions: Is compensating participants in qualitative studies a common practice? Are there any concerns linked to this approach?

Among scholars, there is disagreement about the extension of paying participants involved in a qualitative study. In 2008, Emma Head began her paper[5] by challenging Sonia Thompson's claim that payments for participants in qualitative studies are uncommon.[6] While discussing this issue in depth is beyond the scope of this chapter, recent research indicates that both paid and unpaid methods are being utilized.[7] The more intriguing question, however, is whether it is beneficial to compensate participants in qualitative studies.

Head demonstrated the benefits of compensating participants in a qualitative study.[8] Payments can broaden the pool of individuals willing to engage in the research. It is irrelevant whether the incentive is provided before or after the interview, or whether it takes the form of cash, vouchers, or bonuses, as long as it resembles a mutually beneficial arrangement (contract) or gift exchange. From the researcher's perspective, compensating participants is particularly advantageous, especially in scenarios where garnering interest in a study is challenging. Additionally, payment serves as a fair acknowledgment of the time and effort participants dedicate to answering questions during live interviews or completing questionnaires. Moreover, "omitting to pay participants has sometimes been characterised as unethical, so that making payments (or gift-giving) becomes a mark of ethically sound research ... the act of payment serves to overcome some of the power imbalance between the researcher and the researched so that the former isn't the only one in the relationship to benefit directly."[9] Finally, monetary incentives or gifts can serve as appealing factors for participants who might not have otherwise spent time analyzing the significance of the research topic.

Although these advantages appear appealing initially, several challenges necessitate careful consideration. At times, financial incentives are so substantial and prominent that they may pressure individuals, particularly those in challenging economic circumstances, to participate in a study they might not have joined otherwise – a phenomenon mentioned by Sullivan and Cain in their research on female victims of violence.[10] Another prominent issue concerns the impact of rewards on participants' motivations. Head pointed out the risk of money incentivizing people to imagine what the researcher wants to hear and reply accordingly.[11] Moreover, providing financial rewards for a questionnaire that participants would have filled out for free – maybe due to their belief in the study's significance – might lead to a reduction in their efforts. Scholars at the intersection of social psychology and economics refer to this phenomenon as the crowding-out effect, which occurs when extrinsic motivations diminish or undermine intrinsic motivations.[12] Various factors contribute to motivational crowding-out, such as a diminished sense of autonomy, where the individual perceives extrinsic motivation from incentives as a form of control, or impaired self-expression, which occurs when someone wishes to showcase their intrinsic motivations, but the incentive eclipses them. When participants cut back on replying to questionnaires or participating in interviews, it can really impact the quality of the results that researchers hope to achieve. So, it is important that participants engage fully to ensure meaningful outcomes, and compensation is not always the best means to accomplish that.

The story I am about to present pertains to a qualitative study in which participants receive compensation in the form of monetary payments. Nonetheless, the focus of my discussion shifts to a different issue: the consequences when paid participants fail to engage fully with the qualitative study questionnaire. This is another example of moral problems arising from incomplete contracts.

5.2 Case Study

5.2.1 The Story

After earning a master's degree in international management, a young scholar seeks a PhD. They receive backing from their university and draft a proposal to apply for a grant from a national organization. This research project aims to explore new leadership styles in multinational organizations and understand how employees conceive the qualities of an ideal leader they wish to follow.[13] The proposed methodology is both theoretical and empirical. After a comprehensive literature review of the new leadership styles and their main components, the researcher will conduct a qualitative analysis among the employees of several multinational companies. The funding institution approves the project, leading to the awarding of the scholarship. One of the clauses specifies that a portion of the scholarship may be used to cover expenses related to qualitative research in multinational companies.

The qualitative study is organized as follows. Initially, managerial teams of multinational corporations are contacted. They are informed that the qualitative study does not necessitate employees to assess the leadership style implemented within their respective companies; instead, employees are asked to identify the essential traits deemed crucial for an effective and good leader. After approval is granted, management teams are removed from the process to prevent any pressure on the interviewed employees. The researcher, in fact, successfully persuades top executives at various multinational corporations that new leadership styles enhance not only employee well-being but also productivity – this has already been demonstrated in the literature reviewed by the researcher.[14]

Following the initial phase, the researcher reaches out to employees – previously informed by management – via email, introducing themselves and outlining the research project. They present the study in these terms: If employees agree to participate, they will need to complete a questionnaire that includes demographic questions and five open-ended questions (with responses limited to a maximum of 500 words). The estimated duration required to complete the questionnaire comprehensively is approximately 90 minutes. Although the questionnaire is not anonymous, the researcher ensures that a nondisclosure agreement is in place. This means that the qualitative research results will be shared in an anonymized format, and no personal information will be disclosed to management teams or third parties. Participants will also receive rewards once they agree to participate in the qualitative study. Due to the concerns regarding monetary incentives discussed previously, the researcher has chosen to provide compensation through a $25 gift card to be spent on a well-known online retailer. This means that employees/participants will obtain gift cards they can use freely once they consent to participate. Please notice that the receipt of the gift card is not contingent upon the final outcome, specifically in regard to how each participant completes the questionnaire. The agreement stipulates that the beneficial exchange involves giving gift cards in return for participation in the qualitative survey.

The researcher identified an issue with the results from the analysis of questionnaires completed by employees of the first multinational corporation studied. Approximately 20 percent of participants provided unsatisfactory responses to the open-ended questions. Some clearly relied on generative AI based on large language models, resulting in answers that are so similar and precise that there is minimal doubt. Additionally, other participants provided very brief and generic responses to the open-ended questions. This is evident from the average time taken to complete the questionnaire, which is significantly less than the ninety minutes anticipated by the researcher. As the goal of the qualitative study was to analyze the participants' understanding of leadership in the organizations, the results coming from the questionnaires of the 20 percent cannot be employed. Nevertheless, those participants received the gift card just like the other 80 percent who answered the questionnaires properly. Something went wrong in the process. How to deal with that something pertains to moral issues of incomplete contracts.

5.2.2 The Moral Problem

In a situation like the one mentioned earlier, a researcher's first thought might be related to their research structure. If the gift card had been given after the completion and analysis of the questionnaires instead of beforehand, many of those issues might have been avoided. Nevertheless, defining what constitutes an adequate response to questionnaires is challenging. Setting minimum word counts or time limits could help, but they do not address challenges associated with generative AI, for example. Another immediate reaction might be to simply let it go. After all, 80 percent of respondents completed the questionnaire satisfactorily. Nevertheless, this is the initial group of questionnaires the researcher examines: What happens if the situation resurfaces or deteriorates further in subsequent groups?

The researcher decides to meet participants who provided responses that differed from the questionnaire expectations. Although it requires significant time and effort, this meeting may address issues concerning participants' behavior. The researcher believes that these participants behaved unfairly. Thus, the meeting's objective is to request that they complete the questionnaire once more – without assistance from generative AI and avoiding vague or brief responses. While the researchers' goal is clear, the moral reasons behind it might be different and attached to different moral principles. We return once again to the three economic enlightenments, which present three potential approaches to the meeting and determining what to say during it.

5.3 Applying the Three Economic Enlightenments

In her international management master's program, the researcher studies the three economic enlightenments in their BE course. As I did in the previous chapter, I incorporated this fictional element to illustrate the various directions that the researchers' moral reasoning may follow. The three moral principles are outlined below:

Principle of self-interest and non-tuism: When you are involved in a market transaction that you have freely joined, you should care about your own interest. The interest of the exchange partner should concern you insofar as it promotes your own (no more than that).

Principle of mutual assistance: When you are involved in a market transaction that you have freely joined, you should care about your own interest and, beyond your own interest, to a certain extent, about the interest of your exchange partner.

Principle of honoring the spirit of mutually beneficial contracts: When you have freely signed a mutually beneficial contract, you have the imperfect duty to care about your interest and, beyond your interest, to a certain extent, about the interest of your exchange partner.

Unlike the preceding chapter, I will not illustrate the researcher's and participants' moral reasoning before the meeting. This avoids introducing a further fictional element, such as assuming that participants know the moral principles of the three economic enlightenments. Instead, I assume they learn about these principles from the researcher during the meeting and then use that information to determine which one, if any, should guide their actions – deciding whether to complete the questionnaire again or not.

5.3.1 Researcher

In this story, the three moral principles operate on two distinct levels. At the first level, they justify the researcher's decision to convene a meeting to have 20 percent of the participants complete the questionnaire anew. At the second level, these principles may be utilized to furnish moral reasons and patterns of conduct intended to persuade the participants that this action is appropriate. While the two levels overlap, I shall analyze them individually for clarity in application.

The principle of self-interest and non-tuism justifies the action (meeting) and objective (participants retaking the test) by recalling the agreement's binding nature. Although there was no formal contract or handshake, participants formed a mutually beneficial relationship by agreeing to partake in the study and receiving a gift card. This understanding leads the researcher to believe they are justified in requesting that participants complete the questionnaire again. They are not appealing to the participants' goodwill, nor do they have any prior relationship with them. Instead, the researcher asserts that their interests were overlooked by the 20 percent of participants, making it reasonable to request this additional effort from them.

The remaining two moral principles appear to imply different justifications. The principle of mutual assistance encourages exchange partners to view themselves as a team during market transactions. In this context, the researcher perceived the questionnaire's failure not as their own but as a shared failure involving the researcher and 20 percent of the participants. Thus, requesting them to complete the questionnaire again appears reasonable since participants are naturally concerned about the outcomes of their interaction. If participants lack a natural inclination toward the researcher's interests and are not legally obligated to complete the questionnaire again, Kant's principle of respecting mutually beneficial contracts still applies. They hold an imperfect duty to rise above their feelings and act rightly. In this instance, even though it may require additional time and effort, they should respond to the open-ended questions in alignment with the research expectations. This reasoning might convince the researcher of the righteousness of summoning a meeting and making the request.

The three moral principles offer rules of conduct and courses of action (along with accompanying moral reasons) that researchers can follow during the meeting. Smith's principle may indicate two possible approaches. Firstly, the researcher could prioritize their personal interests, which are jeopardized by the poor quality of answers to the open-ended questions, and threaten participants with disclosure of this issue to the management team. While the nondisclosure agreement safeguards individual identities, it does not prevent the highlighting of a broader issue – complaining to the management about the poor quality of the answers to some questionnaires. Furthermore, anonymity ensures that the remaining 80 percent of participants can be negatively affected by the misconduct of a minority. The researcher intends to invoke participants' apprehension regarding pressures from upper management and their peers to bring them toward the right thing to do. While the gift card reward did not succeed, perhaps another self-interested inclination or reflection, like avoiding shame, could be effective.

This method seems complicated and risky, as it might create further tensions between the researcher and the participants. However, the principle of self-interest and non-tuism suggests another way to handle the situation. In this second scenario, the researcher might appeal to the participants' far-sighted sense of self-interest. As I noted in Chapter 3, this aligns with what Smith discusses in his *Wealth* regarding the virtues of prudence and self-command. The argument can be framed as follows. This study focuses on emerging leadership styles from the employees' perspective. Upon publication, it can potentially enhance a burgeoning field of literature dedicated to boosting productivity and improving workplace conditions. It may seem like a tiny drop in the ocean, but this type of research can truly make a difference for workers in the medium to long term. It is important that participants, who are employees and may be considered "followers," respond to the questionnaire with utmost sincerity and thoroughness. Using generative AI or neglecting the open-ended question may appear advantageous for immediate personal gain, but this choice could be proven misguided in the long run. It's important to note that the researcher is not attempting to convince participants that the primary aim of the qualitative study is solely focused on enhancing workers' well-being. The researcher also has personal interests; a dependable questionnaire would provide valuable material for writing papers, publishing, and ultimately advancing their career. The principle of self-interest and non-tuism suggests that if everyone acts on their self-interested inclinations, ultimately, everyone benefits. This public good argument offers a moral reason to the 20 percent of participants to complete the questionnaire for the second time.

The principle of mutual assistance implies an alternative method. Genovesi's civil economy relies on friendship and mutual trust among individuals. Consequently, the researcher must safeguard their relationships with participants. Instead of resorting to threats or persuasion, the researcher should initiate by expressing regret for any inconveniences caused by the study. Eventually, more precise guidelines for the questionnaire – such as prohibiting generative AI usage and establishing a minimum word count – could have prevented the problem. The researcher might demonstrate consideration for participants' interest by suggesting replacing the questionnaire with in-person interviews to reduce the effort required to answer the questions. In any case, the conversation's tone should emphasize the endeavor's collective nature rather than asking one part to sacrifice for the other. Instead of squandering time and resources on endless blame-shifting discussions, the researcher offers their solution by appealing to the participants' cooperative inclinations and reflections. Genovesi's moral principle also provides a moral reason attached to the common good. The cooperation arising from participants choosing to complete the questionnaire a second time exemplifies the ideal workplace dynamics. The way participants choose to act in the study should be consistent with their typical behavior at work. If the employees view their workplace as a hub for collaboration and support, this creates a compelling moral reason to embrace the principle of mutual assistance and agree to the researcher's suggestion of redoing the questionnaire. The pursuit of the common good must be an integral part of everyone's intentions rather than merely a by-product of self-interested motives.

The researcher might appeal to participants' self-interested or cooperative inclinations and reflections. From Kant's perspective, these are significant, yet not conclusive, moral reasons for agreeing with the researcher's solution. The principle of honoring the spirit of mutually

Unreliable Questionnaires 131

beneficial contracts gives participants a moral reason to retake the questionnaire, regardless of potential benefits. The researcher should approach the meeting by emphasizing that it is everyone's duty to ensure the study's success. While they are willing to fulfill their obligations as part of the agreement by reframing the questionnaires or even providing in-person interviews, the participants must also commit to their responsibilities by dedicating additional time and effort to the study. It's possible that 20 percent of the questionnaire may consist of uninteresting or irrelevant answers, so these responses might not be included in the publications. It is altogether possible that participants do not feel any inclination toward the researcher and, in general, they are not spontaneously willing to abide by mutual assistance in the workplace as well as in the study. In Kant's view, none of this is morally significant. Moral principles take precedence over natural inclinations or expected outcomes. The researcher and participants are expected to fulfill their imperfect duty, as there is no contrast between that and other duties. A contrasting situation would arise if, for instance, the researcher were to request the remaining 80 percent of the participants to retake the examination in pursuit of enhanced results. In that situation, the principle of honoring the spirit of mutually beneficial contracts would conflict with the absolute duty to avoid deception by misrepresenting the inquiry's results. Nothing like that is implied in the researcher's request to the 20 percent of the participants. As rational beings, they must prioritize what is right over what is good.

5.3.2 Participants

The participants learned about the three moral principles during the meeting. However, they might argue that, from their perspective, things stand differently. The same moral principles can suggest different courses of action and moral reasons. Initially, referencing the principle of self-interest and non-tuism, they may contend that any extra effort on their part should warrant additional compensation. The instructions they received did not include any specifics on how the open-ended questions should have been answered. They abide by their part of the deal by completing the questionnaire according to the engagement rules given. Particularly, individuals who utilized generative artificial intelligence could not have anticipated that their actions would inadvertently undermine the validity of the qualitative study's results. The complaints of the researcher and the proposed solution go beyond what they are required to do out of self-interest. If they need to spend more time and effort to take the same or a different questionnaire, they will not do it out of benevolence toward the researcher. Participants can present additional moral reasons to support their request for extra compensation. Having to incur extra costs can be an important lesson for the researcher. Next time, they will take greater care in preparing the guidelines to accompany the questionnaire. This can be framed in the public good argument. By promoting their interest, which means asking for additional compensation, the participants ensure that future studies will be conducted with more attention. Conversely, offering to retake the study at no cost out of goodwill might inadvertently prevent the researcher from reflecting on their actions during the process and committing the same mistake in the future.

Participants can view themselves as teammates with the researcher. The goal is to achieve mutual benefit, meaning while they find value in the gift card, the researcher should appreciate their responses to the questionnaire. Aware of the problems coming from their initial attempt, they might consider returning the gift card's equivalent monetary value. Nevertheless, the principle of mutual assistance encourages them to support their exchange partners' interests. Since the researcher has explicitly requested them to complete the questionnaire again, they have a clear moral reason to do so, even though it would require extra effort. This does not imply that participants become cooperative after the meeting if they were not inclined beforehand. Those who utilized generative AI, for instance, might clarify that they were unaware of the issues with their behavior; otherwise, they would have responded to the question in the first person. Genovesi's view sees human beings as naturally driven to care about the interests of others alongside theirs. Therefore, it can provide valid moral reasons to participants who had this inclination to meet the researcher's request.

Additionally, the principle of mutual assistance may prompt participants to be more open to hearing the researcher's perspective. While it's important to acknowledge that the questionnaire should have included clearer guidelines, participants might consider the researcher's youth and attribute the error to a lack of experience. This kind of disposition signals the difference between Smith's and Genovesi's principles. The former does not require participants to consider the researcher's circumstances, while the latter does so. Should participants choose to embrace the principle of mutual assistance, their actions will not stem from altruism or kindness. Conversely, they would just recognize how valuable it is to nurture relationships and work together to seek intentionally mutual advantage, which are essential moral reasons from the perspective of civil economy.

In line with Kant's moral principle, participants may conditionally agree to the researcher's proposal. They will retake the questionnaire provided two conditions are met. Firstly, clear guidelines must be shared in advance. Secondly, the researcher should supply either a rubric or a sample answer to evaluate the level of the responses. In other words, the participants recognize their duty to honor the spirit of mutually beneficial contracts and are ready to act upon it as long as the researcher does the same. The inclinations or reflections that initially motivated the researcher's and the participants' actions are of no interest. Likewise, the potential need for increased effort from both parties in doing the new questionnaire is also morally insignificant. What truly holds importance is that, as rational beings, they engage in morally appropriate actions driven by morally appropriate principles.

5.4 Discussion

This story differs from the one in the previous chapter. In that case, the contractor and house owners needed to meet to resolve an issue with ongoing work, whereas the researcher and participants had the option to forgo a meeting and discussion. Their decision to meet indicates a moral interest that surpasses personal benefits. The researcher received a significant number of positive responses to the open-ended questions, and those few participants who did not complete the questionnaire properly have already been compensated. Therefore, the meeting in itself is a sign that both parties were interested in doing the right thing. If that was the case, the three economic enlightenments afforded them diverse moral principles and reasons to *frame* their own moral reflections concerning the moral problem pertinent to the qualitative study. I have previously mentioned that the purpose of outlining moral principles for economic agents isn't to offer ready-made solutions but instead to offer, if I may use a common phrase, food for (moral) thought. This does not imply that comparative reflections are impossible or unhelpful.

The choice *among* the three moral principles might depend on many elements. I will mention three of them related to the fictional case of this chapter. The first point relates to external factors, particularly how the participants engaged with the study. As highlighted in the story, management informed participants about the study. Though this was the sole instance of management's involvement, it could have been crucial. Consider if some participants had previously faced issues with management. Then, the 20 percent might have seen their actions as actively boycotting the study to retaliate indirectly toward the management. This explains why, during the meeting, they may be less focused on the researcher's interests. Instead, the researcher might be perceived as part of the management team, leading them to find a moral reason to seek more compensation in line with Smith's moral principle. As I have noted repeatedly, moral reasons are significant and can serve as a motivational force in their own right. However, the connection between moral reasons and moral motivation is not always automatic or guaranteed; instead, it can be shaped by various factors.

Another aspect might stem from the protagonists' pre-reflective inclinations. While online questionnaires encouraged anonymity, the in-person meeting fostered face-to-face interaction. Suppose the researcher and participants had been naturally driven by what Genovesi called *forza diffusiva*, that is, love and care for the other person in front of them. In that case, this element might have played a crucial role mainly, although not exclusively, during and after the meeting. It could have provided moral reasons to follow the principle of mutual assistance and make it the leading moral motivation for their actions.

Another scenario might involve both the researcher and participants embracing Kant's moral economy, influenced by their educational backgrounds. For illustrative purposes, envision the participants as a uniform group who have undergone identical training and education. Kant was educated in a Pietist school, where he understood the significance of adhering to laws and duties in personal conduct. If something similar happened to the participants, they might be less inclined to give moral relevance to their own pre-reflective inclinations or sympathies/antipathies toward the management team. They can view their situation as necessitating the right action for its own sake rather than for any benefit. Even if they haven't read my book or aren't familiar with Kant's moral principle, they can grasp that a certain obligation compels them because they were raised and educated that way. These factors might bring them to favor moral reasons attached to Kant's moral principle and make it the motivation for their actions.

It is simplistic to assume that moral motivations seamlessly convert into actions; just because someone commits to a moral principle does not mean their course of action is predetermined and unchangeable. Conversely, this story makes it evident that actions will arise from moral negotiations between the researcher and the participants. The value of the three economic enlightenments is to broaden the moral perspectives available to the story's protagonists. In my viewpoint, morality is a personal but also a collective endeavor. When determining what is right or what we owe one another, the more moral perspectives we include in the conversation, the more beneficial it will be. If we consider moral principles and reasons as unnegotiable viewpoints to determine our actions, the discussion wraps up even before it begins.

My project does not differ from what is entailed in the classic triad of consequentialism, deontology, and virtue ethics. The reader might have noticed that some of the arguments, both from the researcher's and participants' perspectives, can be framed within the old triad. When the researcher appeals to the far-sighted self-interest of the participants, for example, that is an invitation to focus on the long-term consequences of one's action. Alternatively, emphasizing the goal of building authentic relationships aligns with the Aristotelian interpretation of virtue ethics. I have never asserted that the three economic enlightenments offer complete novelty and clarity in moral discussions. Instead, I have aimed to illustrate how they can broaden the range of moral principles accessible to individuals confronted with a moral dilemma.

Notes

1. Creswell, J. W., & Creswell, J. D. (2018). *Research Design: Qualitative, Quantitative, and Mixed Methods Approaches*. Thousand Oaks, Sage.
2. See Easterlin, R. (1974). Does economic growth improve the human lot? Some empirical evidence. In David, P. A., & Reder, M. W. (eds.), *Nations and Households in Economic Growth: Essays in Honor of Moses Abramovitz*. New York, Academic Press, 89–125.
3. See, for example, Lu, L., & Shih, J. B. (1997). Sources of happiness: A qualitative approach. *The Journal of Social Psychology*, 137(2), 181–187.

4. The same issue is discussed for quantitative studies. See Singer, E., & Kulka, R. A. (2002). Paying respondents for survey participation. *Studies of Welfare Populations: Data Collection and Research Issues*, 4, 105–128.
5. Head, E. (2008). The ethics and implications of paying participants in qualitative research. *International Journal of Social Research Methodology*, 12(4), 335–344.
6. Thompson, S. (1996). Paying respondents and informants. *Social Research Update*, 14, 1–5.
7. See Surmiak, A. (2020). Ethical concerns of paying cash to vulnerable participants: The qualitative researchers' views. *The Qualitative Report*, 25(12), 4461–4481.
8. Head, The ethics and implications of paying participants.
9. Ibid., 337.
10. Sullivan, C. M., & Cain, D. (2004). Ethical and safety considerations when obtaining information from or about battered women for research purposes. *Journal of Interpersonal Violence*, 19(5), 603–618.
11. Head, The ethics and implications of paying participants.
12. Frey, B. S. (1997). *Not Just for the Money: An Economic Theory of Personal Motivation*. Cheltenham, Edward Elgar Publishing.
13. See Anderson, M. H., & Sun, P. Y. T (2017). Reviewing leadership styles: Overlaps and the need for a new "full-range" theory. *International Journal of Management Reviews*, 19, 76–96. In the twenty-first century, new leadership styles have emerged to challenge the hierarchical, authoritarian, and vertical models prevalent in twentieth-century organizations. These earlier styles, often referred to as vertical dyad linkage or authoritarian leadership, neglected workers' autonomy and dignity by focusing on direct commands and strict hierarchies. Contemporary styles, including ethical leadership and servant leadership, favor a horizontal and nonhierarchical framework. Instead of overseeing actions through incentives or commands, these styles seek to inspire followers by recognizing their agency, needs, and desires. Leaders are encouraged to step down from their pedestals to engage collaboratively with their followers, valuing their voices and perspectives. I am very skeptical about these new leadership approaches but, to remain close to the story as I was told, I will put aside my concerns and critiques.
14. See, for example, Nicolae, M., Ion, I., & Nicolae, E. (2013). The research agenda of spiritual leadership. Where do we stand? *Revista De Management Comparat International*, 14(4), 551–566.

6 Armed Banks

6.1 Banks and Morality

The story of this chapter revolves around the relationship between a customer and his bank. This should not come as a surprise. In the Western tradition, every economic reflection that was aimed at becoming an economic theory had to deal with the role and functioning of the banking system. Even in times when economics was not a stand-alone science, such as the Middle Ages, Christian theologians and philosophers who addressed economic issues speculated at length on the liceity or illicitly of interest loans, money borrowing, risk, usury, and so on.[1] Today, in the global economy characterized by free markets, banks are crucial economic institutions. In addition to other functions like secure savings deposits, banks play a crucial role by acting as intermediaries. They connect the liquidity needs of savers with the long-term investment aspirations of investors. Without this intermediary, the varied timing of loan withdrawals and different levels of risk tolerance – reflected in the variability of returns – would hinder savers and investors from effectively meeting each other. This interaction is essential, as it facilitates access to the credit needed for launching new projects, thereby enhancing individual talents and skills. While this is one important aspect of the banking system, it is not the main focus of this chapter or book. Instead, I will examine the moral considerations regarding banks and their functions in modern society. To illustrate my point, I will briefly analyze two contrasting examples.

The 2008 economic crisis marked a pivotal point with the bankruptcy of Lehman Brothers, a major US investment bank. Renowned moral philosopher Michael Sandel discusses this in his book on the moral boundaries of markets:

> The spectacular failure of financial markets did little to dampen the faith in markets generally. In fact, the financial crisis discredited the government more than banks. In 2011, a survey found that the American public blamed the

federal government more than Wall Street financial institutions for the economic problems facing the country – by a margin of more than two to one.[2]

Sandel here expresses a paradox of US society at that time. On the one hand, banks were seen as part of financial institutions guilty of many moral wrongs, such as speculations on their customers' savings, irresponsible money lending, rapacious investments, and so on. On the other hand, people in the United States were still skeptical in expressing negative judgment on private banks, even when their bankruptcy went along with big exit bonuses for their managers (as in the Lehman Brothers case), and preferred to blame public institutions, including the Federal Reserve (the US central banking system). As shown by recent research, the two critiques became one when governments intervened to save banks that were deemed to be too big to fail:[3] "Second, popular resentment of bank bailouts has provided populists the opportunity to claim that bankers, connected with old parties, got away with their mistakes (or alleged crimes)."[4] All of this shows, although it does not prove, that in the social imaginary, banks are not exactly taken as examples of morality and virtuousness.[5]

In contrast to the previous assertion, two notable examples in both Western and non-Western history demonstrate that banks have been seen as leaders in moral conduct. These include the Italian *Monti di Pietà*, early banking institutions established in the fifteenth century by Franciscan friars, and the modern microcredit initiatives, especially the Grameen Bank founded by Muhammad Yunus in Bangladesh. Both examples show the moral nature of the bank's mission: preventing the exclusion of individuals deemed "non-bankable." The *Monti di Pietà* originated from the teachings of the observant Friars Minor, who established hundreds of these institutions beginning in the mid fifteenth century, particularly in central and northern Italy. As cities prospered, wealth accumulation often exacerbated poverty instead of alleviating it. The Franciscans recognized a renewed aspect of Lady Poverty (Madonna Povertà)[6] to love and consequently created new banks, introducing a novel financial approach that catered to those excluded from traditional finance.[7] *Monti*'s moral mission was articulated through distinct procedures: lending money to the poor people (non-bankable) in exchange for a good (pawn); providing long-term loans without expecting repayment within a week or a month, as usurers did; charging only a rate sufficient to cover expenses; lending exclusively for genuine needs; ensuring that if a borrower could not redeem the pledge, they would receive the surplus the *Monte* got from the sale of the pawn; and striving to lend to everyone whenever feasible.[8]

The Grameen Bank's story is similar, yet distinct. Yunus realized this in 1974 while confronting the severe poverty in the villages near Chittagong, one of Bangladesh's largest cities. He recognized the urgent need for alternative solutions to alleviate the hardships faced by these communities. A particularly notable moment was his encounter with Sofia Begum, a Bengali mother of three.[9] She was compelled to create and sell bamboo stools for meager earnings without funds to buy materials on her own. For Sofia, the only alternative to losing most of her profits to the supplier was succumbing to a loan shark. If the conversation between Yunus and Sofia Begum reflects the clients and issues that microcredit tackled, the Grameen model stands out as an exemplary case to address the problem. Originally, the Grameen Bank introduced four innovative features that distinguished it from conventional credit institutions: (1) group lending with dynamic incentives; (2) small loans with prompt, regular, and transparent repayment; (3) trust-based relationships; (4) a focus on lending to women.[10] While not delving into the specifics of the Grameen Bank's achievements, its moral value is recognized globally to such an extent that Yunus was awarded the Nobel Prize, not in economic sciences but in the promotion of peace.

If we imagine inquiries into the morality of the banking system as a spectrum, the examples just mentioned (Lehman Brothers vs. *Monti di Pietà*/Grameen Bank) are at the opposite poles. In the middle, there are many analyses of moral issues surrounding banks' operations, some of which pertain to BE literature.[11] The story of this chapter is framed within one significant moral issue: customers' perceptions of their banks' investments. Though fictional, the story unfolds in a small US town and occurs sometime after 1999. Why are these details important? In 1933, after the economic crisis of 1929, President Roosevelt enacted the Glass–Steagall Act concerning banking legislation. This part of his famous New Deal aimed, among many other things, to differentiate commercial banks from investment banks – the idea was to separate customers' deposits from speculative markets. However, in 1999, US Congress partially repealed the Glass–Steagall Act. Some economists contended that the blending of commercial and investment banking after 1999 contributed significantly to the 2008 economic crisis.[12] Regardless, after 1999, customers who trusted their deposits in banks learned that those same banks were also engaging in investments. The story I am about to share begins here, with a regular customer of an investment bank questioning not whether banks could invest in financial markets but rather the nature of those investments.

6.2 Case Study

6.2.1 The Story

Taylor has served as the council mayor of a small town in the state of Connecticut for two consecutive terms. Prior to this role, he was a well-known local dentist. Geographically, the town is quite isolated, located far from the highway that connects to all major centers in the state. Consequently, basic services, including dental care, are provided within the town, and given the small population, it can be said that everyone knows one another. Taylor's two nearly plebiscitary victories demonstrate that he has earned the trust of his fellow citizens – almost all of them were also his former clients. When our story begins, Taylor is seventy-two years old and has just decided to retire. His willingness is to rest and, at the same time, enjoy the time with his two nieces who, luckily, live in the same town.

The profits from his dental practice and the earnings from two terms in political office allowed him to save a considerable amount of money. As a widower, his primary wish was to leave as much as possible for his son's family, especially his nieces. This is why he decided to transfer his savings from the credit union in town – the historic and only bank in town, established when he was quite young – to a multinational commercial bank that had just opened a branch nearby. The commercial bank, in fact, offered him an excellent deposit interest rate for moving all his life savings. Taylor is an experienced local politician who, accustomed to supervising and signing various types of transactions, conducted thorough research on the commercial bank in advance. Additionally, he meticulously reviewed the contract proposed to him by the commercial bank. At this juncture, he became aware that a provision within the contract mandated the maintenance of his bank account for a minimum duration of ten years from the date of its establishment. Should he decide to transfer to an alternative financial institution prior to that time, he will be liable for a significant fee in addition to the associated transaction costs. The provision will apply only if there are "serious reasons." Instead of specifying what constitutes a serious reason, the provision simply states that the failure of the bank to deliver the services outlined in the contract may qualify under that label. This general statement was deemed sufficient; Taylor signed the contract and moved his money to the commercial bank.

Three years have passed since Taylor joined the commercial bank. Now a retiree, he enjoys spending his ample free time staying informed about national news. One day, he came across an intriguing article about a protest organized by activists in front of the bank's headquarters. Taylor was taken aback by his reading. The activists were demonstrating against the bank's recent decision to invest in the arms and gambling industries through the acquisition of shares in several corporations. This indicates that a portion of the returns generated by the bank was also linked to industries financing what Taylor considered to be two primary social problems in the United States and, additionally, on a global scale: namely, the proliferation of weapons associated with warfare and the issue of gambling addiction. Especially regarding the latter, he witnessed firsthand families devastated by one of their members who was caught in the gambling spiral. Moreover, Taylor established several ethical consumerism labs in his town. His goal was to demonstrate to his fellow citizens that they could wield political influence through their consumption choices in the economic sphere. He started these laboratories by elucidating how seemingly neutral choices, such as the type of milk or meat one decides to buy, carry substantial significance for the future society one aspires to inhabit. The origin of goods or services we seek, their environmental and social impacts, and the working conditions under which they were made; these factors are all disclosed by the labels on the products we buy daily. Being mindful of our consumption is a strong tool, though it requires time and effort. Taylor was very fond of these initiatives and continued promoting them after retirement.

The reader can now grasp Taylor's shock upon discovering that the bank he chose to join was linked to industries he deemed unethical and socially problematic. Ethical consumption extends beyond buying and selling; it also involves choices about where to invest or deposit one's money. Yet, Taylor verified the types of investments the bank made before signing the contract, and, at that moment, nothing could have led him to anticipate such a troubling outcome. This explains why, after the necessary verifications about his bank's investment choices, he opted to visit the bank's office to convey his decision to return to his previous bank. In this context, amid a moral problem related to ethical finance, another moral issue emerged.

6.2.2 The Moral Problem

Taylor scheduled a meeting with the manager of his local commercial bank. Upon entering the bank, he observed numerous familiar faces, as the employees were all residents of the small town. He was acquainted with them, and they were equally familiar with him. During the meeting, he conveyed to the manager his surprise regarding the recent news about the new bank's investments and his readiness to transfer his funds back to his previous bank. He explicitly stated that his decision was not a moral judgment against the individuals employed at the bank nor a naïve battle to reinstate the Glass–Steagall Act. He knew moral matters are complicated and, ultimately, each person has to decide according to their own conscience. He carefully considered his decision, which is why he wanted to meet the manager.

The conversation took a problematic turn and became a matter of incomplete contracts when Taylor made an additional request. He asked the bank manager not to incur the fees and transaction costs associated with his change of bank. In Taylor's view, the bank's investment in the weapon and gambling industries falls within the "serious reason" why a client might want to rescind the contract unilaterally. Upon reflection, it is evident that when signing the contract, Taylor could not have anticipated the bank's investment behavior, and there was nothing within the contract that could have pointed toward such actions. In this case, the contract was incomplete both because of the impossibility of determining future events and for the vagueness of the label "serious reasons."

The manager of the bank found herself in a challenging predicament. Upon being confronted by her superiors, she was informed that Taylor was permitted to transfer his funds; however, no exemption could be granted concerning the payment of fees and transaction costs. Ultimately, the bank fulfilled its obligations under the contract by providing Taylor with all the promised services, which included the benefits associated with a highly favorable deposit interest rate. While Taylor's ethical considerations are commendable, they cannot be utilized as a means to evade fulfilling contractual obligations. After learning about the bank's decision, Taylor chose to arrange a meeting with both local and nonlocal bank managers to discuss his circumstances. He remained confident in the legitimacy of his reasons and was prepared to advocate for them.

Once again, we faced a moral dilemma regarding incomplete contracts. This time, the renegotiation focused not on the economic transaction itself but on its termination. In essence, Taylor was not seeking improved terms or negotiating for personal gain. He was firm in his decision but felt that the contract's conclusion should have differed from the bank manager's expectations. How might the moral principles of the three economic enlightenments come into play? In continuation with the previous two chapters, I shall elucidate how the parties may utilize these frameworks to establish their fundamental moral understanding and prepare for the meeting.

6.3 Applying the Three Economic Enlightenments

In this chapter, I will refrain from introducing any additional fictional elements and will assume that all participants in the story possess knowledge of the content of this book. The three moral principles are outlined below:

Principle of self-interest and non-tuism: When you are involved in a market transaction that you have freely joined, you should care about your own interest. The interest of the exchange partner should concern you insofar as it promotes your own (no more than that).

Principle of mutual assistance: When you are involved in a market transaction that you have freely joined, you should care about your own interest and, beyond your own interest, to a certain extent, about the interest of your exchange partner.

Principle of honoring the spirit of mutually beneficial contracts: When you have freely signed a mutually beneficial contract, you have the imperfect duty to care about your interest and, beyond your interest, to a certain extent, about the interest of your exchange partner.

The reader will observe that the arguments presented here are analogous to those utilized in Chapter 4 and different from Chapter 5. The three moral principles, in fact, will not be applied to determine if Taylor or the bank's manager should join or organize the meeting, given the fact that both parties are interested in finding a resolution to the contract. Conversely, the three economic enlightenments will be used to assess the story protagonists' possible course of actions (how they should approach the meeting) and moral reasons – as it happened in Chapter 4, although that story concerned the continuation and not termination of a contract.

6.3.1 Customer

Smith's principle of self-interest and non-tuism indicates to Taylor a rather assertive course of action. He has tried with good manners to obtain what he thinks is right; now, he is ready to step up and threaten his interlocutors within the limits of law and decency. He plans to address the meeting immediately, pointing out that if no agreement is reached, he is not afraid to go to a court of law and, in parallel, involve the local and national public opinion. Undoubtedly, along the way, there will be troubles for the bank's personnel, whom he has known very well for a long time. But the principle of non-tuism demands ignoring this kind of consideration, at least in the business sphere. This story also elucidates a significant aspect of Smith's political economy: Self-interest transcends mere financial considerations or personal profit and may encompass an individual's own perceptions of value or significance. In other words, Taylor pursues his self-interest by advocating for his perspective on what is right, both in a general context – such as divesting from a bank that invests in the arms and gambling industries – and in a specific context – such as terminating a contract but not renouncing to his own interest. Smith's moral principle does not demand Taylor to ask for preferential treatment but to care about his own interest during the market transaction (including its conclusion).

The moral principles articulated by Genovesi and Kant advocate for a contrasting course of action. It is advisable for Taylor to attend the meeting with a genuine concern for his own interests and, to a degree, consideration for the interests of the other parties involved. Instead of being confrontational, the discussion can focus on proposals that could benefit all parties. For example, they might agree to a significant reduction in fees if Taylor can delay his move by one or two years. Alternatively, Taylor could propose to cover both fees and transaction costs if the bank commits to clarifying the types of investments they make and their future strategic investment sectors for new clients, at least in general terms. They might even consider the bank financing courses on ethical finance to spark vital reflections on a pressing societal issue. Numerous solutions are possible as long as the meeting embodies the moral principles illustrated by Genovesi and Kant. However, Taylor needs to find moral reasons to favor one of these principles over the other and over Smith's principle. How can Taylor choose between those three?

Pre-reflective inclinations may have a significant influence. Based on our understanding of Taylor's story, it appears he is not inherently motivated to prioritize solely his benefit. He engaged in his political endeavors to serve the community and genuinely demonstrated concern for the well-being of others. Smith's principle may not align well with Taylor's perspective on societal good. Smith's concept of the invisible hand suggests that individual self-interest leads to public benefit. In contrast, Taylor emphasized ethical consumerism, asserting that society's well-being can be intentionally pursued through individuals' daily economic decisions. Therefore, Taylor seems to have little or no reason to choose the principle of self-interest and non-tuism. This does not imply that Smith's principle is morally worse than those of Genovesi and Kant. The objective of the three economic enlightenments is to present moral alternatives to shape individuals' moral reasoning. Until now, I have only speculated on which moral principle appears not to provide Taylor's strong moral reasons for being preferred over the others.

One moral reason for choosing Genovesi's principle is the presence of the bank's local manager at the meeting. Taylor knows this person very well; in fact, he might even have been one of his patients in the past or voted for him to become a major. They likely have a friendship and trust built up, making this connection even more meaningful. This may trigger Taylor's instinct to consider the interests of the local bank manager and the staff at the town bank while determining his next steps – what Genovesi referred to as mutual assistance driven by care for others (*forza diffusiva*, see Chapter 3). Taylor values the common good of his community and, aligning with Genovesi, may see the authentic relationships he has developed within the community as integral to this good. If he were to adhere to the course of action proposed by Smith's principle, certain social ties within his community would likely be compromised and harmed. This is why he has strong moral reasons to embrace the principle of mutual assistance. It's important to highlight that this principle doesn't mean he has to sacrifice his own interests for others; rather, it encourages him to consider both his well-being and the well-being of others when making decisions.

Taylor may consider Kant's moral principle as a viable option. The course of action would remain consistent with that of Genovesi; however, the moral rationale underpinning this choice would differ significantly. This distinction is underscored by Taylor's prompt decision to leave the banking institution, reflecting his view of opposition to the weapons and gambling industries as a moral obligation. The notion of rightfulness takes precedence over what may be personally advantageous for him, such as maintaining his commercial bank account and increasing his financial savings for the benefit of his relatives. Yet, like Kant, Taylor recognizes that life presents various duties across different levels. When he signed the contract, he accepted, from a Kantian perspective, the imperfect duty to uphold the mutually beneficial spirit of the agreement. Consequently, he must seek a solution that respects his obligation not to support industries he considers harmful to society while also addressing the interests of his contract partners. This may explain the moral reasons for Taylor's choice to follow Kant's moral principle and the actions that lead him to seek compromise solutions during the meeting.

6.3.2 Bank's Managers

The bank managers can opt for various courses of action recommended by the three economic enlightenments. According to Smith's principle, their focus should be on the bank's interests, and, in this respect, Taylor's requests seem out of place. Banks operate as businesses rather than charitable organizations. They do recognize their social responsibilities, but as outlined by Milton Friedman's (1912–2006) doctrine, which means that they see that responsibility primarily in terms of maximizing profits for shareholders and, in parallel, for stakeholders. In essence, Friedman argues that the only moral obligation of corporations (and most economic participants) is to enhance profits. This perspective aligns seamlessly with Smith's moral principle, which states that economic actors should prioritize their self-interest. By doing so, they inadvertently contribute to societal improvement, benefiting the public good. Although Friedman's stance is widely recognized, its close connection to Smith's theory is less commonly acknowledged. In his presidential address to the American Economic Association, Friedman wrote: "As another example of Smith's relevance to specific issues, here is his comment on the widely proclaimed 'social responsibility of business,' and on those nauseating TV commercials that portray Exxon and its counterparts as in business primarily to preserve the environment: 'I have never known much good done by those who affected to trade for the public good.'"[13] The manager of the bank adopts this perspective; therefore, their course of action is to assert that Taylor has to comply with the provisions of the contract he signed. After all, he enjoyed the benefits of the contract for three years, and during this time, the bank fulfilled all its obligations to its customer. If Taylor chooses to engage a court or sway public opinion, the bank's managers can respond by demonstrating that there is no empirical connection between the weapon industry and warfare, as weapons are also used for public and private security purposes. They can argue that their investment in the gambling industry is primarily in scratch-off games, which are unlikely to cause addiction. Furthermore, they can highlight that Taylor targets specific actions of the bank while overlooking the charitable initiatives the bank supports annually. Smith's principle requires them to do what is necessary to preserve their own interest and do nothing more to accommodate Taylor's requests.

It is evident that the aforementioned course of action may be more readily adopted by nonlocal managers, specifically individuals who possess no prior connection to Taylor or the community. In contrast, the local manager might exhibit a greater inclination toward the moral principles espoused by Genovesi and Kant, striving to identify a compromise that adequately satisfies both parties. Additionally, the local manager can substantiate her arguments by demonstrating to her nonlocal colleagues that, overall, Taylor's complaint enables the bank to formulate improved contracts for the future, thereby presenting an advantage that arises from the situation.

The moral reasons associated with the three principles may carry varying significance for different bank managers. For example, the local bank manager's pre-reflective inclinations may lead her to prioritize the welfare of the former mayor of her town; however, this is less likely to be the case for nonlocal managers, for whom Taylor is merely one customer among thousands. Similar considerations apply to the concerns regarding the good of society. As previously mentioned in the courses of action, nonlocal managers who endorse the Friedman–Smith perspective may perceive a morally sound justification for not adhering to Taylor's request, which includes requiring him to bear both the fees and transaction costs. Making an exception in Taylor's case could establish a potentially hazardous precedent in the bank's relationships with its clients. While they can relate to Taylor's concerns, their primary responsibility is to prioritize the business for the greater good of many other shareholders and stakeholders of the commercial bank. Conversely, the local manager might want to compromise on this issue so as not to affect the social ties of their town with endless polemics, which, in Genovesi's perspective, is something required to preserve the common good.

Local and nonlocal managers might pick Kant's moral principle for different moral reasons. Throughout their training, they recognized the importance of customer care, which became integral to their decision-making process. Happy customers not only enhance the bank's profitability through their loyalty but the bank staff also has a responsibility to treat customers with fairness and kindness. As a result, rather than prioritizing convenience, bank managers might choose to fulfill their imperfect duty toward Taylor by pursuing a balanced solution instead of confronting the concept of "serious reasons." I am unable to engage in further speculation regarding these matters, as our knowledge of the bank's manager and the decision-making process involved in such situations is quite limited. Nevertheless, I consider it essential to reflect on the courses of action and moral reasons associated with the three economic enlightenments. This is because behind every decision-making process lie individuals with their unique histories, moral understandings, and capacities for moral reasoning. It is now the moment to turn into a discussion on how these moral principles might be related to concrete actions and how moral reasons can become moral motivations.

6.4 Discussion

I selected Taylor's and the bank's story because it can facilitate a discussion of several significant issues. Notably, this includes an analysis of the comparative aspects of the triad of moral principles proposed by Genovesi, Kant, and Smith in relation to the traditional triad of consequentialism, deontology, and virtue ethics. To show what I mean, I will compare Kant's principle of honoring the spirit of mutually beneficial contracts with a famous deontological position in BE, that is, moral purism.[14] Moral purism necessitates that Taylor upholds his principles regardless of personal sacrifices or benefits. His calculations regarding justice and rights should be free from any self-interest. Consequently, he should not have requested the cancellation of the fees and transaction costs, but, nonetheless, he should have created a public scandal to put the bank's behavior on the spot. This decision cast a shadow of instrumentality over his noble struggle for a society free from weapons and gambling. Supporters of moral purism argue that when instrumentality is involved, morality becomes irreparably tainted. This would be the real core of Kant's moral philosophy when applied to business: No matter the personal consequences, no matter the desired or actual aims you reach, what counts and should count as moral is only the ground of the principles of your action.

In Chapter 2, I have demonstrated the limitations of moral purism as an interpretation of Kant's moral philosophy. Through Taylor's story, I aimed to emphasize its practical problems. Imagine suggesting to Taylor to choose moral purism's course of action. This would mean that he should have overlooked his responsibilities to the bank's staff, letting them be affected by the public scandal, as well as neglecting his financial support for relatives who would benefit less from him due to the high fees and transaction costs he had to pay. This deontological framework, which emphasizes justice above all else may be intriguing, but I believe it falls short of addressing Taylor's specific obligations in this situation. On the other hand, the principle of honoring the spirit of mutually beneficial contracts can effectively clarify Taylor's duties and obligations in this scenario while not requiring him to abandon his righteous battle for financial ethics.

The advantages of the three economic enlightenments come with certain limitations. Taylor's story illustrates that the scope of the three moral principles is limited to his interactions with the bank's manager and vice versa. Other previously mentioned issues, such as the validity and essence of ethical finance, the connection between deposit and investment banks, and the social challenges posed by the weapons and gambling industries, remain unaddressed. The three moral principles target a limited scope of situations and behaviors. Unlike the classic triad, they aren't applicable to other moral or social issues. For instance, consequentialism can evaluate various subjects, including individual actions, government conduct,[15] AI ethics,[16] and animal ethics.[17] In contrast, the principle of mutual assistance or the principle of self-interest and non-tuism specifically address voluntary market transactions among individuals, and they can hardly be applied beyond that. Therefore, I have stated multiple times that the new triad I suggest should be viewed as complementary rather than a replacement for the classic triad.

A compelling aspect arises when we juxtapose the story of this chapter with those explored in earlier chapters. Analyzing Taylor's options, both through the lens of conduct rules and moral reasoning, uncovers a quasi-natural hierarchy among the moral principles. Smith's principle appears to yield the most adverse consequences for Taylor and the bank's managers, blinding them to their shared responsibilities. In contrast, the cases of the contractor, house owners, and the researcher and participants reveal different viewpoints. I selected Taylor's story specifically because it illustrates that the three moral principles and their corresponding rules of conduct and courses of action are not fixed formulas that can be applied without careful consideration. Analyzing the situation from an external viewpoint differs greatly from experiencing it as one of the characters in the story. If Taylor had decided to approach the meeting with the goal of suing the bank and engaging public opinion, that would have represented a valid moral principle to follow, independently of what an external observer can judge. This does not relegate morality to relativism but, very differently, to pluralism, where, ultimately, personal choices matter.

The moral principles derived from the three economic enlightenments aim to support individuals confronting moral dilemmas in market transactions and external observers who want to comprehend these issues and investigate possible solutions. I believe both perspectives hold equal significance, which is why I have selected fictional case studies distinct from those typically found in business school curricula or BE textbooks.

One final consideration concerns the relationship between moral principles, moral reasons, moral motivations, and actions. I have already explained above that pre-reflective inclinations or considerations for the good of society – two of many elements – can transform moral reasons into moral motivations. What is left to clarify is the connection between the rules of conduct expressed by moral principles and actions. This isn't a straightforward or automatic process; Taylor's hypothetical preference for the principle of mutual assistance does not guarantee he will seek compromises during the renegotiation meetings under all circumstances. Much will depend on the behavior of his interlocutors and how he perceives their intentions as revealed by their actions. It would be foolish, even absurd, for him to pursue compromise when his interlocutors clearly show no interest in doing the right thing and confront him aggressively. Rules of conduct and moral principles do not express ready-made recipes to be applied blindly. Instead, they provide a broad moral guidance that can inspire specific actions and responses.

External circumstances also influence the transition from moral principles to actions. Picture Taylor choosing to prioritize self-interest and non-tuism, preparing to invoke the threats of legal action or public opinion during the meeting. When he communicates his intentions to his son, he learns that the commercial bank's investment funds are part of one of his son's work projects. While this might not alter his choice for Smith's moral principle, it will influence the type of actions he decides to take during the meeting. He might decide to tone down his approach and recur to threats only if it is absolutely necessary. This is just one example of the influence that external circumstances and factors can have in determining what kind of actions one will perform. If one does not keep in mind the transitions between moral principles to course of actions and real actions, including the relationship between moral reasons and moral motivations, then morality is reduced to a set of rules to be followed and applied blindly. This is certainly not what Genovesi, Kant, and Smith envisioned, and it definitely isn't what I envision either.

Notes

1. A recent author who focused his research on medieval debates on this topic is Pierre Januard. He focuses on Thomas Aquinas, but in the course of his arguments, he reconstructs and addresses the principal positions in medieval and pre-medieval debates. See Januard, P. (2021). Analysis risk and commercial risk: The first treatment of usury in Thomas Aquinas's Commentary on the Sentences. *The European Journal of the History of Economic Thought*, 28(4), 599–634. For a reference to a classic study, see De Roover, R. (1954). New interpretations of the history of banking. *Journal of World History*, 2

(1), 38–76. On the relationship between banking and government in the late Middle Ages, see Todeschini, G. (2024). Christian financial government and Jewish political culture in Italy (15th–17th c.): A dialectic of modernity. *Jews and State Building: Early Modern Italy, and Beyond*, 79, 77–94.
2. Sandel, M. (2012). *What Money Can't Buy: The Moral Limits of the Markets.* Farrar, Straus and Giroux (Ebook), 27.
3. Guriev, S., & Papaioannou, E. (2022). The political economy of populism. *Journal of Economic Literature*, 60(3), 753–832.
4. Ibid., 780.
5. For additional evidence, I encourage the reader to conduct a brief research. The objective is to determine how often the word "bank" appears in the constitutional texts of liberal democracies in North America and Europe. A result near zero corroborates my point in this paragraph, eliminating the necessity for indisputable empirical proof.
6. The term employed by Dante in the famous Canto 11 of Paradiso in the Divine Comedy. See Chiarenza, M. (1993). Dante's Lady Poverty. *Dante Studies, with the Annual Report of the Dante Society*, 111, 153–175.
7. The banks of the time lent to the rich, and the poor often ended up in the hands of usurers. The fight against usury was the reason for the birth of the *Monti di Pietà*. See Barile, N. L. (2012). Renaissance Monti di Pietà in modern scholarship: Themes, studies, and historiographic trends. *Renaissance and Reformation*, 35(3), 85–114.
8. To know more, see Bruni, L. (2023). *Capitalism and Christianity: Origins, Spirit and Betrayal of the Market Economy.* Oxon, Routledge.
9. See Yunus, M. (2003). *Banker to the Poor.* New York, Public Affairs.
10. For a more detailed study, see Jain, P. S. (1996). Managing credit for the rural poor: Lessons from the Grameen Bank. *World Development*, 24(1), 79–89.
11. One interesting issue is the relationship between banks and customers. For example, Graafland and De Gelder examine how the trustworthiness of banks affects customer service. They contend that insufficient trust in banks undermines support for free markets, which in turn results in more government regulations. See Graafland, J., & De Gelder, E. (2023). The impact of perceived due care on trustworthiness and free market support in the Dutch banking sector. *Business Ethics, the Environment & Responsibility*, 32(1), 384–400. I have mentioned this study because it intersects, although marginally, the story I will tell in this chapter. For a classic overview of BE and the banking sector, see Green, C. F. (1989). Business ethics in banking. *Journal of Business Ethics*, 8, 631–634.

12. See Crawford, C. (2011). "The repeal of the Glass-Steagall Act and the current financial crisis." *Journal of Business & Economics Research (JBER)*, *9(1)*, 127–134; Nersisyan, Y. (2015). The repeal of the Glass–Steagall Act and the Federal Reserve's extraordinary intervention during the global financial crisis. *Journal of Post Keynesian Economics*, 37(4), 545–567.
13. Friedman, M. (1976). Adam Smith's relevance for 1976. *Selected Paper No. 50*, 7.
14. I presented the main features of moral purism in Chapter 2; therefore, to avoid repetition, I refer the reader to that chapter.
15. Jeremy Bentham established utilitarianism as a guiding principle for personal and governmental actions.
16. See Card, D., & Smith, N. A. (2020). On consequentialism and fairness. *Frontiers in Artificial Intelligence*, 3(34), 1–11.
17. See Singer, *Animal Liberation Now*.

7 Conclusion
The Fourth Economic Enlightenment

7.1 Beyond the Three Economic Enlightenments

Rawls believed that (reasonable) pluralism is a fact of contemporary society, where people live under free institutions.[1] I agree, and I would also add that pluralism is a valuable component of democracy. In a democratic society, people have the opportunity to voice their thoughts on public issues, drawing from their diverse cultural, religious, ethical, and social backgrounds. This rich exchange of perspectives can generate conflicts and disagreement but might also help people come together to reach a thoughtful consensus on the actions that need to be taken. My approach to moral philosophy and BE in this book has been profoundly democratic. Instead of providing prepackaged solutions for moral dilemmas, I have aimed to introduce alternative moral principles for economic agents. Rather than simplifying morality to a mere checkbox approach – where adhering to a principle suffices for being moral – I have illustrated the intricate interplay among moral principles, reasons, motivations, and actions.

I have searched for this pluralism in the history of Western philosophy and economic thought and found it in the eighteenth-century Enlightenment period. This was also the era of what I refer to as the three economic enlightenments, corresponding to the reflections on the market and morality by three of its key figures. Genovesi, Kant, and Smith each offered valuable moral principles that address moral problems that economic agents might encounter during market transactions. My aim has been to look back to look forward. This is why the second part of this book has tried to demonstrate the relevance of the three moral principles for modern issues in BE. Among various topics, I chose incomplete contracts as I believe the three economic enlightenments can offer alternative frameworks for addressing the moral problems arising from contract incompleteness. The moral principles I have drawn from the philosophies of Kant, Genovesi, and Smith hold no hierarchy or priority among them but should instead be regarded as moral tools that can enrich the range of options available for people's moral deliberations.

All these things considered, what is the fourth economic enlightenment? I believe it encompasses at least three meanings. First, it might involve incorporating additional perspectives from the Enlightenment, possibly from the French or English contexts, alongside the three economic insights I have shared. While this integration is practical and advantageous, it deserves more thorough consideration than the one found in the conclusion's limited space. Secondly, the fourth economic enlightenment may refer to the unresolved or overlooked issues related to the three economic enlightenments. If my discussion of the moral principles from Kant, Genovesi, and Smith, along with their application to fictional examples of incomplete contracts, has missed certain issues, then the conclusion should at least acknowledge this reality. Lastly, the fourth economic enlightenment may include various alternative theories that confront the established ideas of the three prior enlightenments. This isn't merely about addressing deficiencies; it presents theories that contest the moral frameworks proposed by Kant, Smith, and Genovesi, while offering substitute theories and methods for tackling ethical dilemmas in BE.

The rest of this chapter is evenly divided between the second and third meanings of the fourth economic enlightenment, namely, expanding the framework of the three economic enlightenments and exploring alternative frameworks. Let me illustrate the difference between the two with an example. After Rawls published *A Theory of Justice*, in 1971, many philosophers engaged with his ideas.[2] Some have sought to clarify the implicit or ambiguous aspects of Rawls's political philosophy. Notably, Rawls himself contributed by publishing *Political Liberalism* in 1993,[3] but also Thomas Pogge, whose cosmopolitan institutionalism came from his attempt of *Realizing Rawls* during his PhD,[4] or all the scholars who worked to understand and develop the difference principle, such as John Harsanyi (1920–2000) and Derek Parfit (1942–2017), to mention two.[5] Others viewed the publication of Rawls's *Theory* as an opportunity to develop a political and social philosophy in opposition to Rawls's contractualism. In this other group, we might recall the tradition of communitarianism, that is a "social philosophy that maintains that society should articulate what is good – that such articulations are both needed and legitimate."[6] MacIntyre's *After Virtue* is often mentioned within this tradition, as it opposes the basic elements of Rawls's theory, such as the idea that a society's basic institutions should not be grounded on one comprehensive doctrine that advances an idea of the good life.[7]

Rawls's *Theory* example illustrates the distinction between expanding the framework from within and developing alternative frameworks. Although I cannot assert that I have introduced a philosophical theory on par with Rawls's, I believe it is a valuable exercise in the conclusion to address some gaps and explore alternatives to my own analysis.

7.2 Expanding the Framework

7.2.1 Third Parties and Externalities

The three economic enlightenments have been illustrated through three fictional stories addressing incomplete contracts. Chapters 4, 5, and 6 outlined three scenarios involving two parties: the contractor and house owners, the researcher and research participants, and a former mayor and bank managers. However, upon closer inspection, all the stories I have considered involved more than two parties. What would happen if the two house owners disagreed on the moral reasons for choosing one of the three moral principles? What if each research participant possessed a distinct understanding of their pre-reflective inclinations? How could local bank managers reconcile their own moral beliefs with those of the nonlocal bank management? These questions indicate that although the three moral principles of economic enlightenments primarily pertain to transactions between two parties, numerous third parties may actually be involved. Thus, it is vital for the proper application of the moral principles discussed in this book, especially when third parties are involved, to have a process for evaluating various moral reasons that could result in the selection of different moral principles. Those can vary from informal procedures, such as a frank conversation between the house owners, to more formal ones, such as participative decision-making within bank personnel. Since I assume that all participants in the three stories care about morality and doing what is right, it is not inappropriate to suggest that they might be interested in finding an effective way to resolve their moral disagreements and find a common moral principle that best fits the situation. This extends beyond the three economic enlightenments;

fortunately, a significant body of BE literature has focused on the ethics of discourse and participative and inclusive decision-making.[8]

We can refer to third parties regarding the moral principles of the three economic enlightenments in at least another respect. I am referencing third parties who, although not directly engaged in the market transaction, are affected by it. This closely relates to the economic concept of externalities, which involves the indirect consequences of the choices made by economic agents. While it could be argued that economic agents capture those externalities by considering the impact their actions may have on the good of society (public good, common good), more can be said about this. A potential risk associated with the perspectives of Genovesi, Smith, and Kant is their evident anthropocentrism. One example is Kant's belief that our responsibilities toward animals are, in essence, responsibilities toward ourselves. He argued that being violent to an animal may encourage a person's propensity to act violently toward other humans.[9] Today, this approach is untenable due to an increasing sensitivity toward animal ethics and ecological matters in general. Thus, it is crucial to broaden the anthropocentric viewpoint of the three economic enlightenments without compromising their fundamental emphasis on moral principles for economic agents.

What is the current relationship between economic science and nature? In 2019, the British Treasury invited economist Partha Dasgupta to address this question. His answer, which resulted from two years of work and synthesized fifty years of development economics research, culminated in a 600-page report titled *The Economics of Biodiversity: The Dasgupta Review*.[10] Dasgupta points out that economists have overlooked or misunderstood a critical area. This realm, which is older than humanity and any economy, simultaneously influences and is influenced by both: the biosphere. For Dasgupta, this intricate term has a specific definition: the ecosystem of all ecosystems, which we commonly call nature.

If Dasgupta wrote a review, literally a re-look, it means that the lenses of observation previously adopted were fogged up. Historically, many economists viewed the biosphere merely as the backdrop for economic activity, treating it as a neutral factor excluded from individual and collective utility evaluations. Others concentrated on the biosphere's natural resources – such as energy, seeds, water, and fish – as commodities to be exploited for human benefit. Even those economists who criticized this indifference versus exploitation dichotomy, according to Dasgupta, adopted a narrow viewpoint: by advocating economic penalties for those who harm the biosphere, they inadvertently suggested that paying for damages legitimizes the exploitation of nature. This thus necessitates a re-evaluation of the connection between economists and nature, or, viewed through the lens of specific fields, economics and ecology.

The biosphere is defined by its biodiversity, meaning the coexistence and equilibrium of various intricate systems. Consequently, economists cannot analyze it from a singular perspective. Dasgupta suggestively outlines at least three viewpoints. Firstly, the biosphere is an asset – essentially, a resource – where we must recognize nature's contributions to our well-being and the numerous functions it fulfills without compensation, such as climate regulation, soil fertility, and ecosystem maintenance. Secondly, the biosphere acts as a partner, involved in both the production and distribution of wealth within the economic system. Therefore, we should adopt a mindset of reciprocity and mutual benefit; akin to how we would not ask an individual to exchange beyond their interest or capacity, we are imposing unfair demands on nature. Our demand far outweighs the supply, leading to the depletion of natural resources, a decline in plant and animal biodiversity, and in the long run, it's evident that, in any mutually beneficial relationship, if one party suffers, both parties will feel the repercussions: This is why we are called to restore our relationship with the biosphere: "Restoration can also help us to address the imbalance between our demands for the biosphere's provisioning services on the one hand and for its regulating, maintenance and cultural services on the other."[11] Finally, Dasgupta emphasizes that the biosphere holds intrinsic value, independent of any benefits we might extract from it. This notion suggest that humans showcase one of their most admirable qualities when they care for others without anticipating a reward in return.

I deeply resonate with Dasgupta's analysis. It can enhance the three economic enlightenments in two different ways. First, it implies that the good of the biosphere must be considered among the moral reasons of economic agents. Secondly, it presents an intriguing challenge for future research. If we view the biosphere as a partner in the exchange, then we can deduce that a reciprocal relationship might exist. Thus, it appears we are assigning intentionality and agency to nature, making it not just a third party but also one of the two economic agents to which the three principles of economic enlightenment should apply. Is it possible to see the biosphere as an agent, an economic agent, and even a moral agent? While this topic goes beyond this book's scope, it deserves a thoughtful discussion in the future.

7.2.2 Initial Conditions

Economic agents are those who can engage in a market transaction with full independence.[12] This implies that, for the moral principles of the three economic enlightenments to be relevant, individuals must be free to select their exchange partner. It's essential to clarify what freedom means: Does it merely signify negative freedom, such as being free from someone else's interference, be it an individual, an organization, or the government? Or does it also include more comprehensive negative freedom, meaning liberation from needs that compel them to participate in a market transaction? I believe that the theories of Kant, Genovesi, and Smith support the latter perspective on freedom and, therefore, call for an institutional framework that enables individuals to be free from need as much as possible.

Herman has argued that Kant's moral philosophy contains this requirement in the concept of true needs:

> The ends which must be realized if a person is to function (or continue to function) as a rational, end-setting agent come from what Kant calls the "true needs" of human agents. They are the conditions of our "power to set an end" that is the "characteristic of humanity." The ends set to meet our true needs are like all other ends we cannot guarantee that we can realize them unaided. But in contrast to all other ends, we cannot, on rational grounds, forgo them.[13]

Although Herman highlighted the significance of imperfect duties in Kant's philosophy – those that permit some flexibility in their execution, like beneficence – the idea of true need suggests that societal institutions should be structured to fulfill these genuine needs. It is not coincidental that Rawls, who examined Kant's perspective on true needs[14] and developed a theory akin to that of Herman, posited in his *A Theory of Justice* that the foundational structures of society ought to be anchored in the two principles of justice that guarantee fundamental freedoms and equal rights alongside the primary social goods to each citizen.

I want to highlight that the moral principles derived from the three economic enlightenments entail considerations that extend beyond their immediate application. These pertain to the starting conditions of the economic agents, indicating their approach to market exchanges with partners. Defining and classifying people's true needs, as well as organizing society to meet those needs, goes beyond the scope of this book. And yet, for the full development of the theory of the three economic enlightenments I am proposing, this element cannot simply be taken for granted, as I have done in the three fictional stories. I contend that Rawls's *Theory* could serve as a suitable framework for organizing the fundamental institutions of society, thereby allowing economic agents the liberty to participate in market transactions. However, due to space limitations, I am unable to elaborate on the rationale supporting this position or the advantages it presents in comparison to alternative approaches. All that can be said here is that inquiring about the political, social, and economic context in which individuals choose to engage in exchanges is crucial to determining whether they are truly free in their decisions.

7.2.3 What Are We Trading?

The moral principles of the three economic enlightenments focus on the proper behavior of people exchanging goods and services but seem to say little or nothing about the goods and services exchanged. Consider the following examples. Arsène Lupin plans a major heist and negotiates a deal with James Moriarty. They agree, through a handshake and the code of thieves, that Moriarty will take half of the profits for his role in disabling the bank's alarm system. During the heist, Moriarty fulfills his part and, when a last-minute issue arises, assists Lupin in fleeing the bank. Consequently, he demands more than half of the earnings. Lupin objects and requests that Moriarty respect their initial agreement. The moral principles of Kant, Genovesi, and Smith are applicable to this situation. I could have spent an entire chapter exploring their pre-reflective inclinations, moral reasons, and moral motivations of Lupin and Moriarty. Nevertheless, there seems to be a lack of moral assessment regarding this situation since the three economic enlightenments do not evaluate the ethical implications of the exchanged item, which, in this instance, are the spoils of a robbery.

There is no need to mention just instances involving the trade of illegal goods or services. We can refer to situations where legal market transactions may be deemed unethical. One example is the right to hunt endangered species, such as the black rhino, which Sandel discusses in his book about the moral limits of the market.[15] Imagine a scenario where hunters strike a deal with the owners of a hunting ground, allowing them to pursue and kill one endangered rhino in exchange for a set amount of money. During the hunt, the hunters accidentally killed a rhino and another animal. As a result, the owners are now demanding an extra fee that was not detailed in the contract, which only referred to such circumstances in general terms. We can apply the moral principles from the three economic enlightenments to assess the situation and the behavior of the economic agents during the renegotiation meeting. However, these moral principles do not address whether it was morally acceptable from the outset to exchange the life of an endangered species for monetary gain.

Given all these factors, examining the moral boundaries of the market is essential to complement the three economic enlightenments. Although Genovesi, Kant, and Smith incorporated assessments of specific goods in relation to human happiness, they overlooked the dangers posed by market expansion in society – viewing it instead as a sign of progress from the feudal premodern societies of their time. Currently, a distinct body of literature is discussing the moral boundaries of the market.[16] Although I expressed skepticism in Chapter 2 regarding their interpretation of Kant's moral philosophy, I still consider them allies in the project put forth in this book. Their perspectives on which goods and services should not be traded, and the inequality issues linked to the progressive expansion of free markets into sectors like health and education, can broaden the three economic enlightenments and enhance their practical application.

7.2.4 Inclinations and Sociality

In Chapter 3, I have delineated two distinct stages: the pre-reflective stage, which pertains to inclinations, and the reflective stage, which relates to reason. This distinction enabled me to elucidate the ethical principles of economic agents that I have deduced from the theories of

Genovesi, Kant, and Smith. Nonetheless, I have neglected a significant issue pertinent to this analytical differentiation regarding human beings. Inclinations may appear as fixed traits of humans, yet they are also influenced by social factors. Rousseau argued that overlooking the social influence on inclinations can lead to wrong conclusions.[17] In discussing theories about the state of nature – how humans would behave without political, social, and economic institutions – Rousseau contended that earlier thinkers erred significantly. They derived fundamental human inclinations from observing their societies and mistakenly applied these assumptions to the state of nature, neglecting the alterations that institutions (like private property) impose on human inclinations. Rousseau's theory of the noble savage states that in the state of nature human beings led a solitary life and that the two basic inclinations would have been *amour-de-soi* (self-love) and *pitié* (pity). Another important inclination, *amour propre* (vanity), emerged only because of the creation of social institutions.[18]

In exploring and applying the three economic enlightenments, I have assumed that individuals can understand their fundamental inclinations simply by observing their instinctive, unreflective responses to specific situations. Rousseau would likely argue against this perspective, as I have failed to consider how society has already influenced those inclinations. The critique could be enhanced by noting that the pre-reflective and reflective stages might not align with people's experiences of their inclinations. The distinctions may blur when considering individuals' encounters with their spontaneous tendencies. Helga Varden contended that this insight is inherent in Kant's ethics, which encompasses his moral philosophy as well as his anthropological, social, and religious insights. In her paper advocating a sympathetic view of Kant's perspective on the nature and role of women, Varden argued that, for Kant, "women should be understood in light of a normative, teleological theory of human nature, related to his view that our sexuality should be understood as profoundly informed also by our unreflective embodied, social natures teleologically informed, and not simply as spheres analyzable through morality (freedom) and empirical science."[19] From my grasp of Varden's paper, Kant would suggest that our reflection on inclinations differs from empirical observations, and while it can be linked to it, it does not coincide with our rational moral reflection. This enables us to comprehend our spontaneous inclinations and separate them from their manifestations within distinct cultural, social, political, religious, and economic contexts. Kant "doesn't simply take himself to be undertaking empirical observations (possibly in combination with scientific explanations). Instead, his aim is to capture how gender inherently concerns the good development of our embodied, social natures, where the goodness involved is seen as of a kind distinct from, but developmentally enabling, freedom, and as involving a teleological, normative understanding of ourselves."[20] According to Varden, this suggests that Kant integrated Rousseau's insights regarding the limitations of empirical observation of human nature.

I argue that this critique enriches rather than undermines my analysis. Investigating the social factors influencing human inclinations and the nonmoral reflections associated with them are critical elements that any serious anthropological study must address and cannot dismiss. However, I am hesitant to attribute the burden of this analysis to economic agents. The ways to correctly engage with one's fundamental inclinations should complement the exploration of the moral principles underlying the three economic enlightenments. To be sure, the objective should not be an internal quest to find one's true self, as this might imply an endless exploration of one's identity. Additionally, one could argue that economic agents often do not see the need to explore the origins of their inclinations; instead, they accept them as they feel and observe them. The protagonists in the three stories examined in this book illustrate individuals who seem to possess sufficient awareness of their own inclinations. Therefore, my theory also needs to accommodate these cases. While it is crucial to acknowledge that inclinations are not fixed truths about human nature, and while it is possible to reflect on them apart from moral considerations, economic agents aiming to do the right thing by exploring alternative moral principles can confidently rely on their own experiences and observations of their inclinations to find moral reasons for choosing one principle over others. BE's theories have to account for the complexity of human beings, but this should not come at the cost of creating moral impasses or dead ends.

7.2.5 The Shadows of the Enlightenments

In Chapter 2, I discussed the Enlightenment project to contextualize the historical and philosophical contributions of Genovesi, Kant, and

Smith. Everything that brings light to an object inevitably casts shadows. This holds true for the Enlightenment. Although it pledged to liberate society from old constraints and biases through reason and science, it largely excluded significant segments of the population. Mary Wollstonecraft (1759–1797) denounced the exclusion of women in her famous *A Vindication of the Rights of Woman* and argued that the educational system, designed by men, made it impossible for women to develop their rationality. Her *Vindication* served as both a denunciation and a rallying cry for women:

> My own sex, I hope, will excuse me, if I treat them like rational creatures, instead of flattering their fascinating graces, and viewing them as if they were in a state of perpetual childhood, unable to stand alone. I earnestly wish to point out in what true dignity and human happiness consists – I wish to persuade women to endeavour to acquire strength, both of mind and body, and to convince them, that the soft phrases, susceptibility of heart, delicacy of sentiment, and refinement of taste, are almost synonymous with epithets of weakness.[21]

Wollstonecraft portrayed the narrow edges of the light brought by the Enlightenment with great skill. Indeed, if we read some pages of Kant and Smith, we might understand that Wollstonecraft's *Vindication* attacked not a straw enlightenment but rather a diffuse attitude toward women.[22]

Others were excluded from the Enlightenment. According to these authors, people in savage and uncivilized regions worldwide could not access the bountiful benefits of reason and science that illuminated European society. Every philosophical movement embodies its unique philosophy of history, and the Enlightenment was no exception. The journey from the darkness of the Middle Ages through the Renaissance to the Enlightenment represents a narrative of ongoing intellectual and civil advancement. This marked a shift into adulthood for humanity, allowing individuals to live freely and autonomously. The Enlightenment authors eradicated many prejudices and discriminatory practices, but they failed to get rid of racial discrimination and philosophical justifications for colonialism and imperialism. Although some Enlightenment thinkers exhibit tension regarding this topic, it frequently resolves inappropriately. I will illustrate this by referring to Smith and Kant, since Genovesi was less influenced by these first-world biases due to geographical factors.

Smith is frequently hailed as an opponent of colonialism and as an author who prioritizes the well-being of the colonized populace. Nonetheless, a recent article by David Williams provided new evidence indicating that Smith's position was more nuanced: "To put the argument very briefly, Smith's opposition to colonial rule derived largely from its impact on the metropole, rather than on its impact on the conquered and colonised. Second, Smith recognised that colonialism had brought 'improvement' in conquered territories, and that such progress might not have occurred without this intervention."[23] Here, we see the Enlightenment philosophy of history in action as a justificatory veil for political, social, and cultural domination. Williams continues: "Third, the reading of Smith as non-judgemental about other cultures hinges on an account of the basis upon which Smith made (or thought it was possible to make) judgements about other cultures. And here, Smith struggles to balance recognition of moral diversity with a universal moral framework and a commitment to a particular interpretation of progress through history."[24] Enlightenment authors believed that if society was progressing and European men had reached maturity, it was natural for those who differed from them to be considered at a lower stage of development within the universal moral and civil framework.

Kant's works on race were full of racial discrimination and prejudices.[25] Pauline Kleingeld mentioned one of the most evident, where Kant compared the Native Americans to the "Negro" in a race to the bottom, whereas white men are at the top.[26] Reporting the pages of Kant's work serves little purpose; something must be said instead. In his transcendental philosophy, Kant viewed humanity as an "end in itself," asserting that the rational a priori realm should ground and transform empirical reality observed a posteriori. This philosophy holds the potential to challenge various forms of prejudice and discrimination. Although Kant himself did not take that step or did not take it fully, it should not deter others from doing so. More broadly, the Enlightenment's shadows represent lost opportunities for many thinkers to truly embrace the concept of *sapere aude* and have the courage to explore the full implications of their ideas.

The comments here may not directly relate to the application of the moral principles of Kant, Genovesi, and Smith. Nonetheless, I feel they improve our comprehension of the three economic enlightenments and their ideas, which is equally important as their practical application. By identifying those marginalized by the Enlightenment movement of the eighteenth century, this subsection paves the way for the subsequent section, where I will explore alternative perspectives on the three economic enlightenments I have described so far.

7.3 Alternative Frameworks

7.3.1 Masculine and Feminine Approaches

Are the three economic enlightenments contributing to the projects of feminist economics and feminist BE? When we reflect on Genovesi, Kant, and Smith – three white men with distinct opinions about women's societal roles – the conclusion seems evidently negative. However, it is essential to clarify what the term "feminist" signifies in relation to economics and BE. The economist Julie Nelson characterized feminist economics as distinct from masculine economics, which represents a male-dominated field. This male-centric approach emphasizes certain topics, methodologies, and teaching styles prevalent in eighteenth-, nineteenth-, and twentieth-century economics. According to Nelson, "objectivity, separation, logical consistency, individual accomplishment, mathematics, abstraction, lack of emotion, and science itself have long been culturally associated with rigor, hardness – and masculinity. At the same time, subjectivity, connection, 'intuitive' understanding, cooperation, qualitative analysis, concreteness, emotion, and nature have often been associated with weakness, softness – and femininity."[27] Nelson argued that feminist economics is different from feminine economics, as the former entails an openness to both masculine and feminine methods and a progressive overcoming of these outdated gender divide. In this respect, Genovesi's anthropology and certain interpretations of Smith's moral philosophy might be connected to the project of feminist economics. However, I would refrain from pushing this argument so far. I think feminist economics and BE offer a distinct framework for analyzing the issues addressed by the three economic enlightenments. I will illustrate how these approaches can represent the fourth (and fifth, sixth, and so on) economic enlightenments by referencing Mary Wollstonecraft's works once again.

In 2024, Catherine Packham released a book with a revealing title: *Mary Wollstonecraft and Political Economy: The Feminist Critique of Commercial Modernity*.[28] In this context, Packham showed that

Wollstonecraft's economic reflections developed through continuous discourse with philosophers like Smith, Rousseau, and Edmund Burke (1729–1797), among others. In my opinion, the significant contribution of Packham's book lies in the assertion that to uncover the originality of Wollstonecraft's "feminist critique" of commercial society, it is necessary not only to examine the substance of her reflections but also to consider the conceptual framework within which they are presented. Wollstonecraft's use of literary genres reflects her alternatives to political economy and commercial society. In contrast to systematic investigations like Smith's *Wealth* she draws on lived, engaged, and partial experiences found in letters, correspondences, political invectives, contextual and situated essays, and so on. In response to the shortcomings of commercial society, she seeks alternative models of social relationships and community: "A community founded on sympathetic feeling, whether of readers or listeners, offers a different model of society from that founded on the rational exchanges of civil society's public sphere, which constituted one eighteenth-century self-image."[29] This does not merely serve as a sentimental escape from the logic of commercial society. Wollstonecraft transcends the Romantic retreat into a pastoral poetic realm. Her perspective prompts a profound challenge to the foundations of political economy. Different writing styles themselves attempt to push back against commercialism, freeing feelings and passions from the constraints of property, money, and wealth to uncover genuine human affections. Although this aspiration may seem appealing, Packham's work demonstrates that such efforts inherently lack any universal or systematic guidelines for behavior and living. Resistance and alternatives can be discovered through the reader's engagement with the stories of the protagonists in Wollstonecraft's novels, as well as her first-person voices found in many of her writings.

Approaches such as Wollstonecraft's can interrogate the three economic enlightenments, whose moral principles governing economic agents and their application reside within a rationalistic framework of moral reflections. Additionally, Wollstonecraft's literary genre aligns more closely with my approach to narratively presenting case studies in the book's second part. In all honesty, the rationale for not titling this book "The Four (or Five, Six) Economic Enlightenments" stems from my insufficient familiarity with this literature to effectively conduct a comprehensive comparison between Wollstonecraft (and others) and Kant, Genovesi, and Smith. The only appropriate action at this juncture is to direct this matter to future researchers, who will critically examine the three economic enlightenments from feminist perspectives.

7.3.2 Base and Superstructure

In Section 2.4, I pondered what Rousseau would think about my differentiation between the pre-reflective stages of inclinations and the reflective stage of reason. In the following, I will conduct a similar thought experiment to explore how Karl Marx (1818–1883) and Marxist thinkers would judge and critique the entire project of the three economic enlightenments. In my view, they would present two interrelated critiques: one concerning the contextualization of my analysis and the other related to the methodology employed. The former would clarify that my inquiry into the moral principles for economic agents reflects the material determinants of the society in which I live and my position within it. In other words, I have approached moral issues from a WEIRD perspective, meaning the viewpoint of a person living in a Western, Educated, Industrialized, Rich, and Democratic society.[30] Individuals from varying social backgrounds or holding different roles than mine – a full-time Italian employee in Dutch academia – might approach fundamental moral questions in different ways, maybe choosing other authors or viewpoints. Marx articulated a comparable argument when he critiqued political economists such as Smith for failing to comprehend that their investigations into markets and society, which featured assertions of universality (human nature, propensities, inclinations), were also reflective of the interests of the emerging bourgeois class of the eighteenth century. This critique is valid and intriguing; however, I will defer my response until the next subsection, where I will address non-Western approaches.

The second critique Marx would probably move to this project is that the chosen methodology is unsuitable for achieving the intended results. If people genuinely wish to engage ethically in market transactions, they should be furnished with a theory that examines the underlying material structure responsible for injustices in economic exchanges rather than presenting them with varied moral principles. Marx would argue that my analysis is not scientific but ideological because it focuses on the level of the superstructure while ignoring the base:

In the social production of their existence, men inevitably enter into definite relations, which are independent of their will, namely relations of production appropriate to a given stage in the development of their material forces of production. The totality of these relations of production constitutes the economic structure of society, the real foundation, on which arises a legal and political superstructure and to which correspond definite forms of social consciousness.[31]

This captures the core of Marx's critique of Hegel's philosophy, presented in the preface of his aptly titled book *A Contribution to the Critique of Political Economy* (1859).

Kant, Genovesi, and Smith's three moral principles are expressed within the superstructure framework; therefore, they can be seen as derived concepts. To understand the core of morality for economic agents, as my book proposes, examining material factors like economic relationships, wealth and income disparities, demographics, geography, and more is essential: "In studying such transformations it is always necessary to distinguish between the material transformation of the economic conditions of production, which can be determined with the precision of natural science, and the legal, political, religious, artistic, or philosophic, in short, ideological forms in which men become conscious of this conflict and fight it out."[32] My analysis seems to hide the conflicts that can arise among various economic agents behind an ideological, moral veil influencing their behavior.

The Marxist critique of the three economic enlightenments must be separated from the examination of the initial conditions, which I have outlined in Section 2.2 as an expansion of this book's analysis. The former seems to imply a form of determinism according to which not only all our actions but also all our moral reflections are determined by the material conditions of our social reality. While the Marxist perspective is significant and merits attention, I suggest that its main purpose in this context is to provide an alternative lens for examining the same issues I am approaching through the three economic enlightenments. Reconciling the two viewpoints is desirable, but I fear it is nearly impossible due to the differing methodological frameworks.

7.3.3 Non-Western Approaches

This book aims to diversify the Western tradition of philosophical and economic thought to show its relevance in tackling modern problems. Nonetheless, one could contend that this effort to diversify the Western canon is confined to narrow limits. As I have illustrated in Chapter 1, there are many approaches to BE, and categorizing some as non-Western may reflect a Western-centric perspective. Beyond the lexical issue, I believe that more can be said about the difficulty of embedding other perspectives within the three economic enlightenments. For instance, Kant, Genovesi, and Smith, despite their differing views, suggest that economic agents are individuals capable of transcending their natural inclinations through moral reasoning. Many of the diverse constellations of Indigenous approaches would challenge this assumption. In her attempt to understand Indigenous views on relationality, Allison Weir engaged the position of Aileen Moreton-Robinson, who aimed to describe the features of an Australian Indigenous view on relationality.[33] Weir's analysis of Moreton-Robinson's stance is especially beneficial for grasping the difficulties of broadening the framework to incorporate Indigenous viewpoints.

Weir begins by acknowledging that her effort to analyze Moreton-Robinson's thought is inextricably linked to her identity as a member of a former colony state: "settler colonial academics, activists, governments, and societies need to work on a politics of listening: to engage in a politics of self-transformation through listening, to become capable of a politics of mutual recognition."[34] What was Weir attempting to hear? Essentially, she aimed to grasp how Moreton-Robinson distinguished Indigenous views on relationality from those presented by eco-feminist philosophy. Both perspectives challenge Western individualism, particularly through their shared critique of Locke's philosophy.[35] However, Moreton-Robinson's Indigenous perspective uniquely addresses the bodily–earthly divide that persists in feminist analysis. This entails recognizing the intrinsic connection between humans and their lands and understanding that these lands are not merely physical spaces but are imbued with historical, cultural, and political significance. Weir engages Moreton-Robinson's view that Australian Indigenous relationality deeply impacts human beings' ways of being, knowing, and acting.

One point Weir finds very difficult to engage with is the idea of relational knowing, which entails "not prioritizing human knowledge: listening to the knowledge of rivers and trees, recognizing those other beings as co-knowers, collaborators, and sometimes recognizing their knowledge as primary, and superior to ours. For some Indigenous thinkers, it is self-evident that stones have the most knowledge, because

Conclusion: The Fourth Economic Enlightenment   171

they have been there for the longest time."[36] This viewpoint appears to support the suggestion discussed in Section 2.1, where I mentioned the idea of treating the biosphere as an exchange partner and moral agent. Yet, I want to emphasize the point that Weir made regarding the Western academic potential for comprehension:

> The idea that knowledge is dispersed among multiple knowers in an entirely animate universe is of course very difficult for Western secular academics to comprehend, let alone accept. What does it mean to say that a stone or a river has knowledge? The impulse is to see these ideas as primitive and prescientific, or, if we are more generous, romantic and beautiful but not real: not accurate representations of reality. It may be possible to see this as "Indigenous knowledge," but it's much more difficult to accept it as knowledge.[37]

The same issue arises concerning the moral implications of this Indigenous framework, which implies a reciprocal relationship between humans and nonhuman entities, including land, animals, plants, and others. It appears that there is a dead end that various frameworks reach when discussing the same issue.

The conclusion drawn appears disheartening, as it seems to hinder reciprocal engagement among various frameworks. Nevertheless, I want to identify at least one general way forward and a more specific one pertinent to this book's project. The general direction pertains to the politics of listening that Weir introduced at the start of her analysis, which I believe aligns with the approach of Moreton-Robinson when she analyzed the philosophy of Locke, for instance. This means that one must first be aware of their situatedness, avoiding overly rapid essentialist or universal claims while also engaging with very distant perspectives. Since I read Weir and Moreton-Robinson, I have continuously asked myself what it means for rocks to have knowledge. I have not come to any conclusion, but I see the value of the road taken.

The moral principles of the three economic enlightenments are situated in two contexts: the situation of the authors whose theories I have derived from and my own situatedness. At the same time, I believe the three economic enlightenments can transcend these two levels. This is because I have aimed not to impose a universal theory devoid of historical context that everyone should adhere to. In a markedly distinct manner, I envision a grassroots approach to the moral principles underlying economic enlightenment. If readers are interested in the moral issues discussed and find the three moral principles relevant, I do not see why geographical, cultural, social, or other differences should create an unbridgeable gap. Revisiting Dickens's *A Christmas Carol* in Chapter 1, along with the three fictional stories in Part II, has allowed me to emphasize this point. Novels achieve universality not by dictating messages to an average reader model but through readers' spontaneous and personal connections with specific stories and characters, even those far removed from their own experiences. This is how timeless novels have thrived through the centuries and continue to be read globally. While I do not expect the same level of success for this book, I hope it encounters no undue prejudices against its content.

Notes

1. See Rawls, *Political Liberalism*.
2. See Rawls, *A Theory of Justice*.
3. See Rawls, *Political Liberalism*.
4. Pogge, T. (1989). *Realizing Rawls*. Ithaca, Cornell University Press.
5. See Harsanyi, J. C. (1975). Can the maximin principle serve as a basis for morality? A critique of John Rawls's theory. *American Political Science Review*, 69(2), 594–606; Parfit, D. (1995). *Equality or Priority? The Lindley Lecture*. University of Kansas: Department of Philosophy.
6. Etzioni, A. (2003). Communitarianism. In Rossel, S. A. (ed.), *Encyclopedia of Community: From the Village to the Virtual World*. Ottawa, Carleton University Press, 224.
7. MacIntyre, *After Virtue*; see also Sandel, M. (1982). *Liberalism and the Limits of Justice*. New York, Cambridge University Press.
8. See Beschorner, T. (2006). Ethical theory and business practices: The case of discourse ethics. *Journal of Business Ethics*, 66, 127–139; Kaner, S. (2014). *Facilitator's Guide to Participatory Decision-Making*. San Francisco, Wiley & Sons.
9. See Korsgaard, C. M. (2013). Kantian ethics, animals, and the law. *Oxford Journal of Legal Studies*, 33(4), 629–648.
10. For an overview, see the short version: Dasgupta, P. (2021). *The Economics of Biodiversity: The Dasgupta Review (Abridged Version)*. London, HM Treasury.
11. Ibid., 71.
12. See Chapter 1, note 30.
13. Herman, B. (1984). Mutual aid and respect for persons. *Ethics*, 94(4), 586.

14. Rawls, *Lectures on the History of Moral Philosophy*, 232–234.
15. Sandel, *What Money Can't Buy*.
16. See Anderson, *Value in Ethics and Economics*; Sandel, *What Money Can't Buy*; Satz, *Why Some Things Should Not Be for Sale*.
17. See Rousseau, J. J. ([1755] 1997). *Discourse on the Origins and Foundations of Inequality Among Men*, in Gourevitch, V. (ed.), *The Discourses and Other Early Writings*,Cambridge, Cambridge University Press.
18. See Chazan, P. (1993). Rousseau as psycho-social moralist: The distinction between amour de soi and amour-propre. *History of Philosophy Quarterly*, 10(4), 341–354.
19. Varden, H. (2017). Kant and women. *Pacific Philosophical Quarterly*, 98(4), 655.
20. Ibid., 658.
21. Wollstonecraft, M. ([1792] 2019). *The Feminist Papers: A Vindication of the Rights of Women*. Layton, Gibbs Smith Publisher, online edition, 30.
22. I am referring to Kant's pages on women as connected to beauty but incapable of appreciating the sublime and as an object of contemplation by men. See Kneller, J. (2007). *Kant and the Power of Imagination*. Cambridge, Cambridge University Press. For Smith, I have referred in Chapter 2 about the gendered nature of his interpretation of feminine passions versus masculine virtues.
23. Williams, Adam Smith and colonialism, 285.
24. Ibid.
25. See Mikkelsen, J. M. (2013). *Kant and the Concept of Race: Late Eighteenth-Century Writings*. Albany, State University of New York Press.
26. Kleingeld shows an internal evolution in Kant's thought on the subject. See Kleingeld, P. (2011). *Kant and Cosmopolitanism: The Philosophical Ideal of World Citizenship*. Cambridge, Cambridge University Press.
27. Nelson, J. A. 1995. Feminism and economics. *Journal of Economic Perspectives*, 9(2), 133.
28. Packham, C. (2024). *Mary Wollstonecraft and Political Economy: The Feminist Critique of Commercial Modernity*. Cambridge, Cambridge University Press.
29. Ibid., 210.
30. See Henrich, J., Heine, S. J., & Norenzayan, A. (2010). The weirdest people in the world? *Behavioral and Brain Sciences*, 33(2–3), 61–83.
31. Marx, K. ([1859] 2002). Preface: A contribution to the critique of political economy. In Raines, J. (ed.), *Marx on Religion*. Philadelphia, Temple University Press, 109.

32. Ibid.
33. Weir, A. (2017). Decolonizing feminist freedom: Indigenous relationalities. In Mclaren, M. A. (ed.), *Decolonizing Feminism: Transnational Feminism and Globalization*. London, Rowman & Littlefield, 257–287.
34. Ibid., 258.
35. See Shiva, V., & Mies, M. (2014). *Ecofeminism*. London, Bloomsbury Publishing.
36. A. Weir, Decolonizing feminist freedom, 264.
37. Ibid.

Bibliography

Anderson, E. (1995). *Value in Ethics and Economics*. Cambridge, MA, Harvard University Press.

Anderson, M. H., & Sun, P. Y. T. (2017). Reviewing leadership styles: Overlaps and the need for a new "full-range" theory. *International Journal of Management Reviews*, 19, 76–96.

Aristotle (1984). *Complete Works of Aristotle, Volume 2: The Revised Oxford Translation*, ed. by J. Barnes. Princeton, Princeton University Press.

Aristotle (2014). *Nicomachean Ethics*, ed. by R. Crisp. Cambridge, Cambridge University Press.

Arnold, D. G., & Harris, J. D. (eds.) (2012). *Kantian Business Ethics: Critical Perspectives*. Cheltenham, Edward Elgar Publishing.

Baker, K. M., & Reill, P. H. (2001). *What's Left of Enlightenment? A Postmodern Question*. Stanford, Stanford University Press.

Barile, N. L. (2012). Renaissance Monti di Pietà in modern scholarship: Themes, studies, and historiographic trends. *Renaissance and Reformation*, 35(3), 85–114.

Bee, M. (2021). The pleasure of exchange: Adam Smith's third kind of self-love. *Journal of the History of Economic Thought*, 43(1), 118–140.

Bee, M., & Desmarais-Tremblay, M. (2023). The birth of Homo Œconomicus: The methodological debate on the economic agent from JS Mill to V. Pareto. *Journal of the History of Economic Thought*, 45(1), 1–26.

Bellamy R. (1987). "Da metafisico a mercatante": Antonio Genovesi and the development of a new language of commerce in eighteenth-century Naples. In Pagden, A. (ed.), *The Languages of Political Theory in Early-Modern Europe*. Cambridge, Cambridge University Press, 277–300.

Bentham, J. ([1790] 2007). *An Introduction to the Principles of Morals and Legislation*. New York, Dover Philosophical Classics.

Beschorner, T. (2006). Ethical theory and business practices: The case of discourse ethics. *Journal of Business Ethics*, 66, 127–139.

Bird, F. (2009). Why the responsible practice of business ethics calls for a due regard for history. *Journal of Business Ethics*, 89, 203–220.

Boltanski, L., & Chiapello, E. (2018). *The New Spirit of Capitalism*. London, Verso Books.
Bonica, M. J., & Klein, D. B. (2021). Adam Smith on reputation, commutative justice, and defamation laws. *Journal of Economic Behavior & Organization, 184*, 788–803.
Borgerson, J. L. (2023). On the harmony of feminist ethics and business ethics. In Panter, M., & Werhane, P. H. (eds.), *Leadership, Gender, and Organization*. Cham, Springer International Publishing, 37–62.
Bowie, N. (2000). A Kantian theory of leadership. *Leadership & Organization Development Journal, 21*(4), 185–193.
Bowie, N. (2002). A Kantian approach to business ethics. In Donaldson, T., Werhane, P. H., & Cording, M. (eds.), *Ethical Issues in Business: A Philosophical Approach*. New Jersey, Prentice Hall, 61–71.
Bowie, N. (2017). *Business Ethics: A Kantian Perspective*. Cambridge, Cambridge University Press.
Brenkert, G. G. (2016). Business ethics and human rights: An overview. *Business and Human Rights Journal, 1*(2), 277–306.
Broadie, A. (2012). *The Scottish Enlightenment*. Edinburgh, Birlinn Limited.
Bruni, L. (2007). The "technology of happiness" and the tradition of economic science. In Bruni, L., & Porta, P. L. (eds.), *Handbook of Economics of Happiness*. Cheltenham, Edward Elgar, 24–52.
Bruni, L. (2012). *The Genesis and Ethos of the Market*. Basingstoke, Palgrave Macmillan.
Bruni, L. (2017). On the concept of economia civile and "Felicitas Publica": a comment on Federico D'Onofrio. *Journal of the History of Economic Thought, 39*(2), 273–279.
Bruni, L. (2023). *Capitalism and Christianity: Origins, Spirit and Betrayal of the Market Economy*. Abingdon, Routledge.
Bruni, L. (2024). *Capitalismo meridiano: alle radici dello spirito mercantile tra religione e profitto*. Bologna, Il Mulino.
Bruni, L., & Porta, P. L. (2003). Economia civile and pubblica felicità in the Italian Enlightenment. *History of Political Economy, 35*(5), 361–385.
Bruni, L., & Santori, P. (2018). The plural roots of rewards: Awards and incentives in Aquinas and Genovesi. *The European Journal of the History of Economic Thought, 25*(4), 637–657.
Bruni, L., & Santori, P. (2022a). The Adam Smith problem theologically reconsidered. In Ballor, J. (ed.), *Theology, Morality and Adam Smith*. London, Routledge, 258–275.
Bruni, L., & Santori, P. (2022b). The other invisible hand: The social and economic effects of theodicy in Vico and Genovesi. *The European Journal of the History of Economic Thought, 29*(3), 548–566.

Bruni, L., Santori, P., & Zamagni, S. (2021). *Lezioni di Storia del Pensiero Economico. Dall'Antichità al Novecento*. Rome, Città Nuova.

Bruni, L., & Sugden, R. (2008). Fraternity: Why the market need not be a morally free zone. *Economics & Philosophy*, 24(1), 35–64.

Bruni, L., & Sugden, R. (2013). Reclaiming virtue ethics for economics. *Journal of Economic Perspectives*, 27(4), 141–164.

Bruni, L., & Zamagni, S. (2007). *Civil Economy: Efficiency, Equity, Public Happiness*. Oxford, Peter Lang.

Card, D., & Smith, N. A. (2020). On consequentialism and fairness. *Frontiers in Artificial Intelligence*, 3(34), 1–11.

Cassirer, E. ([1865] 1981). *Kant's Life and Thought*. New Heaven, Yale University Press.

Chan, G. K. Y. (2008). The relevance and value of Confucianism in contemporary business ethics. *Journal of Business Ethics*, 77, 347–360.

Chazan, P. (1993). Rousseau as psycho-social moralist: The distinction between amour de soi and amour-propre. *History of Philosophy Quarterly*, 10(4), 341–354.

Chiarenza, M. (1993). Dante's Lady Poverty. *Dante Studies, with the Annual Report of the Dante Society*, 111, 153–175.

Ciulla, J. B. (2020). *The Search for Ethics in Leadership, Business, and Beyond*. Cham, Springer Nature.

Crane, A., Matten, D., Glozer, S., & Spence, L. (2019). *Business Ethics: Managing Corporate Citizenship and Sustainability in the Age of Globalization*. Oxford, Oxford University Press.

Crawford, C. (2011). The repeal of the Glass-Steagall Act and the current financial crisis. *Journal of Business & Economics Research (JBER)*, 9(1), 127–134.

Creswell, J. W., & Creswell, J. D. (2018). *Research Design: Qualitative, Quantitative, and Mixed Methods Approaches*. Thousand Oaks, Sage.

Dal Degan, F. (2018). Antonio Genovesi and Italian economic thought: When ethics matters in economics. *The European Journal of the History of Economic Thought*, 25(4), 524–530.

Dasgupta, P. (2021). *The Economics of Biodiversity: The Dasgupta Review (Abridged Version)*. London, HM Treasury.

Davis, P. (1990). *Lives and Times of Ebenezer Scrooge*. New Haven, Yale University Press.

De Cruz, A. F. (2024). *Business Ethics: An Institutional Governance Approach to Ethical Decision Making*. Singapore, Springer Nature Singapore.

De Pierris, G., & Friedman, M. (2024). Kant and Hume on causality. In *The Stanford Encyclopedia of Philosophy*. https://plato.stanford.edu/archives/fall2024/entries/kant-hume-causality/. Last access: February 12, 2025.

De Roover, R. (1954). New interpretations of the history of banking. *Journal of World History*, 2(1), 38–76.
Derry, R., & Green, R. M. (1989). Ethical theory in business ethics: A critical assessment. *Journal of Business Ethics*, 8, 521–533.
Dickens, C. (2010). *A Christmas Carol and Other Christmas Writings*. London, Penguin.
D'Onofrio, F. (2015). On the concept of "felicitas publica" in eighteenth-century political economy. *Journal of the History of Economic Thought*, 37(3), 449–471.
Dragonetti, G. (1788). *Origine dei feudi nei regni di Napoli e Sicilia*. Naples, Nella Stamperia Regale.
Dubbink, W. (2018). The bystander in commercial life: Obliged by beneficence or rescue? *Journal of Business Ethics*, 149, 1–13.
Dubbink, W, & van der Deijl, W. (2023). Corporate responsibility and the morality of the market. In Dubbink, W., & van der Deijl, W. (eds.), *Business Ethics: A Philosophical Introduction*. Cham, Springer.
Dubbink, W., & Van Liedekerke, L. (2014). Grounding positive duties in commercial life. *Journal of Business Ethics*, 120, 527–539.
Dubbink, W., & Van Liedekerke, L. (2020). Rethinking the purity of moral motives in business: Kant against moral purism. *Journal of Business Ethics*, 167(3), 379–393.
Dubbink, W., & Slegers, R. (2022). The trolley dilemma and the art of making judgments on concrete situations. *Ethical Perspectives*, 29(3), 313–334.
Dumez, H. (2015). What is a case, and what is a case study? *Bulletin of Sociological Methodology*, 127(1), 43–57.
Duska, R. F. (1993). Aristotle: A pre-modern post-modern? Implications for business ethics. *Business Ethics Quarterly*, 3(3), 227–249.
Easterlin, R. (1974). Does economic growth improve the human lot? Some empirical evidence. In David, P. A., & Reder, M. W. (eds.), *Nations and Households in Economic Growth: Essays in Honor of Moses Abramovitz*. New York: Academic Press, 89–125.
Etzioni, A. (1987). Toward a Kantian socio-economics. *Review of Social Economy*, 45(1), 37–47.
Etzioni, A. (2003). Communitarianism. In Rossel, S. A. (ed.), *Encyclopedia of Community: From the Village to the Virtual World*. Ottawa, Carleton University Press, 224–228.
Evensky, J. (2005). "Chicago Smith" versus "Kirkaldy Smith." *History of Political Economy*, 37(2), 197–203.
Fatima, T., & Elbanna, S. (2023). Corporate social responsibility (CSR) implementation: A review and a research agenda towards an integrative framework. *Journal of Business Ethics*, 183(1), 105–121.

Ferrara, F. (1852). Preface. In *Biblioteca dell'Economista*, vol. 3. Turin, Cugini Pomba ed Editori Librai.

Fiorentino, F. (1887). *Manuale di Storia della Filosofia a Uso dei Licei, Diviso in Tre Parti. Seconda Edizione*. Naples, Morano.

Fleischacker, S. (1991). Philosophy in moral practice: Kant and Adam Smith. *Kant-Studien*, 82(3), 249–269.

Fleischacker, S. (1996). Values behind the market: Kant's response to the "Wealth of Nations." *History of Political Thought*, 17(3), 379–407.

Fleischacker, S. (2013). *What Is Enlightenment?* London, Routledge.

Freeman, R. E. (2023). Foreword. In Painter-Morland, M., & Ten Bos, R. (eds.), *Business Ethics and Continental Philosophy*. Cambridge, Cambridge University Press.

Frey, B. S. (1997). *Not Just for the Money: An Economic Theory of Personal Motivation*. Cheltenham, Edward Elgar Publishing.

Friedman, M. (1976). Adam Smith's relevance for 1976. Selected Paper No. 50, 1–19.

Fukuyama, F. ([1992] 2006). *The End of History and the Last Man*. New York, Simon and Schuster.

Galanti A. M. (1772). *Elogio storico dell'abate Antonio Genovesi*. Naples, Androsio.

Galiani, F. ([1750] 1803). *Della Moneta, Collezione Custodi di Scrittori Classici di Economia Politica. Parte Moderna*. Milan, De Stefanis.

Gauthier, D. (1986). *Morals by Agreement*. Oxford, Oxford University Press.

Genovesi, A. ([1753] 1984). *Discorso sopra il vero fine delle lettere e delle scienze*. Naples, Istituto Italiano per gli Studi Filosofici.

Genovesi, A. (1757). "Ragionamento sul commercio universale." In Cary, J., *Storia del commercio della Gran Brettagna scritta da John Cary mercatante di Bristol, tradotta in nostra volgar lingua da Pietro Genovesi giureconsulto napoletano. Con un Ragionamento sul commercio in universale, e alcune annotazioni riguardanti l'economia del nostro regno, di Antonio Genovesi*. Naples, Benedetto Gessari, vii–cviii.

Genovesi, A. ([1765–1767] 1824–1825). *Lezioni di commercio o sia d'economia civile con un ragionamento sull'agricoltura e un altro sul commercio in universale di Antonio Genovesi*. Milan, Società Tipografica dei Classici Italiani.

Genovesi, A. ([1766] 1973). *Della diceosina o sia della filosofia del giusto e dell'onesto*. Milan, Marzorati.

Genovesi, A. (1775). *Istituzioni di metafisica per li principianti del signor abbate Antonio Genovesi. Ad uso delle scuole pubbliche di Venezia*. Venice, Tommaso Bettinelli Editore.

Genovesi, A. ([1777] 1838a). *Lo spirito delle leggi di Carlo Secondat Barone di Montesquieu con le annotazioni dell'abate Antonio Genovesi. Tomo Primo*. Milan, Giovanni Silvestri.

Genovesi, A. ([1777] 1838b). *Lo spirito delle leggi di Carlo Secondat Barone di Montesquieu con le annotazioni dell'abate Antonio Genovesi. Tomo Secondo*. Milan, Giovanni Silvestri.

Genovesi, A. (1835). *Logica e Metafisica di Antonio Genovesi*. Milan, Società Tipografica dei Classici Italiani.

Genovesi, A. (1962). *Autobiografia e altri scritti*. Milan, Feltrinelli.

Gentile, G. ([1903] 2003). *Storia della filosofia italiana. Dal Genovesi al Galluppi*. Florence, Le Lettere.

Gibson, K. (2023). *Ethics and Business: An Introduction*. Cambridge, Cambridge University Press.

Gordon, L. R. (2019). Decolonizing philosophy. *The Southern Journal of Philosophy*, 57, 16–36.

Graafland, J. (2022). *Ethics and Economics: An Introduction to Free Markets, Equality and Happiness*. Oxon, Routledge.

Graafland, J., & De Gelder, E. (2023). The impact of perceived due care on trustworthiness and free market support in the Dutch banking sector. *Business Ethics, the Environment & Responsibility*, 32(1), 384–400.

Gray, J. (2007). *Enlightenment's Wake: Politics and Culture at the Close of the Modern Age*. London, Routledge.

Green, C. F. (1989). Business ethics in banking. *Journal of Business Ethics*, 8, 631–634.

Guasti, N. (2006). Antonio Genovesi's Diceosina: Source of the Neapolitan enlightenment. *History of European Ideas*, 32(4), 385–405.

Guriev, S., & Papaioannou, E. (2022). The political economy of populism. *Journal of Economic Literature*, 60(3), 753–832.

Haakonssen, K. (1996). *Natural Law and Moral Philosophy: From Grotius to the Scottish Enlightenment*. Cambridge, Cambridge University Press.

Hamowy, R. (1987). *The Scottish Enlightenment and the Theory of Spontaneous Order*. Carbondale, Southern Illinois University Press.

Hansen, R. (2011). The Cratchits on film: Neo-Victorian visions of domesticity. In Kohlke, M., & Gutleben, C. (eds.), *Neo-Victorian Families*. Amsterdam, Rodopi, 175–196.

Harsanyi, J. C. (1975). Can the maximin principle serve as a basis for morality? A critique of John Rawls's theory. *American Political Science Review*, 69(2), 594–606.

Hart, O. (2017). Incomplete contracts and control. *American Economic Review*, 107(7), 1731–1752.

Hart, O., & Moore, J. (1988). Incomplete contracts and renegotiation. *Econometrica: Journal of the Econometric Society*, 56(4), 755–785.

Head, E. (2008). The ethics and implications of paying participants in qualitative research. *International Journal of Social Research Methodology*, 12(4), 335–344.

Heath, E. (1995). The commerce of sympathy: Adam Smith on the emergence of morals. *Journal of the History of Philosophy*, 33(3), 447–466.

Henrich, J., Heine, S. J., & Norenzayan, A. (2010). The weirdest people in the world? *Behavioral and Brain Sciences*, 33(2–3), 61–83.

Herman, A. (2003). *The Scottish Enlightenment: The Scots' Invention of the Modern World*. London, Fourth Estate.

Herman, B. (1984). Mutual aid and respect for persons. *Ethics*, 94(4), 577–602.

Herman, B. (1993). *The Practice of Moral Judgment*. Cambridge, MA, Harvard University Press.

Herman, B. (2016). *Morality as Rationality: A Study of Kant's Ethics*. London, Routledge.

Herzog, L. (2013). The Community of Commerce: Smith's rhetoric of sympathy in the opening of the Wealth of Nations. *Philosophy & Rhetoric*, 46(1), 65–87.

Herzog, L. (2014). Adam Smith on markets and justice. *Philosophy Compass*, 9(12), 864–875.

Hetherington, N. S. (1983). Isaac Newton's influence on Adam Smith's natural laws in economics. *Journal of the History of Ideas*, 44(3), 497–505.

Hooker, B. (2023). Rule consequentialism. *The Stanford Encyclopedia of Philosophy*. https://plato.stanford.edu/entries/consequentialism-rule/. Last accessed Oct. 15, 2023.

Iannaccone, L. R. (1991). The consequences of religious market structure: Adam Smith and the economics of religion. *Rationality and Society*, 3(2), 156–177.

Israel, J. (2006). Enlightenment! Which Enlightenment? *Journal of the History of Ideas*, 67(3), 523–545.

Jain, P. S. (1996). Managing credit for the rural poor: Lessons from the Grameen Bank. *World Development*, 24(1), 79–89.

Januard, P. (2021). Analysis risk and commercial risk: The first treatment of usury in Thomas Aquinas's Commentary on the Sentences. *The European Journal of the History of Economic Thought*, 28(4), 599–634.

Joyner, B. E., & Payne, D. (2002). Evolution and implementation: A study of values, business ethics and corporate social responsibility. *Journal of Business Ethics*, 41, 297–311.

Kaner, S. (2014). *Facilitator's Guide to Participatory Decision-Making*. San Francisco, Wiley & Sons.

Kant., I. ([1781] 1998). *Critique of Pure Reason*. Cambridge, Cambridge University Press.
Kant, I. ([1783] 2004). *Prolegomena to Any Future Metaphysics*. Cambridge, Cambridge University Press.
Kant, I. ([1784] 1991). An answer to the question: "What is Enlightenment?" In Reiss, H. S. (ed.), *Kant: Political Writings*. Cambridge, Cambridge University Press.
Kant, I. ([1785] 2012). *Groundwork of the Metaphysics of Morals*, ed. by M. Gregor & J. Timmermann. New York, Cambridge University Press.
Kant, I. (1996). *The Cambridge Edition of the Works of Immanuel Kant*, ed by Gregor, M. J. Cambridge, Cambridge University Press.
Kant, I. (2016). Natural right course lecture notes by Feyerabend. In Rauscher, F. (ed.), *Lectures and Drafts on Political Philosophy*. Cambridge, Cambridge University Press.
Keller, J., & Kittay, E. F. (2017). Feminist ethics of care. In Garry, A., Khader, S. J., & Stone, A. (eds.), *The Routledge Companion to Feminist Philosophy*. New York, Routledge, 540–555.
Kennedy, G. (2011). The hidden Adam Smith in his alleged theology. *Journal of the History of Economic Thought*, 33(3), 385–402.
Kirchgässner, G. (2000). *Homo oeconomicus*. Tübingen, Mohr Siebeck.
Kleingeld, P. (2011). *Kant and Cosmopolitanism: The Philosophical Ideal of World Citizenship*. Cambridge, Cambridge University Press.
Kleingeld, P. (2017). Contradiction and Kant's formula of universal law. *Kant-Studien*, 108(1), 89–115.
Knell, M. (2025). Isaac Newton, Robert Simson and Adam Smith. *Homo Oeconomicus*, 41(1)1–16.
Koehn, D. (2023). Narrative business ethics versus narratives within business ethics: Problems and possibilities from an Aristotelian virtue ethics perspective. *Journal of Business Ethics*, 189(4), 1–17.
Korsgaard, C. M. (1985). Kant's formula of universal law. *Pacific Philosophical Quarterly*, 66(1–2), 24–47.
Korsgaard, C. M. (1996). *Creating the Kingdom of Ends*. Cambridge, Cambridge University Press.
Korsgaard, C. M. (2013). Kantian ethics, animals, and the law. *Oxford Journal of Legal Studies*, 33(4), 629–648.
Liedman, S. E. (ed.). (1997). *The Postmodernist Critique of the Project of Enlightenment*, vol. 58. Amsterdam, Rodopi.
Liedtka, J. M. (1996). Feminist morality and competitive reality: A role for an ethic of care? *Business Ethics Quarterly*, 6(2), 179–200.
Lu, L., & Shih, J. B. (1997). Sources of happiness: A qualitative approach. *The Journal of Social Psychology*, 137(2), 181–187.

Luban, D. (2012). Adam Smith on vanity, domination, and history. *Modern Intellectual History*, 9(2), 275–302.

Lurie, Y., & Albin, R. (2007). Moral dilemmas in business ethics: From decision procedures to edifying perspectives. *Journal of Business Ethics*, 71, 195–207.

MacIntyre, A. ([1981] 2007). *After Virtue*. London, Duckworth.

Magnusson, L. (1992). Economics and the public interest: The emergence of economics as an academic subject during the 18th century. *The Scandinavian Journal of Economics*, 94, 249–257.

Malthus, T. R. ([1798] 1966). *An Essay on the Principle of Population*. London, Macmillan.

Marx, K. ([1859] 2002). Preface: A contribution to the critique of political economy. In Raines, J. (ed.), *Marx on Religion*. Philadelphia, Temple University Press, 107–112.

Marx, K. (2005). *Grundrisse: Foundations of the Critique of Political Economy*. London, Penguin.

McCloskey, D. (2008). Adam Smith, the last of the former virtue ethicists. *History of Political Economy*, 40(1), 43–71.

Meijer, K., & Smit, M. (2024). The status of business ethics teaching, research and training: The Netherlands. In Robinson, B., & Enderle, G. (eds.), *Global Survey of Business Ethics: 2022-2024: Teaching, Research and Training – Europe*. Geneva, Globethics Global Series, 340–373.

Meld Shell, S. (1980). *The Rights of Reason*. Toronto, University of Toronto Press.

Melé, D. (2020). *Business Ethics in Action*. London, Bloomsbury.

Melé, D. (2024). *The Humanistic Person-Centered Company*. Cham, Springer International Publishing.

Micewski, E. R., & Troy, C. (2007). Business ethics–deontologically revisited. *Journal of Business Ethics*, 72(1), 17–25.

Michaelson, C. (2005). Dealing with swindlers and devils: Literature and business ethics. *Journal of Business Ethics*, 58, 359–373.

Michaelson, C. (2010). Revisiting the global business ethics question. *Business Ethics Quarterly*, 20(2), 237–251.

Mikkelsen, J. M. (2013). *Kant and the Concept of Race: Late Eighteenth-Century Writings*. Albany, State University of New York Press.

Mill, J. S. ([1861] 2017). *Utilitarianism: With Related Remarks from Mill's Other Writings*, ed. by B. Eggleston. Indianapolis, Hackett Publishing Company.

Montes, L. (2003). The Adam Smith problem: Its origins, the stages of the current debate, and one implication for our understanding of sympathy. *Journal of the History of Economic Thought*, 25(1), 63–90.

Montes, L. (2008). Newton's real influence on Adam Smith and its context. *Cambridge Journal of Economics*, 32(4), 555–576.

Montes, L. (2019). Adam Smith's foundational idea of sympathetic persuasion. *Cambridge Journal of Economics*, 43(1), 1–15.

Mulsow, M. (2015). *Enlightenment Underground: Radical Germany, 1680–1720*. Charlottesville, University of Virginia Press.

Myint, H. (1977). Adam Smith's theory of international trade in the perspective of economic development. *Economica*, 44(175), 231–248.

Nelson, J. A. (1995). Feminism and economics. *Journal of Economic Perspectives*, 9(2), 131–148.

Nersisyan, Y. (2015). The repeal of the Glass–Steagall Act and the Federal Reserve's extraordinary intervention during the global financial crisis. *Journal of Post Keynesian Economics*, 37(4), 545–567.

Nicolae, M., Ion, I., & Nicolae, E. (2013). The research agenda of spiritual leadership: Where do we stand? *Revista De Management Comparat International*, 14(4), 551–566.

Niekerk, C. (2003). "Spätaufklärung": Rethinking the late eighteenth century in German literary history. *The Journal of English and Germanic Philology*, 102(3), 317–335.

Norman, J. (2018). *Adam Smith: Father of Economics*. New York, Basic Books.

O'Neill, O. (1975). *Acting on Principle: An Essay on Kantian Ethics*. Cambridge, Cambridge University Press.

Oncken, A. (1877). *Adam Smith und Immanuel Kant*. Leipzig, Duncker & Humblot.

Otte, J. T. (2009). Virtuous enterprises: The place of Christian ethics. *Finance & Bien Commun*, 33(1), 87–98.

Oz-Salzberger, F. (1995). *Translating the Enlightenment: Scottish Civic Discourse in Eighteenth-Century Germany*. Oxford, Oxford University Press.

Pabst, A. (2018). Political economy of virtue: Civil economy, happiness and public trust in the thought of Antonio Genovesi. *The European Journal of the History of Economic Thought*, 25(4), 582–604.

Pabst, A., & Scazzieri, R. (2019). Virtue, production, and the politics of commerce: Genovesi's "civil economy" revisited. *History of Political Economy*, 51(4), 703–729.

Pabst, A. & Scazzieri, R. (2023). *The Constitution of Political Economy*. Cambridge, Cambridge University Press.

Paganelli, M. P. (2015). Recent engagements with Adam Smith and the Scottish enlightenment. *History of Political Economy*, 47(3), 366–367.

Paganelli, M. P. (2022). Adam Smith and economic development in theory and practice: A rejection of the stadial model? *Journal of the History of Economic Thought*, 44(1), 95–104.

Paganelli, M. P., & Simon, F. (2022). Crime and punishment: "Adam Smith's theory of sentimental law and economics." *Journal of the History of Economic Thought*, 44(2), 268–287.

Pagden, A. (2013). *The Enlightenment: And Why It Still Matters*. Oxford, Oxford University Press.

Parfit, D. (1995). *Equality or Priority? The Lindley Lecture*. University of Kansas: Department of Philosophy.

Pihlström, S. (2003). On the concept of philosophical anthropology. *Journal of Philosophical Research*, 28, 259–286.

Pinker, S. (2018). *Enlightenment Now: The Case for Reason, Science, Humanism, and Progress*. London, Penguin.

Pirson, M. (2017). *Humanistic Management: Protecting Dignity and Promoting Well-Being*. Cambridge, Cambridge University Press.

Pogge, T. (1989). *Realizing Rawls*. Ithaca, Cornell University Press.

Porta, P. L. (2018). From economia civile to kameralwissenschaften: The line of descent from Genovesi to Beccaria in pre-Smithian Europe. *The European Journal of the History of Economic Thought*, 25(4), 531–561.

Pozzo, R. (2016). Review of J. Colin McQuillan, Immanuel Kant: The very idea of a critique of pure reason, *Notre Dame Philosophical Reviews*, 17, 1–3.

Provis, C. (2020). Business ethics, Confucianism and the different faces of ritual. *Journal of Business Ethics*, 165(2), 191–204.

Racioppi, G. (1871). *Antonio Genovesi*. Naples, Morano.

Rao, A. M. (2005). Enlightenment and reform: An overview of culture and politics in Enlightenment Italy. *Journal of Modern Italian Studies*, 10(2), 142–167.

Raphael, D. D. (1988). Newton and Adam Smith. In Sweet-Stayer, M. (ed.), *Newton's Dream*. Montreal, Queen's Quarterly, 36–49.

Rawls, J. (1971). *A Theory of Justice*. Cambridge, MA, Harvard University Press.

Rawls, J. (2000). *Lectures on the History of Moral Philosophy*. Cambridge, MA, Harvard University Press.

Rawls, J. (2005). *Political Liberalism*. New York, Columbia University Press.

Reill, P. H. (1975). *The German Enlightenment and the Rise of Historicism*. Berkeley, University of California Press.

Reinert, S. A. (2011). *Translating Empire: Emulation and the Origins of Political Economy*. Cambridge, MA, Harvard University Press.

Reisman, D. A. (1998). Adam Smith on market and state. *Journal of Institutional and Theoretical Economics (JITE)*, 154(2), 357–383.

Rickless, S. C. (2018). Brief for an inclusive anti-canon. *Metaphilosophy*, 49 (1–2), 167–181.

Robertson, J. (1997). The Enlightenment above national context: Political economy in eighteenth-century Scotland and Naples. *The Historical Journal*, 40(3), 667–697.

Robinson, R. M. (2022). *Business Ethics: Kant, Virtue, and the Nexus of Duty – Foundations and Case Studies*. Cham, Springer Nature.

Robinson, B., & Enderle G. (2024). *Global Survey of Business Ethics 2022–2024: Teaching, Research and Training*, vol. 3, Europe. Geneva, Globethics Publications.

Rosile, G. A. (ed.). (2016). *Tribal Wisdom for Business Ethics*. Bingley, Emerald Group Publishing Limited.

Rosmini A. ([1865] 1993). *The Philosophy of Right: The Essence of Right*, vol 1. Durham, Rosmini House.

Rosmini, A. (1883). *The Origin of Ideas by Antonio Rosmini Serbati. Translated from Fifth Italian Edition of the Nuovo Saggio sull'Origine delle Idee*. London, Kegan Paul.

Ross, I. S. (2010). *The Life of Adam Smith*. Oxford, Oxford University Press.

Rothschild, E. (1994). Adam Smith and the invisible hand. *The American Economic Review*, 84(2), 319–322.

Rousseau, J. J. ([1755] 1997). *Discourse on the Origins and Foundations of Inequality Among Men*. In Gourevitch, V. (ed.), *The Discourses and Other Early Writings*, Cambridge, Cambridge University Press.

Sandel, M. (1982). *Liberalism and the Limits of Justice*. New York, Cambridge University Press.

Sandel, M. (2012). *What Money Can't Buy: The Moral Limits of the Markets*. Farrar, Straus and Giroux (Ebook).

Santori, P. (2019). The foundation of the right of property: Rosmini as Genovesi's interpreter. *International Review of Economics*, 66(4), 353–367.

Santori, P. (2020). Donum, exchange and common good in Aquinas: The dawn of civil economy. *The European Journal of the History of Economic Thought*, 27(2), 276–297.

Santori, P. (2021). *Thomas Aquinas and the Civil Economy Tradition: The Mediterranean Spirit of Capitalism*. London, Routledge.

Santori, P. (2022). Is relationality always other-oriented? Adam Smith, catholic social teaching, and civil economy. *Philosophy of Management*, 21(1), 49–68.

Santori, P. (2022). Idleness and the very sparing hand of God: The invisible tie between Hume's Dialogues Concerning Natural Religion and Smith's

Wealth of Nations. *Journal of the History of Economic Thought*, 44(2), 246–267.

Santori, P. (2024). The market in the kingdom of ends: Kant's moral philosophy for business ethics. *Philosophy of Management*, 23, 239–256.

Santori, P. (2024). The curious case of the three Adam Smiths: Women and the Nobel Prize in economics. *Journal of Contextual Economics–Schmollers Jahrbuch*, 1–16.

Satz, D. (2010). *Why Some Things Should Not Be for Sale: The moral Limits of Markets*. Oxford, Oxford University Press.

Schabas, M., & De Marchi, N. (2003). Introduction to oeconomies in the age of Newton. *History of Political Economy*, 35(5), 1–13.

Schapiro, T. (2009). The nature of inclination. *Ethics*, 119(2), 229–256.

Schultz, B. (2024). Henry Sidgwick. *The Stanford Encyclopedia of Philosophy*. https://plato.stanford.edu/archives/fall2024/entries/sidgwick/. Last accessed Oct. 15, 2024.

Schumpeter, J. A. ([1954] 1986). *History of Economic Analysis*. Taylor & Francis e-library.

Schwartz, T. (1972). Rationality and the myth of the maximum. *Noûs*, 6(4), 97–117.

Sen, A. K. (1977). Rational fools: A critique of the behavioral foundations of economic theory. *Philosophy & Public Affairs*, 317–344.

Sen, A. (1980). Equality of what? In *Tanner Lectures on Human Values*, vol. 1. Cambridge, Cambridge University Press.

Sen, A. (2011a). *The Idea of Justice*. Cambridge, The Belknap Press.

Sen, A. (2011b). Uses and abuses of Adam Smith. *History of Political Economy*, 43(2), 257–271.

Shaw, W., & Miller, D. (2024). *Business Ethics: A Textbook with Cases*. Boston, Cengage Learning.

Shiva, V., & Mies, M. (2014). *Ecofeminism*. London, Bloomsbury Publishing.

Singer, P. (2023). *Animal Liberation Now: The Definitive Classic Renewed*. New York, Harper Perennial.

Singer, E., & Kulka, R. A. (2002). Paying respondents for survey participation. *Studies of Welfare Populations: Data Collection and Research Issues*, 4, 105–128.

Slegers, R. (2024). Vanity and social media: Adam Smith reassures us that we are not all narcissists. *Journal of Contextual Economics–Schmollers Jahrbuch*, 1–14.

Smith, A. ([1776] 1976). *An Inquiry into the Nature and Causes of the Wealth of Nations*. In Campbell, R. H., Sranner, A. S., & Todd, B. (eds.), *The Glasgow Edition of the Works and Correspondence of Adam Smith*, vol. 2. Indianapolis, Liberty Fund.

Smith, A. ([1896] 1982). *Lectures on Jurisprudence*. In Meek, R. L., Raphael, D. D., & P. G. Stein (eds.), *The Glasgow Edition of the Works and Correspondence of Adam Smith*. Indianapolis, Liberty Fund.

Smith, A. ([1759] 2012). *The Theory of Moral Sentiments*. New York, Dover Publication.

Solomon, R. C. (2004). Aristotle, ethics and business organizations. *Organization Studies*, 25(6), 1021–1043.

Sorensen, R., & Proops, I. (2024). Kant and the king: Lying promises, conventional implicature, and hypocrisy. *Ratio*, 37(1), 51–52.

Stapelbroek, K. (2006). Preserving the Neapolitan state: Antonio Genovesi and Ferdinando Galiani on commercial society and planning economic growth. *History of European Ideas*, 32(4), 406–442.

Stigler, G. J. (1971). Smith's travels on the ship of state. *History of Political Economy*, 3(2), 265–277.

Stigler, G. J. (1976). The successes and failures of Professor Smith. *Journal of Political Economy*, 84(6), 1199–1213.

Stobart, J., & Van Damme, I. (2016). Introduction: Markets in modernization – Transformations in urban market space and practice, c. 1800–c. 1970. *Urban History*, 43(3), 358–371.

Sugden, R. (2002). Beyond sympathy and empathy: Adam Smith's concept of fellow-feeling. *Economics & Philosophy*, 18(1), 63–87.

Sugden, R. (2018). *The Community of Advantage: A Behavioural Economist's Defence of the Market*. Oxford, Oxford University Press.

Sullivan, C.M., & Cain, D. (2004). Ethical and safety considerations when obtaining information from or about battered women for research purposes. *Journal of Interpersonal Violence*, 19(5), 603–618.

Surmiak, A. (2020). Ethical concerns of paying cash to vulnerable participants: The qualitative researchers' views. *The Qualitative Report*, 25(12), 4461–4481.

Thompson, S. (1996). Paying respondents and informants. *Social Research Update*, 14, 1–5.

Throop, C. J. (2012). Moral sentiments. In Fassin, D. (ed.), *A Companion to Moral Anthropology*. Chichester, Wiley-Blackwell, 150–168.

Tirole, J. (1999). Incomplete contracts: Where do we stand? *Econometrica*, 67(4), 741–781.

Todeschini, G. (2024). Christian financial government and Jewish political culture in Italy (15th–17th c.): A dialectic of modernity. *Jews and State Building: Early Modern Italy, and Beyond*, 79, 77–94.

Toenjes, R. H. (2002). Why be moral in business? A Rawlsian approach to moral motivation. *Business Ethics Quarterly*, 12(1), 57–72.

Tonelli, G. (1974). Kant's Critique of Pure Reason within the tradition of modern logic. In Funke, G. (ed.), *Akten des 4. Internationalen Kant-Kongresses: Mainz, 6.–10. April 1974, Teil 3: Vorträge*. Berlin, De Gruyter.

Tonelli, G. (1994). *Kant's Critique of Pure Reason within the Tradition of Modern Logic*, ed by Chandler, D. H. Zürich, Georg Olms.

Tribe, K. (2016). The German reception of Adam Smith. In Mizuta, H. (ed.), *A Critical Bibliography of Adam Smith*. London, Routledge.

Van der Deijl, W. (2023). Moral reasons. In Dubbink, W., & van der Deijl, W. (eds.), *Business Ethics: A Philosophical Introduction*, Cham, Springer, 67–86.

Varden, H. (2017). Kant and women. *Pacific Philosophical Quarterly*, 98(4), 653–694.

Venturi, F. (1962). *Riformatori napoletani*. Milan, Ricciardi.

Vickers, M. R. (2005). Business ethics and the HR role: past, present, and future. *Human Resource Planning*, 28(1), 26–33.

Villari, L. (1959). *Il pensiero economico di Antonio Genovesi*. Florence, Le Monnier.

Viner, J. (2015). *The Role of Providence in the Social Order: An Essay in Intellectual History*. Princeton, Princeton University Press.

Wahba, M. (1990). Ideals of the enlightenment for today. *Social Philosophy Today*, 3, 13–20.

Walschots, M. (2022). Achtung in Kant and Smith. *Kant-Studien*, 113(2), 238–268.

Watkins, E., & Stan, M. (2023). Kant's Philosophy of Science. *The Stanford Encyclopedia of Philosophy*. https://plato.stanford.edu/archives/fall2023/entries/kant-science/. Last accessed Feb. 12, 2025.

Weber, M. (2005). *Protestant Ethic and the Spirit of Capitalism*. London, Routledge Classics.

Weir, A. (2017). Decolonizing feminist freedom: Indigenous relationalities. In Mclaren, M. A. (ed.), *Decolonizing Feminism: Transnational Feminism and Globalization*. London, Rowman & Littlefield, 257–287.

Weiss, J. W. (2021). *Business Ethics: A Stakeholder and Issues Management Approach*. Oakland, Westchester Publishing Services.

Werhane, P. H. (1999). *Moral Imagination and Management Decision-Making*. New York, Oxford University Press.

White, M. D. (2010). Adam Smith and Immanuel Kant: On markets, duties, and moral sentiments. *Forum for Social Economics*, 39, 53–60.

Wicksteed, P. H. ([1910] 1933). *The Common Sense of Political Economy*. London, Routledge.

Williams, D. (2014). Adam Smith and colonialism. *Journal of International Political Theory*, 10(3), 283–301.

Wollstonecraft, M. ([1792] 2019). *The Feminist Papers: A Vindication of the Rights of Women*. Layton, Gibbs Smith Publisher.
Yunus, M. (2003). *Banker to the Poor*. New York, Public Affairs.
Zafirovski, M. (2010). *The Enlightenment and Its Effects on Modern Society*. New York, Springer.
Zamagni, S. (2020). On the birth of economic science during the Italian-Scottish Enlightenment: Two paradigms compared. *Roczniki Nauk Społecznych*, *48*(2), 5–28.
Zambelli, P. (1972). *La formazione filosofica di Antonio Genovesi*. Naples, Morano.
Zambelli, P. (1978). Antonio Genovesi and eighteenth-century empiricism in Italy. *Journal of the History of Philosophy*, *16*(2), 195–208.

Index

absolute monarch, 36, 56
Adam Smith Problem, 22, 48, 50, 51, 52
Anderson, Elizabeth, 59, 60, 61
Aristotle, 5, 7, 9
   friendship based on utility, 83
   Nicomachean Ethics, 11
autonomy, 37, 46, 57

banks and morality, 139
benevolence, 79, 80, 82
Bentham, Jeremy, 4
Bruni, Luigino, 52, 55, 56
butcher, brewer, baker, 80, 81, 86

care ethics, 5, 6
Chair of Commerce and Mechanics, 25, 32
A Christmas Carol, 1, 2
civil economy, 7, 8, 12, 35, 40, 53, 55, 56, 86, 130
common good, 40, 55, 86
   formal aspect, 56
   material dimension, 56
Confucian ethics, 6
consequentialism, 3, 5, 8, 149
   act-consequentialism, 4
   rule-consequentialism, 4
contradiction in conception, 89
contradiction in will, 89
corollaries
   Genovesi's principle, 86
   Kant's principle, 90
   Smith's principle, 83
courses of action, 3, 105, 106
criticism, 30, 31, 37, 42
Critique of Pure Reason, 30, 46, 88

Dasgupta, Partha, 157, 158
deontology, 3, 4, 5, 8, 57, 118
determinism, 78, 169

Dickens, Charles, 1, 2, 16, 172
dignity, 57, 58
Dragonetti, Giacinto, 40
duty, 88
   conflict of duties, 91

economic agents, 14, 93
   externalities, 157
   incomplete contracts, 107
essentialism, 75, 77, 78
ethical finance, 142, 149

feminist business ethics, 6, 166
feminist economics, 166
Ferrara, Francesco, 53
feudal societies, 9, 39
   hierarchy, 29
fictional case study, 15, 16
First Industrial Revolution, 27, 34
Friedman, Milton, 146

Galiani, Ferdinando, 29
Genovesi, Antonio, 7, 8, 9
   anthropology, 55, 84
   church, 32
   civic virtues, 40, 56
   Enlightenment, 28, 36
   forza concentriva and *forza diffusiva*, 29
   homo homini natura amicus, 55
   incivilmento, 53
   influence on Kant, 42, 43
   life, 21, 25, 40
   markets and reciprocity, 55
   monarchy, 56
   mutual assistance, 55
   Neapolitan Enlightenment, 39, 40
   Newton, 29
   on inclinations, 77
   on markets and reciprocity, 85

Genovesi, Antonio (cont.)
 Practical Knowledge, 41
 pubblica felicità, 55, 56
 religious controversies, 32
 sensism, 54
 we-rationality, 87
Gentile, Giovanni, 42
German Enlightenment, 9, 36
good will, 46
Grameen Bank, 139
Groundwork of the Metaphysics of Morals, 25, 44, 45, 46, 58, 62, 76, 90

happiness studies, 122
Herman, Barbara, 78, 159
Hobbes, Thomas, 55, 84, 108
human nature, 48, 50, 79, 162
Hume, David, 30, 31, 33, 38
 Dialogues Concerning Natural Religion, 33

imperfect duties, 90, 91, 95, 128
incentive, 107, 123, 124, 126
incomplete contracts, 101, 107, 108
 third-parties, 156
independence, 81, 83, 159
Indigenous frameworks, 6, 170
inequalities, 8, 93
interest in morality, 92, 118
Italian Enlightenment, 21, 39, 40, 84

Kant, Immanuel, 4
 academic career, 25
 censorship, 33
 criticism, 30, 36
 Critique of Pure Reason, 46, 88
 deontology and business ethics, 9, 57
 discrimination and prejudices, 165
 duty, 88
 duty and categorical imperative, 5, 88
 Enlightenment, 28
 ethics, 62
 German Enlightenment, 37
 Lectures on Natural Right, 7, 90
 life, 25
 moral principle for economic agents, 90
 on Hume and Wolff, 31
 on inclinations, 76
 on Rousseau, 162

rational impartial spectator, 46
reader of Newton, 30, 31
reader of Smith, 26
Smith's division of labor, 45
true needs, 159
works, 35
kingdom of ends, 7, 58
Korsgaard, Christine, 88

Lezioni di Commercio o sia d'Economia Civile, 26, 32, 35, 40, 53, 55
Locke, John, 32, 38, 43, 170, 171

MacIntyre, Alsdair, 5, 156
Malthus, Thomas Robert, 47, 48
market transactions, 8, 13
Marx, Karl, 168
maxim of human action, 88
Mill, John Stuart, 4
Monti di Pietà, 138
moral economy, 7, 9, 12, 35, 63, 90
moral law, 10, 45, 63
moral limits of the market, 58, 59, 60, 62
moral motivations, 12, 106, 135
moral purism, 58, 149
moral reasons, 2, 12, 150
morality as ticking boxes, 11
morally free zone, 3, 119
Moreton-Robinson, Aileen, 170, 171
mutual assistance, 55, 85, 86

Neapolitan Enlightenment, 39, 40, 41
Nelson, Julie, 166
neoclassical economic theory, 26, 49
Newton, Isaac, 29
normative ethical theories, 3
 application, 10
 presence in business ethics courses, 4
 classic triad, 9
 decolonizing, 6
 expanding, 7
 new triad, 7
 two triads, 8
novels and business ethics, 103, 172

Oncken, August, 44

Packham, Catherine, 166
Pietism, 37

Index 193

Plato, 84, 109
political economy, 7, 8, 12, 35, 47, 53, 76, 83
pre-reflective stage, 76, 77, 78, 86, 105, 161, 162
principle of mutual assistance, 7, 86, 90, 94, 113, 127, 143
principle of self-interest and non-tuism, 7, 83, 90, 112, 127, 143
public trust, 55

qualitative research, 122

Rawls, John, 5, 159
  A Theory of Justice, 102, 155, 159
  reasonable pluralism, 11, 154
reflective stage, 76, 78, 86, 105, 161, 162
renegotiation, 108, 111, 112, 113, 116, 143
representativity, 102
Rosmini, Antonio, 43, 53, 54
Rousseau, Jean-Jacques, 108, 162, 163, 167

Sandel, Michael, 137, 161
Satz, Debra, 61
Scottish Enlightenment, 9, 38
self-interest, 80, 81, 82, 85
self-love, 80, 81, 84, 88
Sen, Amartya, 44
  interpretation of Smith, 50
Sidgwick, Henry, 4
Smith, Adam, 7
  "True Adam Smith," 23
  Calvinism, 33
  Chicago Smith, 49
  colonialism, 53, 165
  division of labor, 27, 45
  gender issue, 52
  impartial spectator, 47
  influence on Kant, 44
  invisible hand, 49, 51, 73
  invisible hand and public good, 81
  life, 25, 26
  Malthus on Smith, 48
  moral philosophy, 38, 50

  mutual advantage, 80
  nature and Providence, 39
  on inclinations, 76
  on Newton, 29
  persuasion, 51
  political economy, 50, 55, 79
  propensity to truck, barter, and exchange, 48, 77
  prudence and self-command, 48, 52
  religion, 32
  Scottish Enlightenment, 38
  self-love and self-interest, 49
  sympathy, 50, 77, 79
  Wicksteed's interpretation, 81
  Wollstonecraft's critique, 167
  works, 35
spirits of capitalism, 34
Sugden, Robert, 52

the principle of honoring the spirit of mutually beneficial contracts, 131, 149
Theory of Moral Sentiments, 35, 38
Thomasius, Christian, 37, 38
Tirole, Jean, 107
Tonelli, Giorgio, 42, 43

utilitarianism, 4, 11, 54

Varden, Helga, 162
virtue ethics, 3, 5, 8, 118
  Aristotelian virtue ethics, 6, 11
voluntary exchanges, 8, 9, 13

Wealth of Nations, 25, 26, 27, 35, 39, 44, 48, 49, 52, 79
Weir, Allison, 170, 171
WEIRD perspective, 168
What Is Enlightenment, 21
Wicksteed, Philip Henry, 82
  non-tuism, 82
Wolff, Christian, 30, 37
Wollstonecraft, Mary, 164, 166, 167
  feminist critique to commercial society, 167

Zamagni, Stefano, 55, 56

For EU product safety concerns, contact us at Calle de José Abascal, 56–1°,
28003 Madrid, Spain or eugpsr@cambridge.org.

www.ingramcontent.com/pod-product-compliance
Ingram Content Group UK Ltd.
Pitfield, Milton Keynes, MK11 3LW, UK
UKHW020716211125
465240UK00022B/812